THE BILINGUAL BRAIN

Neuropsychological and
Neurolinguistic Aspects of Bilingualism

PERSPECTIVES IN
NEUROLINGUISTICS and PSYCHOLINGUISTICS

Harry A. Whitaker, Series Editor
DEPARTMENT OF PSYCHOLOGY
THE UNIVERSITY OF ROCHESTER
ROCHESTER, NEW YORK

HAIGANOOSH WHITAKER and HARRY A. WHITAKER (Eds.).
Studies in Neurolinguistics, Volumes 1, 2, and 3

NORMAN J. LASS (Ed.). Contemporary Issues in Experimental Phonetics

JASON W. BROWN. Mind, Brain, and Consciousness: The Neuropsychology of Cognition

SIDNEY J. SEGALOWITZ and FREDERIC A. GRUBER (Eds.). Language Development and Neurological Theory

SUSAN CURTISS. Genie: A Psycholinguistic Study of a Modern-Day "Wild Child"

JOHN MACNAMARA (Ed.). Language Learning and Thought

I. M. SCHLESINGER and LILA NAMIR (Eds.). Sign Language of the Deaf: Psychological, Linguistic, and Sociological Perspectives

WILLIAM C. RITCHIE (Ed.). Second Language Acquisition Research: Issues and Implications

PATRICIA SIPLE (Ed.). Understanding Language through Sign Language Research

MARTIN L. ALBERT and LORAINE K. OBLER. The Bilingual Brain: Neurophysiological and Neurolinguistic Aspects of Bilingualism

In preparation

HAIGANOOSH WHITAKER and HARRY A. WHITAKER (Eds.).
Studies in Neurolinguistics, Volume 4

THE BILINGUAL BRAIN

Neuropsychological and Neurolinguistic Aspects of Bilingualism

MARTIN L. ALBERT
LORAINE K. OBLER

Aphasia Research Center
Department of Neurology
Boston University Medical School
Veterans Administration Hospital
Boston, Massachusetts

ACADEMIC PRESS
New York   San Francisco   London   1978
A Subsidiary of Harcourt Brace Jovanovich, Publishers

ACADEMIC PRESS, INC.
111 Fifth Avenue, New York, New York 10003

United Kingdom Edition published by
ACADEMIC PRESS, INC. (LONDON) LTD.
24/28 Oval Road, London NW1 7DX

Library of Congress Cataloging in Publication Data

Albert, Martin L
   The bilingual brain.

   (Perspectives in neurolinguistics and psycholinguistics)
   Bibliography: p.
   1.   Aphasia.   2.   Bilingualism--Physiological aspects.
3.   Bilingualism--Psychological aspects.   4.   Brain--
Localization of functions.   I.   Obler, Loraine K., joint
author.   II.   Title.   [DNLM: 1.   Language development.
2.   Brain--Physiology.   3.   Neurophysiology.
4.   Psycholinguistics.   WL335 A333b]
RC425.A43   ·   616.8'552   78-51243
ISBN 0-12-048750-0

PRINTED IN THE UNITED STATES OF AMERICA

80 81 82 83   9 8 7 6 5 4 3 2

To the memory of Benjamin Albert

and to

Alice Albert, Miriam Dworsky Obler, and Edward Obler

Contents

Preface

Working in Jerusalem in behavioral neurology and neurolinguistics, we began to make clinical observations that could not be explained by recourse to traditional teachings. For example, we were seeing more aphasia in right-handers with right hemispheric lesions than we had come to believe was "normal." We also saw a brain-damaged multilingual patient who had a clinical picture of Broca's aphasia in one language and a clinical picture of Wernicke's aphasia in another. This pattern of two different types of aphasia in one patient at the same time, we had been taught, was theoretically impossible. Either our clinical observations were erroneous, or the standard theories of cerebral organization for language needed to be modified.

Since very few adults in Israel speak only one language, we wondered whether the fact of being bilingual influenced cerebral organization for language, thereby causing the unusual clinical situations we were encountering. Perhaps the traditional theories of cerebral organization for language were correct, but only for monolinguals. As Dr. Phyllis Albert suggested, perhaps "an accident of history" had determined that most neurobehavioral investigations of language had been carried out in monolingual societies. It was possible that traditional theories needed to be modified or expanded to account for the facts of bilingualism.

We did not start out with the intention of writing a book. We set out to discover what had been done by others to study the neurological bases of bilingualism, and to conduct some studies ourselves. We discovered much excellent work that had been done by linguists, psychologists, and neurologists on the neurological bases of bilingualism. We also found that most of this work was widely scattered in diverse publications, and that brought together, the evidence provided a coherent and compelling picture. We decided to bring the evidence together; the result was this book.

At the outset we posed the following question: How is language organized in the brain of a bilingual? Is it the same as in the brain of a monolingual, as most people suppose, or is it somehow different? To answer these questions we collected and analyzed research in various disciplines as they relate to bilingualism. Reflecting this procedure, we consider in separate chapters three main approaches to the study of bilingualism—linguistic, psychological, and neuropsychological. In the chapter on neuropsychological aspects of bilingualism, we present a detailed review of our own research. Following the chapters that consider studies in bilingualism by research field, we select key issues of bilingualism and synthesize data from the various fields in relation to each key issue. By this means we hope to clarify the relationship of neurologic organization to linguistic organization.

We conclude by suggesting that the fact of learning a second language seems to distinguish the bilingual from the monolingual, not only in language skills but also in perceptual strategies and even in patterns of cerebral organization. The facts of bilingualism indicate that the right hemisphere plays a major role in the learning of a second language, even in the adult. The brain is seen to be a plastic, dynamically changing organ which may be modified by processes of learning.

Acknowledgments

Our own experiments were carried out for the most part in Jerusalem in the Aranne Laboratory for Human Psychophysiology of the Department of Neurology, Hadassah Hospital and Hebrew University Medical School (Professor S. Feldman, Chairman). Professor T. Najenson opened the facilities of the Beit Loewenstein Rehabilitation Hospital of Tel Aviv Medical School to us. I. Schechter, the aphasia specialist, was most helpful in aiding our research there.

We completed this work with the help of numerous friends and colleagues, whom we take this occasion to thank again. Tirca Gaziel, and Drs. Harold Gordon and Ruth Silverberg contributed considerable professional expertise to collaboration in our research. Joel Walters, Dr. Margaret Fearey, and Professors Norman Geschwind, Harold Goodglass, and D. Frank Benson generously provided critical challenge and insightful comment. For sharing his thoughts about the neurolinguistics of bilingualism, as well as his work on polyglot aphasia, and for critical reading of the manuscript, we thank Dr. Michel Paradis. Dr. Phyllis Albert and David and Michael Albert contributed a series of stimulating questions and several thoughtful answers. Professor W. Lambert kindly supplied us with prepublication manuscripts of current findings from his own laboratory. The support of our editor, Professor Harry Whitaker, is also greatly appreciated.

Errol Baker, Jerry Levinson, Peter Soloman, and Gil Stern aided us in collecting and/or analyzing data. Dr. Israel Nachshon, Dr. Robert Cooper, and Joel Walters opened their personal libraries to us, and aided our bibliographic search. Gaila Obstfeld and Claire Sybertz contributed excellent typing services.

Other friends and colleagues, especially from the Aphasia Research Center of the Department of Neurology, Boston University Medical School and Boston Veterans Administration Hospital, provided constructive comments, theories, and disagreements. In particular, we thank Dr. Edgar Zurif for his time, concern, and constructive advice.

We wish to advise the reader that our policy on pronoun gender deviates slightly from standard practice. In order that the reader may bear in mind that third person pronoun reference may apply to both females and males, we have chosen to alternate use of the male and female pronouns, insofar as this will not lead to confusion.

THE BILINGUAL BRAIN

Neuropsychological and
Neurolinguistic Aspects of Bilingualism

1

Introduction

Statement of the Problem

Many people know more than one language; entire societies are bilingual or multilingual. Yet, perhaps by an accident of history, neurobehavioral studies have been conducted mainly in societies that are predominantly monolingual. As a result, much pertinent information about natural language behavior and its neurological basis has been largely ignored. Scientists concerned with the organization of language in the brain should, therefore, consider the neurological implications of bilingualism.

The weight of evidence collected over many years by able scientists in different disciplines has convincingly demonstrated that the left cerebral hemisphere is dominant for language in most humans, that is, that language in some way has a special dependence on the anatomical structures and physiological activity of the left hemisphere. This evidence, however, has been collected almost exclusively from monolinguals. There is no special reason to assume on an a priori basis that the second language sits in the brain of a bilingual in exactly the same manner as does the first and only language in the brain of a monolingual. The hypothesis could be proposed that the learning of a second language in some way influences the subtle interactions between left and right hemispheres, and between cortical and subcortical structures, so that cerebral function is different for monolinguals and bilinguals.

The facts known to date cannot confirm or deny the validity of such a hypothesis. Nevertheless, a number of psychological, linguistic, and neurological investigations have been carried out on subjects who know and speak more than one language. These studies provide some clues for answering the question of how language is organized in the brain of the bilingual. This question is the focus of our monograph.

Background

The history of studies on bilingualism does not fall into a neat, continuous line. Several threads, rather, can be identified, and these threads are seen to intersect with each other during periodic surges of research activity into mechanisms of bilingualism.

Studies on aphasia in polyglots constitute one strand. Such studies have dealt primarily with patterns of recovery. Ribot's (1882) general theory of memory disorders was that earlier-learned items are better preserved in brain damage, and that, in recovery from memory loss, earlier-learned items return before later-learned items. His hypothesis with respect to polyglot aphasics, then, was that the earlier-learned language recovers first. Pitres (1895) suggested that the language to recover first would be the one that has been used most in the extended period prior to the onset of aphasia. Krapf (1957) and Minkowski (1965) felt that affective factors help determine which language will return first.

These theories were proposed to explain the clinical observation that often a polyglot aphasic patient recovers one language before another. Some authors have suggested that differential recovery may result from different premorbid patterns of anatomical organization of the languages (Scoresby-Jackson, 1867; Gloning & Gloning, 1965; Albert & Obler, 1975). Pitres (1895) and others have argued against the possiblility that different languages may be organized differently in the brain. Their position is supported by studies of groups of brain-damaged patients (e.g., Charlton, 1964; L'Hermitte, Hécaen, Dubois, Culioli, & Tabouret-Keller, 1966) that suggested that the majority of aphasic polyglots lose and then recover their languages in proportion to the premorbid degree of fluency in the language. Goldstein (1948) attempted to provide a single explanation for the two divergent sets of studies—those focusing on differential recovery, and those focusing on parallel recovery. He suggested that a cognitive mechanism responsible for switching between the two languages might be impaired in cases of differential recovery.

Whereas aphasiologists have dealt with various forms of behavioral and anatomical distinction between the two languages, linguists and psychologists have focused on various forms of interference between languages. Epstein's (1916) dissertation, *Pensée et Polyglossie*, spoke of the "inhibition" of one language on a second language, and of the "antagonism" between two languages, especially at the phonological and lexical levels. Vildomec's volume *Multilingualism* (1963) provided numerous examples of interference at all linguistic levels, in writing as well as in speech. Within the American structuralist framework, Weinreich's *Languages in Contact* (1953) systematized the notion of bilingual interference at all linguistic levels. In emphasizing the importance of the manner in which a second language is learned, Weinreich paved the way for the Osgood and Ervin (1954a) model of compound as opposed to coordinate bilingualism. In their scheme, the manner in which a second language is learned determines whether the two languages are "stored" as a single, compound system or as a dual coordinate system. Over the past two decades many studies have been conducted to test the viability of the compound–coordinate model. Studies, such as those by Lambert and his colleagues (e.g., 1956a,b,c, 1969), have measured interference in word-list learning or in word association tasks and have correlated this measure with the different language histories of their bilingual subjects.

In other studies (e.g., Riegel, 1968; Diller, 1974) the compound–coordinate notion has not been viewed as a clear-cut dichotomy, but, rather, as a continuum. A new perspective on bilingual interference has developed as a result. Authors interested in how interference is **avoided** have posited a switch mechanism (which would be functionally the same as that proposed by Goldstein, 1948). Macnamara and Kushnir (1971) and Kolers (1966), for example, have developed instruments for measuring the facility and timing involved in forced switching from one language to another.

The majority of psychological and linguistic studies of bilingualism have focused on language production. Only in recent years have researchers begun to investigate systematically the capacity of a bilingual to perceive and comprehend verbal information. Most psycholinguistic tests (e.g., Caramazza, Yeni-Komshian, Zurif, & Carbone, 1973) have focused on phonological perception as well as on production. Various psychological tests—using dichotic, tachistoscopic,

evoked potential, electroencephalographic, and reaction time measures—have also compared perception of stimuli in one language to
that in the other (e.g., Genesee, Hamers, Lambert, Mononen, Seitz, &
Starck, 1978; Obler, Albert, & Gordon, 1975).

Such studies bring us full cycle to the clinical aphasiological
concerns of the last century, since they speak to the issue of how two
languages can be housed in one brain.

Definition of Terms

We shall first define bilingualism, then the factors that have been
considered to play a part in the development of the bilingual state, and,
last, the evaluation measures which have been used to determine the
linguistic consequences of bilingualism for the individual.

BILINGUALISM

The range of meaning of the term **bilingualism** varies throughout
the literature on the topic. Some authors focus on equal passive competence in both languages (listening and perhaps also reading equally
well), whereas others focus on equal productive competence (speaking
and perhaps also writing). Researchers also differ on the degree of
proficiency necessary to bilingualism; for some a person is bilingual
only if she "knows" both languages equally; others may include third-
year students of the second language within their definition of the
bilingual. Some experimental tests are designed to exclude speakers of
more than the two languages in question, whereas others unquestion-
ingly consider polyglots to be "bilinguals."

Bilingualism is broadly defined by Weinreich (1953) as "the practice of alternately using two languages." This phrasing starts to serve
our purposes as it includes the widest possible population. It should be
noted, however, that it leaves unresolved several issues:

1. Is **multilingualism** merely an extension of the bilingual state, or
   might it be qualitatively different?
2. How does one judge whether two distinct languages are under
   consideration (i.e., do bidialectalism, diglossia, or even wide
   register control come under the same rubric?)
3. Does "use" of a language entail any minimal fluency criterion?
   (To take an extreme example, does the use of "OK" imply that
   its worldwide users are English speaking? If it does not, then
   what parameters are to determine fluency?)

4. What modalities (e.g., speaking, comprehension, writing, reading) are to be considered in the evaluation of "using languages alternately?"

We subscribe to Weinreich's purposely vague definition with the conscious stipulation that any research done on bilinguals must specify the more detailed criteria considered in subject selection, since it is reasonable to expect that distinctive subgroups are to be found among all the people who "alternately use two languages."

THE BILINGUAL STATE

A **balanced bilingual** has, theoretically, native language proficiency in both languages. The term **dominant bilingual** describes someone who is more fluent in one language than in another; **second language learners** are the subgroup who are somehow actively involved in improving their second language skills. **Fluency** must be considered for the various *skills*: Reading and auditory understanding are not necessarily interdependent, nor are writing and speaking, although it is likely that the abilities to speak and to write a language are dependent, respectively, on the abilities to understand and to read it.

The question of **interference** between the two languages begs that of the existence of a true balanced bilingual. The speech of a bilingual will often manifest influences of one language on the other, whether this be at the phonological level (accent), the lexical level (word borrowings), or the syntactic level (inappropriate phrase translation or use of grammatical morphemes). At the same time, it is clear that there is some measure of independence between the two languages of a bilingual, that one can speak quite fluently in one language without the obvious intrusion of the other language. It has, thus, been claimed (e.g., Macnamara & Kushnir, 1971) that the bilingual has a more or less voluntary **output switch**, which inhibits one language while permitting the other to be produced. An automatic **input switch** is hypothesized, as well, which alerts or sets the language-processing system to deal with the different languages which it hears or reads. This input switch must be at work in those confusing first seconds of a received telephone call or discovered radio station, in which one initially does not understand a known language, not knowing which language is being spoken.

The psycholinguistic concepts of language independence and language interdependence are related to the concepts of **compound** and **coordinate bilingualism**. A true compound bilingual is assumed to have the two languages organized as a single system, whereas the true coordinate bilingual has the two organized as two separate systems.

These theoretical categories have been much debated. Beyond questioning whether a true compound or coordinate bilingual may exist, one may ask if the two categories are sufficient to account for all cases of bilingualism. For example, one might need to posit a case of **subordinate bilingualism** in which the second learned language is processed not directly but rather via the first. In operationalizing the terms for purposes of defining experimental groups, one must decide whether to choose as a criterion for definition the age of learning the second language (e.g., those who had learned the second language before age 6 would be compounds; those who had learned the second language after age 13 would be coordinates), the manner of learning the second language (e.g., one-parent, one-language situations would result in coordinate bilinguals; teaching in school by a translation method would result in compound bilingualism), or usage patterns (e.g., people in a community which regularly mixed languages would be compounds; jet-setters between monolingual societies would be coordinates).

For the neurolinguist, all the terms discussed in this section must correspond to some mechanism or organizational principle in the brain. Thus, in neurolinguistic research the same questions of independence or interference could be phrased around the (unsatisfactory) notions of **separate** or **same language centers**. Our own studies indicate that factors of cerebral dominance may prove to be relevant in understanding specific parameters and mechanisms of bilingualism (e.g., degrees of cerebral dominance may differ for each language). The issue of switch mechanisms may be seen in the inhibition caused by the assumed breakdown of a switch after brain damage; bilingual aphasics may lose their previous flexibility in appropriately shifting from one language to the other.

PARAMETERS OF LANGUAGE ACQUISITION

The following factors have been proposed as conditioning either the state of the healthy bilingual, or the pattern of recovery from aphasia after brain damage:

THE AGE OF LEARNING THE SECOND LANGUAGE

It would appear that after puberty the likelihood of learning a second language with native accent is reduced (Lenneberg, 1967; Guiora, Brannon, & Dull, 1972). Curtiss (1977) reports a case of difficulty in learning a first language after puberty. Language teachers often subscribe to the theory that the younger the learners are, the better they will learn a foreign language. Little systematic work, however, has been done to compare age-dependent differences in learning capacities and strategies across the continuum from birth to puberty, or across that from adolescence to senescence.

THE MANNER OF LEARNING THE SECOND LANGUAGE

The second language is learned either like the first, in the home, or from peers (as in the case of the children of immigrant parents who make an effort to speak the new language but have an accent; the children eventually learn the unaccented speech of their peers), or in the more artificial situation of the educational system. In the last case, either an **auditory** or a **visual method** may be used, perhaps with different consequences, as may a method encouraging translation, or one discouraging it. It is important to emphasize that second language learning can occur naturally in an individual with little or no translation of the new language to the older or better known one. This is obviously likely to occur in children who are learning both languages simultaneously, and are possibly applying a general language-learning strategy to each language separately (most strongly at the lexical and idiomatic levels, less obviously at the phonological level, and perhaps later at the grammatical level), and among illiterate immigrants, isolated from other speakers of their language, who pick up a new language from their new surroundings.

It is not unreasonable to hypothesize that different manners of acquisition may determine different patterns of organization of the two languages in the brains of the bilinguals, and that different organization systems may result in different language competence and performance patterns. For example, we would expect that someone who learned a second language by a word and sentence **translation method** would be better at translation or interlingual association tasks than someone who learned the second language directly, with no drill in referring second language words and forms to first language. The indirect method might also enhance **transfer** of structures in L_1 to L_2. Such transfer, however, may occur spontaneously in any person who knows one language well at the time he starts to learn a second language.

As we have already noted, where the languages of the bilingual seem to share a single system, the bilingual can be considered **compound**; where the languages seem to be two separated systems, **coordinate**. But what exactly do we mean by "language system"? Most of the experimentation that applies the notion of a compound–coordinate categorical dichotomy has been done at the lexical level. Although this level provides the most clear-cut stimulus items and offers the best chance of choosing equivalent stimuli across languages (by meaning, function, morphological shape, and/or frequency of occurrence), it must not be concluded that the question of separate versus merged systems occurs only at that level. For example, one would want to measure the nature of phonological perception and production systems to see if they were unified or not. One would also wonder whether the systems for various levels of grammatical rules are unified or separate. Thus the notion of a language system must include at least its phonological items and rules, its morphological items and rules, its lexical items, and its grammatical rules.

Another question then arises: Can there really be a clear-cut dichotomy between compound bilinguals and coordinate bilinguals? At any linguistic level, it is possible that a part of the subsystem under discussion would most efficiently be shared by the two languages (i.e., the principles of speech production, phonemes common to both languages, cognate words in both languages, common grammatical rules and structures), whereas another part would include those items or rules that occur only in one language. It is therefore unlikely that an individual could be labeled either entirely compound or entirely coordinate.

Moreover, the compound and coordinate dichotomy is usually taken to be a synchronic state in the head of a bilingual, while Riegel (1968) has discussed the possibility that one may develop from a coordinate to a compound state. Perhaps, under different usage patterns (e.g., rigid delineation of situations in which one or the other language is appropriate), one might also develop from a more compound to a more coordinate state.

USAGE PATTERNS

A bilingual may use her two languages interchangeable in all situations, or one or the other language may be appropriate on certain occasions, in certain places, or with certain people. Furthermore, she may develop and practice certain skills in one language (reading, writing, speaking, aural understanding, translation, interpretation) and not in another. After long disuse of a language, it may be "lost" or rendered difficult. Disuse may impair only active production or may also impair passive understanding.

SOCIAL–EMOTIONAL FACTORS

The attitudes toward the two cultures, which are identified with the languages or to known speakers of the languages, are expected to have influence on both language learning and language usage situations. For example, some people claim to maintain deliberately an accent in their second language. Such attitudinal variation is considered to be in the realm of **affective** factors. It is unclear as yet what the neuroanatomical or physiological correlates of these affective factors might be.

THE LINGUISTIC RELATIONSHIP BETWEEN THE TWO LANGUAGES

This relationship is little researched, but the following points must be considered: People show more lexical interference on similar items (e.g., French–English *bleu*–blue versus *blanc*–white, Lambert & Preston, 1967); so it may follow that languages with more similar items (e.g., English and French) are more susceptible to mutual interference than languages with fewer similar features (e.g., English and Japanese). On the other hand, we might also expect more learning difficulties, and thus more likelihood of performance interference at those points in a second language which are most distant from the first language.

In both cases the interference may result from a strategy on the part of the learner which assumes equivalence, both formally and functionally, of two items or rules sharing either function or form. More advanced learning of the second language may involve a greater number of rules or marking features for distinguishing between the two languages. Pairs of languages which share features at different levels might, perhaps, induce different organizational systems in the brains of the bilinguals.

Structure and Limitations of This Monograph

In preliminary research for this monograph, we soon realized that work in bilingualism has been undertaken for many purposes. We decided to limit ourselves to the relationship between bilingualism and cerebral function. We have excluded works that deal with bilingualism from its societal perspectives. This means that we set aside questions of language change engendered by a bilingual society, of sociological patterns within the bilingual society, and of prescriptive pedagogy based on research or speculation into the intellectual or attitudinal repercussions of bilingualism on various elements of the society. Readers interested in a more complete picture of these facets of bilingualism are referred to the extensive bibliographies of Weinreich (1953), Darcy (1953), Vildomec (1963), Haugen (1974), and Hornby (1977).

Our study considers the question of how the bilingual brain manages its two languages. In treating the question we have turned to several disciplines that have dealt with the issues of bilingualism, each from its particular perspective. Neurologists for the most part have viewed the problem as one of patterns of impairment and recovery following aphasia in polyglots. Neuropsychologists and psycholinguists have tested bilingual performance—especially in its perceptual aspects—in groups of brain-damaged or healthy subjects. Experimental psychologists have devised measures for inducing language interference, especially at the lexical level. Linguists have studied patterns of productive performance both in children acquiring bilingual competence and in adults acquiring a second language.

We have chosen to start by grouping studies and reports by field (linguistics, psychology, and neurology) insofar as possible. Given the multifaceted nature of each field, such an arbitrary division has not always been easy. Even a reduction to the cross-disciplines of neurolinguistics and neuropsychology did not facilitate categorization. For each discipline we present an interpretive review and analysis of representative literature. In the chapter on neuropsychological studies of bilingualism, we present an extensive report of our own research on Hebrew–English bilinguals.

Following the review and analysis of studies by discipline, we cut across the arbitrary limits of each discipline to consider key issues of bilingualism. Thus, in the fifth chapter, we attempt to synthesize data and hypotheses from the various fields in such a way as to clarify the relationship of neurologic organization to linguistic organization. A final chapter outlines our general conclusions.

2

Linguistic Studies of Bilingualism

Introduction

Linguistic methodology commonly involves observing speech (in others or in the linguist), determining alternative forms the speech unit in question might have taken, and then abstracting a rule or system of rules (a model) that could explain simply the phenomenon in question. Emphasis is on the ideal system underlying the individual utterances, and, indeed, this system, known as the speaker's competence, may be of greater interest to the theoretical linguist than is the speaker's performance, which is often interfered with by nonlinguistic factors. Few linguists would claim that the grammar that is formally best (simplest or most elegant) corresponds directly with the neuronal system in the language area of the brain of the speaker; rather, the grammar is assumed to represent the knowledge that neuronal systems must store.

In the sections which follow, we will see that the linguist's understanding of how language is structured contributes to the way he thinks about the dynamics of bilingualism. We consider aspects of interference, language acquisition, and perceptual processing of language.

Interference

Bilingual interference involves unintentional usage of one language in the course of using the other. The existence of the phenomenon raises the question of interdependence, or compounding, of storage of the two languages. Categorization of the types of interference, and of the environments in which they occur, may provide evidence for distinguishing linguistic subsystems in human language. Relating types of interference to the sorts of people who exhibit them provides evidence of the effects of language acquisition parameters on the eventual organization of the languages of the bilingual.

Three volumes present extensive discussions of interference phenomena in bilinguals: Epstein (1916), Weinreich (1953), and Vildomec (1963). Each book is the unique product of a time and place. Epstein, writing in France in 1916, dealt with the relations between thought and language before the conceptual tools of modern psycholinguistics were available. His data were based on his personal observation of multilingual Europeans, on a review of the previous literature related to his topic, and on a questionnaire he sent to 10 scholars and 13 Swiss university students.[1] Weinreich, in contrast, wrote as an American structural linguist. He carefully separated sociological and psychological factors from his linguistic analyses of bilingualism. Weinreich's data were based on analysis of his personal observations in the United States and on his review of the literature, particularly that from the half-century since Epstein's book. Vildomec again represented a European approach. Like Epstein, he focused on multilingualism in the educated. His book *Multilingualism* comprised a review of the European literature of the century, a statement of his own observations as a language teacher in Great Britain and Germany, and an analysis of responses to a questionnaire given to friends. As opposed to Weinreich's book, the two European books relied perhaps too heavily on the self-evaluation of subjects who were not linguists. American structuralists have often taken such intuitive evidence to be suspect. The European works, especially that of Vildomec, included analysis of interference that was evidenced in the written mode, whereas Weinreich focused on interference occurring in speech.

All three studies are of value because they describe in detail patterns of interference. The assumptions on which the studies are based influence the author's selection and presentation of the material, how-

---

[1] It is important to note how many of the European studies deal with bilingualism in the educated elite rather than in uneducated bilinguals or polyglots. One wonders what effect this focus on the language of the educated may have had on linguistic analyses.

ever. Precisely because emphasis is on the topic of interference, discussion of points in which interference does not obtain is rare. (This is unfortunate, in our opinion. It would be valuable to go beyond descriptions of interference phenomena, where they do occur, and contrast those linguistic realms in which interference occurs with those in which the same speaker is not subject to interference.) A second underlying assumption is that there are two entirely different language systems which interfere with each other in various ways. The authors ignore the possibility that these two systems may share certain elements. Of course it must be kept in mind that the two linguistic "systems" that are postulated in these studies of bilinguals belong to the hypothetical realm of grammar. Linguists would hesitate to claim that they have a precise anatomical correlation. Another limitation to the linguistic perspective of these authors is that it is generally restricted to the study of speech production. The possibilities for interference in speech perception remained unexamined. Thus linguists seem to assume a priori that the two comprehension systems of the bilingual are separate and that a bilingual listener will never experience interference that would cause her to process the speech of one language differently from a monolingual listener of that language.

Epstein considered linguistic phenomena of interference at the phonological, lexical, and syntactical levels, but he employed psychological terminology to describe them. Interference between the languages was seen as a type of "antagonism"; difficulty in learning the accent of a new language resulted from phonological "inhibition" of the mother tongue. Syntactical interference was, for Epstein, interference in the rules pertaining to ideas.

Weinreich (1953) divided interference into three types: phonic, syntactic, and lexical. One example of interference at the phonic level is substitution of "equivalent phonemes." For example, the /r/ of one language might be substituted for the /r/ in another language. Weinreich considered such a substitution to be an instance of underdifferentiation of phonemes. An example of overdifferentiation would be an instance in which a single phoneme in a second language is produced by the speaker with various other allophones appropriate to the first language. Both these examples imply some form of compound language system in the bilingual. In the first case an actual item is borrowed into the second language; in the second case, the phonological rules for realizing an item are borrowed from one language and applied to the second. At the grammatical level, Weinreich discussed the transfer of morphemes. This occurs when inflectional or derivational morphemes are affixed to lexical items from another language. Similarly, function words can be translated, resulting in inappropriate usages (e.g., *How long are you here?*). Co-occurrence constraints on word category features that are not present in the better known language are sometimes ignored or difficult to learn in a new language. At the lexical level, words may be borrowed from one language into the other. Weinreich suggested that lexical borrowing may occur particularly where "structural weak points obtained in the recipient vocabulary." We note that even fluent bilinguals often report feeling inadequate in both their languages. This may result from their awareness that certain words or idioms in one language cannot be expressed as a single word in the second language.

In 1957, Weinreich wrote a modification of his 1953 analysis of phonological interference. This newer treatment of the topic adopted two positions that have only recently become widely accepted in linguistics: One is the distinction between perceptive and productive language systems; the second is the importance of considering free and not so free variation in constructing precise grammars. In this article, Weinreich suggested that the speaker's internal analysis of the second language may or may not result in producing audibly nonnative language. Nevertheless, if the speaker is basing his production of the form on a nonnative understanding of its deep structure, we must consider this nonnative perception as interference of the structure of L_1 on L_2. For example, the English word *hopscotch* contains two separate phonemes, /p/ and /s/ for the native speaker of English, that might be considered a single phoneme /ps/ by the speaker of Hebrew. It is a common phoneme in that language. The rules which govern permissible phoneme sequences and impossible phoneme sequences in one language will influence the expectations a speaker of that language has for phoneme sequencing in a second language. For example, the /ŋ/ which can occur initially in Indonesian should not be too difficult for English speakers to produce, as it does occur in English words like *singing*. The fact that /ŋ/ cannot occur in word-initial position in English, however, makes it difficult for the English speaker learning Indonesian to pronounce the sound in word-initial position.

The rules for realizing distinctive features in one language may influence their realization in a second language. For example, a feature that is distinctive in one language may be optional in another language. The speaker whose native language is the one in which the feature is in free variation (i.e., either of two alternate forms may occur) will have difficulty learning the rules which constrain the occurrence of the feature in the second language.

Vildomec (1963) discussed structural distance between the two languages of the bilingual, noting that if the languages are very similar, learning will be facilitated. Eventually, however, this similarity will lead to greater interference between the two languages. Thus cognate words might be expected to cause greater phonological problems for a bilingual speaker and to induce semantic confusion if they do not bear exactly the same meaning in both languages. Vildomec also discussed the influence of a foreign language on the mother tongue, noting that nouns, especially, are borrowed. In fact his discussion restricted itself to lexical borrowing, although he admitted the possibility that the borrowed item may be fitted into the morphology and phonology of the language into which it is borrowed. He made little mention of the potential influence on the mother tongue of frequent use of a second language. It is our observation, yet to be systematically verified, that phonological and syntactic patterns can be tangibly influenced by interference of a second language with the mother tongue. When this is the case and a language learned late in life interferes with the earliest language, we may conclude that for this particular language phenomenon the brain is operating a single-language system that is ever open to modification by new stimuli.

Vildomec went on to speak of interference in the foreign language, caused either by the mother tongue, especially with respect to sentence patterns and concepts, or by another foreign language. He suggested that influence of a second foreign language on a third comes about when the two languages are genetically close. In such cases, phonemes, bound morphemes, particles, and lexical items are likely to be similar. This similarity would cause interference in the most recently acquired language.

The studies cited in the preceding provide compendia and categorizations of instances of interference in bilingualism. Two further papers must be discussed for their theoretical contributions. Mackey (1965) dealt with the issues of analysis and measurement of bilingual interference. He defined instances of interference as "a divergence from the local standard as a result of the inclusion in the message of features from another code." The data collected from extended taping of 97 subjects in Acadia were subjected to analysis along the following parameters: proportion of units (sentences, clauses, etc.) in one language to those in the other, and rate of alternation. He further divided all interference into either **combinatory** (an interleaving of units) or **modificatory** (a superimposition of units). Interference by combination was seen to be a horizontal or surface mixing (if at least one of the immediate constituents of an item contained elements from the other language). For example,

1. SENTENCE LEVEL MIXING
   Çe n'est pas leur faute si leur père est runné out of business.
2. PHRASE LEVEL
   est runné
3. LEXICAL LEVEL
   /rə̣ne/   [ə] is English, [r] and [ṇ] are French.
4. PHONEMIC LEVEL
   a /t/, pronounced with English aspiration, but with dental articulation as in French.

Modificatory interference obtains when any linguistic unit contains some of the features characteristic of the other language. Thus, literal translation of idioms is an example of modificatory interference, as is extension borrowing of semantic field (e.g., *Père* for all the religious uses the word *Father* can connote in English). Structural modification may involve reordering elements in one language by the rules of the other, adding or deleting constituent elements (e.g., pronouncing *wire* as two syllables, deleting articles), reclassifying items as to grammatical class (gender, ± declension), applying phonological rules of L_1 to L_2 (e.g., assimilation of /–ps–/ by French speakers on English *observation*, whereas English speakers may mistakenly pronounce /–bz–/ in the French *observation*).

It is unclear why the pronunciation of /t/ with English aspiration and French dental articulation was considered an instance of combinatory interference. Were that case not given, one might abstract a definition of productive simultaneity, or overlap of patterns, for Mackey's modification instances, as distinguished from a linear mixing of elements in the combinatory interference. With this definition, his distinction might prove useful for correlating with compound and coordinate subjects, since one would expect those with single compound language systems to produce more modificatory interference, while coordinates might exhibit more linear interweaving.

Hasselmo (1969) discussed interference as a phenomenon to be distinguished from code switching. The former involves some overlapping of the two languages (at a given instant of time), while code switching means a linear interweaving of the two languages. (We refer to interference as a mixing problem in our section on aphasic speech and to inappropriateness or inflexibility of code switch as a switching problem.) Hasselmo stressed the fact that interference can occur at many linguistic levels, and in either production or perception. He pointed out that code switch regularly occurs at the boundaries of constituent units (words, phrases), rather than within them. He referred to a notion (personally communicated to him by M. Clyne) that code switch may be triggered when an item in the context of speech is ambiguous between the two languages. The existence of such ambiguity would provide support for some degree of compound lexical storage.

It is not unreasonable to evaluate a grammar in the light of what is known about the neural mechanisms that must form its substrate. We may thus expect that any neuropsychological model of bilingualism must justify the patterns of interference described in this section, and the related pattern of transfer discussed in second language learning studies. A model must account for the fact that interference occurs differently at different linguistic levels and that it may even affect various word classes differently. The fact that interference may be unidirectional between two languages or may be asymmetrical, influencing one language in one way and the other language in different ways, must also be explained. Individual differences in interference patterns and even in the sociological context in which they occur must be explainable within a model of bilingualism. The linguistic notion that a single competence for language may underlie the variable performance of the speaker might be expanded to account for the bilingual. Just as the monolingual's competence can master different registers of speech, so the bilingual may differentiate the two languages. Where differentiation proves inefficient, for whatever reason, interference may be expected.

Models of Second Language Acquisition

In order to draw conclusions about the neuropsychology of bilingualism, we may ask how the learning of a second language takes place. One might eventually want to determine neurological implications, whether L_2 is learned like L_1, or whether it is learned differently. Perhaps certain subsystems of a language will be learned more as they are in L_1, whereas others may be learned differently. Different patterns may obtain, depending on who the learners are, how old they are, and what psychological and neuropsychological characteristics they bring to the L_2 learning process. Various methodologies have been applied to study the question of how a second language is learned and what the characteristics are of persons learning a second language.

Dulay and Burt (1974a) analyzed errors in the speech of 179 Spanish–English speaking children and found that only 4.7% of the errors made by the children could be considered to be errors resulting from interference. The authors hypothesized that the errors that came about in the process of acquisition of the second language occurred simply because it was a language to be learned by a child. It was therefore treated by the child with the basic cognitive strategies for language learning that a native learner would use. Indeed, 87.1% of the second language errors made by these children were like the morphological errors made by monolingual learners of the language. On the basis of this finding, Dulay and Burt (1974b) predicted that the order of acquisition of the different function markings in English would be parallel for all groups of child learners, whether they were learning English as a first or second language. Their study of 55 Chinese and 60 Spanish learners of English aged 6–8 confirmed this hypothesis.

Bailey, Madden, and Krashen (1974) carried out a parallel study on adult learners with similar results. That is, the order of acquisition of morphemes in the second language paralleled that of children learning their first language. It therefore appears likely that language-specific structures do have some influence on the learning of a language, no matter what the previous linguistic knowledge of the learner is. We should note, however, that these studies restricted themselves to acquisition of morphological rules, and that no claims were made against the possible occurrence of phonological or semantic types of interference, as Cancino, Rosansky, and Schumann (1974) point out. Furthermore, the measure of acquisition in these studies was that of consistently producing morphs in obligatory contexts. No measure was made of ability to comprehend or process them.

In a subsequent study, Dulay and Burt (1974c) tested the hypothesis that the complexity of elements of the second language determines the relative difficulty of learning these elements. They discovered that neither measure of complexity employed (semantic or derivational) could account for the hierarchy of acquisition of morphemes. They concluded that complexity by linguists' measures probably has nothing to do with complexity for the learner and that an analysis of learners' strategies must take into account the mechanisms of perception of the second language.

In fact, models of interference could be expanded to account for perceptual interference, but they rarely are. Perceptual interference would involve difficulties in distinguishing distinctive elements and processing them for meaning, difficulties which have come about because processing procedures were used in L_1 that were not appropriate to L_2.

Kessler (1972) did deal with comprehension of syntactic and morphological elements, and proposed a diachronic interference effect to account for differential comprehension abilities. She tested 12 Italian–English children aged 6–8 by asking the children to point to the picture (out of three) that best represented the spoken stimulus. For example, the child might be asked to point to the picture described by the English sentence *The boy has been hit by the ball*, and also to point to the picture described by the sentence, *The ball has been hit by the boy*. Although the subject's command of the two languages was equal overall, more errors were seen with Italian pronouns and possessive adjectives than with English, and more errors were seen with English reflexive and reciprocal structures than with Italian. These difficulties in English were probably due to the additional complexity of the English forms, since two different structures in English correspond to a single structure in Italian (*The girls see themselves* and *The girls see each other* are expressed by *Le regazze si vedono*). Kessler concluded that those structures that are shared by the two languages are acquired in the same order in each language. She suggested that structures are acquired in the same order because they are of equal transformational difficulty. One might infer from Kessler's study that the two languages are being learned independently by these simultaneous learners and it is only because shared syntactic rules are of equal difficulty in the two languages that they are mastered in the same relative order.

Kessler's work complemented that of Jakobovits (1968b, 1969). He assumed that there must be "transfer" from an earlier learned language to a later one. His notion of transfer implies that previously learned structures facilitate or inhibit later learned structures. His theory then is a theory of learning strategies, which are not necessarily controllable on the part of the learner. Tremaine (1975) might well have incorporated this notion in her theory of speech perception in second language acquisition. She proposed a two-stage learning system (more likely a continuum) in which the beginning learner processes cues such as word order and emphasis and takes context greatly into account in understanding any individual item. By her model, the learner's strategy amounts essentially to intelligent guessing (a process native speakers must use under some noise conditions). The intelligence behind the guessing still comes from prior linguistic knowledge; the speaker has learned that word order or emphasis are significant in language processing and that one can disambiguate by taking context into account. In any case, her theory of slowly refining strategies in language comprehension explains why passive knowledge of the language precedes active proficiency.

A model of bilingual speech production that takes into account both language-inherent structures and learner's strategies is Selinker's (1972a) theory of interlanguage. He proposed that the learner abstracts rules for L_2 as well as she can (and probably on the basis of previous language experience) and then creates a new system which falls between the previous language and the new target language. Over the course of study, this new interlanguage may progressively approach the L_2. Some stages, however, become fossilized and are then characteristic of the idiolectal interlanguage of the nonnative speaker.

The studies discussed so far as based on the assumption that learners of a second language share certain dynamics. In addition to analyzing errors in acquisition of the second language, it is also important for researchers in bilingualism to study the developmental process of learning the correct structures. Two basic types of interference are suggested by these studies: One is the synchronic, unchanging type of interference. Synchronic interference will include the accent that remains with a speaker, or idiolectal syntactic uses influenced by the L_1. The second, but earlier, type of interference is dynamic interference which comes about in progressive approximation of a second language.

Another assumption would be that different people learn their second language differently. Hartnett (1974), cited in Krashen (1975) and in Diller (1975), conducted a study which spoke to the relative merits of teaching a language "inductively" (by presenting structures to students by way of conversation drill and letting them draw their own conclusions) as opposed to teaching it "deductively" (by presenting a rule and then drilling students to illustrate the rule).

Hartnett selected 29 students who were at the top of their classes. All subjects were native English speakers who were in Spanish classes taught by two different methods. Thirteen students had succeeded with what the author called the inductive method (conversational) and 16 were selected from the class that had been taught by a method which the author called deductive (the more "traditional" method). Hartnett hypothesized that learning style would be related to the cerebral hemisphere used for learning. Someone who was using more left-hemisphere approaches would have a more analytic style of language learning, while someone who was using more right-hemisphere approaches would have a more synthetic style. A simple test was employed to determine for each subject which hemisphere was the one that dealt with verbal cognition. In this test, subjects were posed with problems like "How many letters are in the word Mississippi?" A note was made of the direction subjects' eyes drifted while they were thinking of the problem. On the basis of Kinsbourne's (1974) work relating direction of eye movement to hemispheric activity, subjects whose eyes consistently drifted to the right were considered to have a "left-hemisphere," or analytic style of language acquisition. Subjects whose eyes drifted to the left were considered to have a "right-hemisphere" or synthetic style. Much more right than left movement was seen in students who had been successful with what Hartnett called the "deductive" method, in which drills were given, and students were expected to deduce the appropriate grammatical rules. Among the students who had succeeded under Hartnett's "inductive" method, there were equal numbers of consistently right, and consistently left movers. It would appear that anyone may succeed in learning a second language when rules are presented and then drilled, whereas left movers are unlikely to succeed when expected to abstract rules from drills and conversation. People who are strongly left lateralized for language should do better in a class that is taught "deductively." They may actually prefer to be given a number of items that exemplify a rule and then discover the rule themselves.

Sodhi (1969) considered the question of language "set." Comparison was made between successful and unsuccessful learners of French at the college level. One hundred sixty subjects were labeled "good" or "bad" learners on the basis of reading and listening comprehension tests. The two groups were then compared with respect to the number of trials necessary to fixate a "set" (after Uznadze's, 1966, definition of set fixation), and no significant difference was found, although good language learners, surprisingly, averaged slightly more trials before their set was fixated. On the test of set extinction, however, a test of the facility in shifting from one language to another, the good learners were significantly better than the poor learners. They needed fewer trials in order to get into the new set. These data may bear relevance to a model of bilingual language switching; perhaps the ability to switch set effectively is entailed in appropriately switching between languages.

The studies we have reviewed here leave unresolved the question of whether learning a second language in adulthood follows any, some, or all of the same patterns as learning it (or for that matter, a first language) in childhood. Even within the period of childhood, it may be important to distinguish instances of simultaneous learning of two languages from instances in which one is learned from the beginning and the second is learned later. Although we predict that all children who learn a second language in childhood will eventually be fluent in it, the stages of acquisition and the sources of interference which occur in the process of acquisition may differ depending on the age of second language learning. Much work remains to be done on the factors influencing individual differences in style and success of second language learning at any age.

Studies of Childhood Bilingualism

In this section we treat several modes of approach in studying childhood bilingualism. A number of linguist–parents persevered in documenting the development of bilingual language in their children. This research provides us with invaluable case studies. Other researchers (e.g., Kessler, 1972) tested groups of bilingual children in order to compare their linguistic attainments in each language. There has been a long pedagogical debate about whether bilingualism retards a child's development, enhances it, or has no effect on it. The case studies we present speak to this issue, as do preliminary findings of Trites and Price (1976), whose study was based on a multifaceted evaluation of a wide-scale second language immersion program. With childhood bilingualism we may also consider the questions of when and how the child develops awareness that he is dealing with two distinct language systems. We would then go on to ask what the linguistic repercussions of this awareness would be, and whether various linguistic systems are differentially affected.

The monumental work in this field is Leopold's four-volume *Speech Development of a Bilingual Child* (1939–1949). None of the works that preceded it (Ronjat, 1913; Velten, 1943) obtained the linguistic sophistication or the systematization of this work. It contains a detailed analysis of the first 2 years of speech of the author's first daughter, Hildegard, studied from the phonetic, phonological, lexical, and morphological points of view, with notes on the points of difference in the development of the language of his second daughter, Karla. The final volume is a looser follow-up in the form of a diary, extending through Hildegard's sixteenth year and Karla's tenth. Both girls were brought up for the most part in the United States where only their father intentionally and regularly spoke German with them. It is important to note that there were speech differences between the two children that were apparently not predictable simply on the basis of the fact that the second daughter was exposed to slightly less German. Also of interest is the fact that nonlinguistic development of both daughters took place at the normal rate.

While Leopold's research is of value for the general study of language development, we will refer here to those aspects that pertain to the development of the bilingual systems. For Leopold the first 2 years of language development showed a single-system strategy; there was no separation maintained between the two languages. Thus Hildegard is described as having a single phonological system (containing two /l/s, one the German of *Ball*, the other the English of *ball*) and a single, mixed, lexicon, for both function and content words, with occasional combined use of cross-language synonyms (*please–bitte*). The only likely instance of true interference was in the morphological system; the German infinitive regularly lacked its suffix. All other features of the child's speech could be attributed to the monolingual development of child language. Hildegard displayed no instances of morphological blending like her sister's *byewiedersehen*.

Only after the beginning of the third year did some concept of the existence of two different languages show itself; Hildegard would turn to her father asking the name of an object, and then to her mother. At around this time, English began to predominate in her lexicon, with German serving mostly for nouns and a few verbs. Her passive understanding of German, however was as good as that of English; indeed, throughout the rest of the history, whatever language may have been the predominant one in production, the two languages were equally well comprehended.

At the beginning of the fourth year, her father instituted his policy of encouraging Hildegard to speak only German with him. He noticed that she often chose German cognates of English words, and had lost a previously good /x/ sound. She remained quite willing to speak German, nevertheless, until puberty. At this earlier period she spoke with some hesitation, and made some obvious transferences from English (*candle* for *Kandl*) and confused translations between the two languages (the response to *ich glaube* was *he glaubs*, then *he thinks*? It should have been *he thinks so*). A few German words were used when she was with English-speaking friends with no awareness on Hildegard's part that they were inappropriate. While we get the impression that her English improved constantly, her German improved in fits and starts. The fact that it always ended up equally proficient to the English at these early stages might suggest a steady cognitive development on which language could be overlaid, or some transference of development in English to that in German.

When Hildegard was 5 the family made a half-year trip to Germany. Left in an entirely German-speaking environment for a month, Hildegard quickly progressed from brief sentences to a reasonable fluency, and could discuss remembered American situations in German. Her parents returned to her to find that Hildegard would speak only German, even with her native English-speaking mother. At this point she might embed English nouns in sentences with German function words, and she used the German /l/ in English. Nevertheless some English influence remained in her German throughout the half-year she spent in Germany. This influence exhibited itself in subordinate clause word order, diphthongs for the long vowels, and *haben* for *sein* as a past marker. Returning to the United States at the end of the half-year period, Hildegard again evidenced 2 to 3 weeks of relative taciturnity, some hesitation when speaking English, and idiomatic translation influence. After 2 months her German became halting, as her English improved, although in any long session with her father, it regained some fluency.

By age 6 she was more comfortable in both languages, and associated German clearly with her father. After learning arithmetic patterns in school, in English, she was found by her father vocalizing them in German. By age 7 her German began to deteriorate phonetically, and she lost her facility in finding words, although when pressed to search, she could find them after some time. She became more unwilling to speak German, but had in no way lost passive comprehension, even by her sixteenth year.

From Hildegard's case we see clearly the division between her comprehension ability, which appeared to develop smoothly in both languages, and her fluctuating production ability. Her case also raises the possibility of positive, or facilitative, interference. Since her progress in English was to some extent transferable to German, we might postulate a facilitative factor in developmental bilingualism, whereby progress in learning one language necessarily advances the learning of the other language.

The case of Burling's son Stephen (1959) is of interest because his language immersion from age 1:4 to 3:4 was in Garo, a language more distant, both historically and structurally, from English than is German. Garo relies heavily on morphological affixation rather than word order to express syntactic relationships, and Stephen's development reflected this structural difference; he had mastered the niceties of Garo morphological substitution patterns when his English still consisted of unbreakable phrases. Unfortunately it is unclear from the report how much English Stephen was exposed to, although it would appear that his mother was the main source of English and we know that she was absent for some months during the first year of the trip. His father frequently spoke Garo to Stephen and the environment they were in permitted mixing of the two languages by the adults.

Stephen would often fit English words into Garo morphological patterns. Later, when his progress in English "exploded," he would incorporate Garo words into English syntax, but his father claimed it was always clear whether the underlying sentence framework was Garo or English. Burling noted some parallels of "semantic" development: Stephen first used the word for *swallow* in both languages on the same day and he first began applying learned color words correctly in both languages at the same time. Burling took Stephen's rapid expansion of English after a few months' association with his mother as another sign of parallel development.

The child's awareness of the fact that he controlled two languages might be seen in his early insistence on speaking English with his father. In his third year, he would intentionally use translation synonyms redundantly together (as with Hildegard's *bitte–please*). When his father did not understand the son's poor English, Stephen condescended to translate from English to Garo. However, if asked a question in English, he might answer unhesitatingly in Garo. Thus, his preference for production at this time was Garo, but he had not altogether differentiated the two languages. Six months after having left the Garo-speaking environment, by then age 3:10, Stephen was having trouble with producing the simplest Garo words. It is not stated in the report to how great an extent his comprehension of Garo had been lost.

Kinzel (1964) documented and categorized bilingual interference in the speech of his 6-year-old daughter, Anne. Most important in her history was the fact that she had no exposure to mixed speech, since her parents had always spoken French to each other and to her at home, whereas English had been the environmental language for the most part. Both parents understood English, and the child was not pressured to speak French with her parents. During the period of the study it was noted that when she spoke with the parents there was no obvious factor predicting Anne's language of response, except topic of discussion. Her utterances in both languages were analyzed.

Although her primary place of residence was the United States, prior to the period under question she had made short trips to France. At the beginning of each of these trips she would inappropriately speak English, and complain of difficulties in understanding French, but upon return to the United States her French seemed as fluent as that of a French child. Then her English might be halting for a while but would soon recover fluency, and what lexical and syntactic interference was reported in her seventh-year French must be viewed as deterioration of her French. By her eighth year, with only one short additional trip to France, Anne's French had stabilized and was without interference, except that it was less fluent than her English (cf. Leopold's daughter, whose German deteriorated from this age). Phonological interference did occur in her Spanish and it was from French rather than English.

It must be noted that the child's verbal performance in school was at least normal, and that she had a positive attitude to bilingualism in general and to the specific French–American biculturalism of her case. She was given instruction in Spanish from age 7:6 and displayed no strategies different from those of a monolingual child, except perhaps a greater willingness to name familiar objects in new words.

During her seventh year note was made by Anne's parents of all examples of French–English interference. No phonological and little morphological interferences were evidenced, only lexical and syntactic interferences. It is unclear whether this discrepancy came about because phonology and morphology are simpler systems (in terms of clear-cut contrast between the two languages, or limited elements per system), or whether they are somehow more basic to language, or whether they are simply mastered earlier for developmental–cognitive reasons. Only a very few instances of code switch, that is, of language mixing within sentences, were evidenced (e.g., *On va use these cups?*), and apparently Anne permitted herself such mixing only in bilingual company.

But lexical interference was evidenced in both languages and could occur in instances in which the correct item was clearly known by the child. Such interference was of two sorts: outright borrowings (e.g., *we're droles*) and semantic extensions (e.g., *quel nombre?* for what number, instead of *quel numéro?*). In the case of word borrowing, 26 instances were reported of English into French, and 23 of French into English. A further 10 French items were borrowed and adapted to English morphology (e.g., *I am not rouspete + ing*). The converse, English items with French morphology, did not obtain. The most commonly borrowed morpheme was the participle ending -*ing*, but cases of plural /z/, third-person present verb inflection /z/, and the causal /en/ (to have the sleeves *longue* + /nd/) did obtain. Examples were given of nouns, verbs, adjectives, adverbs, borrowed from each language, and of prepositions borrowed from English. When English nouns were borrowed, they invariably became masculine in French.

Anne's semantic extensions involved interference of grammatical features. A noun like *poisson* could take on the noun–verb character of the English *fish*. Verbs could switch from transitive to intransitive in

French when their translation equivalents in English could (*Elle regarde mieux maintenant*, 'She looks better now'). Phonological closeness could give greater motivation for the borrowing (e.g., *Elle juste vient d'arriver*, 'She just arrived', or, *Doris can eat the restovers*, '*les restes*'). More examples were seen of extension errors in French than in English. Seven cases of English inanimate nouns being referred to as *she* were recorded however (e.g., *I got her* [the napkin]).

Anne would sometimes translate English prepositions which co-occur with English verbs, and add them incorrectly to the corresponding French verb, for example, *Je cherche pour le livre*, 'I'm looking for the book' (cf. Kinzel's correct French: *Je cherche le livre*). Translation of the English article, or lack of it, was sometimes mistakenly made into French (*C'était été*, 'It was summer', cf. correct: *C'était l'été*). In English there were fewer such errors, and they involved different categories. For example, two errors involved adverbs (e.g., *since one year*, 'for a year') and two involved the genitive construction (*three balls of tennis*, cf. French, *balles de tennis*).

Clear-cut cases of borrowing word order patterns occurred from English to French. The 25 instances could be seen as lack of control over several major rules: Five involved splitting of the causative *faire* + infinitive (e.g., *tu fais ce pistolet marcher*, 'you are making that pistol shoot', cf. correct French: *Tu fais marcher ce pistolet*). Six instances involved misplacement of an adverb, and all were intensity adverbs (*vraiment, mieux,* etc.) (*J'aime ça mieux*, 'I like that better'). Five instances were expression of the indirect object by means of a preposition instead of by word order (*J'attends pour toi*). In English such cases as: *You suggested me yesterday*, '*Tu m'as suggéré cela hier*' indicated that, for Anne, indirect object formation permitted free variation of the rules of both languages. Finally, a number of examples of application of the English rule that employs added stress for emphasis were recorded, where French would use additional morphemes (e.g., *C'est **sa** main*, 'It's **his** hand', cf. correct French: *C'est sa main à lui*).

Noun–adjective order, which is regularly opposite in French and in English, was at times incorrect, but French noun–adjective agreement never was. This is another instance of the apparent selective nature of the compounding system, as evidenced by interference in Anne's speech. Some rules had been carefully sorted out by age 6—especially those involving phonological and morphological production. Other language-specific constraints, especially ones relating to lexical and syntactic features, were not yet differentiated for the two languages.

Hakuta (1974) analyzed the speech of a 5-year-old Japanese girl who was brought to America. Here she entered kindergarten although she continued to speak Japanese at home. The author concentrated on order of acquisition of morphemes in the child, and discovered that in many respects this order did not parallel that seen in native learners of English (contrary to the findings of Dulay & Burt, 1974b). For example, in the case of this girl, the plural rule for nouns was acquired after the possessive rule. Even though the two rules are essentially the same, (/əz/ after sibilants, /z/ after other voiced consonants, /s/ elsewhere), other studies of English monolingual children show the plural rule to be mastered before the possessive rule. Hakuta proposed that his subject's learning the rules in inverse order may have been due to the fact that the notion of plurality is not formally expressed in Japanese. A related phenomenon was seen in the fact that the child mastered use of the copula *be* relatively early compared to monolingual English children, but even after about a year did not use the plural form *are* (except in a frozen phrase, after *these*). The regular past marker (/əd/ after /t/ or /d/, /d/ after voiced consonants, /t/ elsewhere), as well as the irregular past forms, were learned relatively late in her acquisition sequence. Hakuta suggested that this delay may have been due to the Japanese phonological constraint against stops occurring in word-final position (all forms of the regular English past tense require a final stop).

In the preceding instances, an item (phonological or conceptual) not existing in Japanese was late to be mastered in English. A contrary example was the child's apparent overuse of *in*, often in place of other prepositions (especially *on* and *at*), and also perhaps more frequently than normal for native speakers in optional positions. Hakuta pointed out that Japanese requires a single postposed syllable, *ni*, for many of these instances. Thus we can assume semantic category interference by overextension from Japanese. This semantic interference was perhaps reinforced by the shared phonetic elements.

Major (1977) detailed the process of phonological differentiation in his bilingual daughter, up to age 2:8. Sylvia was born in Brazil and addressed in Portuguese by her Brazilian mother and American father until the age of 1:2. During that first year, however, Sylvia heard some English because her parents spoke that language with each other. When the family moved to the United States at age 1:2, her father began to address her in English. At 2:1 she began to attend an English-language day-care center, and by 2:8 she was speaking more English and less Portuguese.

From 1:9 to 2:1, Sylvia began to use utterances of more than one word. In these utterances, Sylvia freely mixed words from both languages. She would answer questions in the same language in which they were asked, however. At this early age, she began to differentiate between Portuguese and English at the phonetic level. For example, in English diphthongs developed, whereas in Portuguese they could be pronounced alternately as monophthongs and diphthongs. After the age of 2:1, utterance length was three or more words, and Sylvia was no longer mixing words from the two languages. The "same" phonemes in each language became more differentiated. This phonological differentiation was particularly obvious for voiceless stops, liquids, and vowels. Between 2:1 and 2:3, Sylvia gradually mastered the rule which aspirates voiceless stops where they should be aspirated in English, and she avoided altogether aspiration of these stops in Portuguese. After age 2:3, Major described what he now called "borrowings" from one language to the other. The items that were borrowed were ones that Sylvia had only experienced in one language, e.g., *bala*, (ball) (p. 11). Major pointed out that Sylvia pronounced this particular Spanish word differently (by making a diphthong of the first vowel) when it was in an English sentence context. He suggested that a certain supersegmental articulatory "posture" was associated with speaking each language, and that the child mastered the different postures in the third year.

The study of Collins-Ahlgren (1974) provides an interesting confirmation of the assimilation of a later-learned language to earlier structure in the young child. A deaf girl born of English-speaking deaf parents first learned manual–visual sign language, a system in which a single motion carries the weight of a full semantic unit equivalent to a word. She was then introduced to manual English signs, a closer translation of oral English, which includes such function items as articles, auxiliaries, and inflections. In a transitory stage these functions signals were optional for her. Furthermore, as many adult deaf speakers do, she would superimpose speech on her signs, especially when speech provided greater specification; and she would manipulate fingerspelling (the alphabet of which was learned by age 2:2) productively (e.g., she might turn *fun* sign into *funny* by adding a sign for the letter Y). It would appear that the mixing of the three systems was still going on at age 5.

A study of childhood bilingualism was conducted by Rosenbaum and Obler (unpublished data) on three American families who had moved to Israel. All three families had been in the country at least 4 years, and their 12 children ranged in age from 2 to 12. While English was spoken at home, the children attended school or day-care kindergartens in Hebrew. Preliminary analyses of samples of spontaneous speech stimulated by pictures revealed no phonological interference. The younger children, however, evidenced more unmarked lexical borrowing errors, whereas the older children managed to avoid these, or at least to mark them with pauses. The older children, however, would make more unconscious idiom translation and syntactic interference errors. Thus it is clear that even within childhood, later learning of a second language is more likely to induce syntactic transfer errors. We cannot claim that phonological errors do not obtain, only that they may be mastered earlier than lexical and syntactic errors.

No morphological errors were evident in the spontaneous speech of the children (perhaps a sign that they were aware enough of what they knew and what they did not know to avoid circumstances that would produce errors, because what they knew was that which is most frequently used). On a nonsense test patterned after the Berko (1958) test, however, more severe problems were seen on the part of all the children in Hebrew than in English. Although none of the children had formal training in Hebrew, the older children had a better grasp of the correct patterns permissible in Hebrew, while the younger children had apparently abstracted mistaken forms not unlike those that native child learners of Hebrew might mistakenly use.

As mentioned, Kessler (1972) tested the level of morphosyntactic development for comprehension in 12 Italian–English bilingual children aged 6–8. In reviewing her results, one must bear in mind that her final criterion for fluent bilingualism in selection of the subjects was a test of repetition of grammatical and ungrammatical sentences in each language. Taped sentences were played to the children, who were asked to match them either to pictures (in the case of inflectional endings or syntactic constructions like passive, possessive) or to synonymous sentences (in cross-language or same-language conditions).

Statistical analyses of the data indicated that structures that were shared in both languages were mastered in the same order and at the same rate by the bilingual children, less complex structures (on a case grammar measure) being acquired first. The hardest task for these children was identifying synonymous structures when syntactic form varied. This was true both within and across languages. The children were more likely to label as synonymous *The truck pushes the car* and *Il camion spinge la macchina* than they were to label either sentence as synonomous with *The car is pushed by the truck* or *La macchina e spinta dal camion*. If this difference could not be explained as an artifact of the difficulty of the test, it implied a level of shared structure at a syntactic level.

Tremaine (1975) extended Kessler's methods to test syntactic comprehension in French–English bilingual children aged 6–10. The major hypothesis tested was that stabilization of syntax comprehension for the more complex syntactic rules in a language would correlate with achievement of the Piagetian stage of concrete operational reasoning. Also studied was the effect of study of French on level of comprehension of English syntactic structures. Tremaine's 60 subjects were children for whom English was the dominant language; half were in a French immersion program; the other half studied French 75 min a day.

In this study, as in that of Kessler, the rate and order of acquisition of shared syntactic structures was seen to be approximately parallel. Three out of five of the tests of having passed into the stage of concrete operations correlated highly with the mastery of syntax in both English and French. (The most highly correlated task was the test of numeration, of figuring out the number of steps a man would have to climb from a given position to reach the top of the staircase. Mass and weight conservation problems also correlated; volume and seriation did not.) The children with intensive study of French performed better on the English syntax subtest. This result may be attributed a sampling distortion, since parents chose one or the other course for their children, or to a higher degree of linguistic–cognitive stimulation engendered in the intensive bilingual situation.

Bain (1976) tested response to command in 48 infants between 22 and 24 months of age, at which age, he reported, a clear-cut distinction of language by addressee first manifests itself in bilingual children whose parents speak only one or the other language to them. He divided the subjects into three groups by means of a task of taking messages from one parent to the other in another room. The 15 subjects of Group A were bilinguals (French–Alsatian) whose parents each regularly addressed the child in a different language. He called this the one-person–one-language condition. The 17 subjects of Group B were bilinguals whose parents used both languages interchangeably. Group C consisted of 16 monolinguals. The mother was instructed to carry out the task of telling the child the location of a marble hidden secretly (and randomly across 100 trials) under one of two opaque containers.

Several conditions of repeating the instructions to the child, and of delaying their response by distracting them for 10 sec, were tried. In all cases the bilingual group from the one-person–one-language families outperformed the other two groups which were quite similar. This group, Group A, totalled 69.7% correct responses, whereas the other bilinguals totalled 55.0%, and the monolinguals 55.7%. Since the results could not be proven significant, Bain admitted that these results constituted only suggestive support of the hypothesis that bilinguals from a one-person–one-language (i.e., coordinate) environment have accelerated cognitive development over the other two groups, and noted that the bilinguals exposed to mixed language environment are no worse off than monolinguals.

Two other articles of Bain (1975a,b) concluded that balanced bilingual children display more cognitive flexibility than do monolinguals. In one (1975b) he divided 40 French–English bilinguals into balanced bilinguals and monolinguals on the basis of home history, teacher and experimenter judgment of fluency, and vocabulary tests. Additionally, 20 subjects were classified as preoperational by Piagetian standard (these subjects averaged age 7), whereas 20 were seen to operate at a level of concrete operations (average age around 11). Within the two age levels, bilingual and monolingual subjects were matched for IQ, socioeconomic level, and school grades. The task was to abstract mathematical patterns (e.g., 1,3,7,15,31, _____) and to carry over the rules learned for such tasks in the first session to the second session 2 days later.

Only in the younger group was there a significant difference between bilinguals and monolinguals in the time necessary to abstract the rules (26.25 min for the bilinguals, 37.35 min for the monolinguals). This trend, however, held for the older group as well. It is interesting to note that in the second session bilinguals and monolinguals took equal amounts of time, at both age (or maturational) levels, so the difference seen was in **grasping** the rules and not in generalizing or transferring them. Bain concluded that "different language experiences give different direction and meaning to cognitive development."

Trites and Price (1976) ran a battery of neuropsychological tests and language tests on 32 children who had diffculty in a French immersion program. These children were native speakers of English who were receiving all instruction, including reading instruction, in French, for kindergarten and first grade. The authors tested 224 matched controls as well, in groups that differed along language and nonlanguage lines. These groups included hyperactive children, dyslexic children, functionally maladjusted children, and children with minimal brain dysfunction. They found that positive parental attitudes correlated with children's success in the immersion program, and that hyperactive children might succeed in the program. The test which best differentiated the unsuccessful children from the other groups (except the minimally brain damaged and the anglophones in exclusively francophone schools) was a test of tactile performance. On the tests of verbal and performance IQ, however, these children performed better than the controls. Included were tests of psychomotor problem solving, memory, and spatial location. The authors suggested that this specific disability on tactual performance could point to a maturational lag in the temporal lobes of children who experienced difficulty in the immersion program. They implied that this temporal lobe immaturity was related to the difficulty of the children in the French immersion program. It must be noted that these data are considered preliminary, and are presently in the process of being validated. It seems to us an extreme claim for the authors to derive temporal lobe maturation lag from the three tests listed. Nevertheless, it remains of interest to note that high IQ is not a predictor of success in a second language immersion program.

These studies of acquisition of language in bilingual children suggest that any child sets out to acquire a unified language system. Although by age 3, the child may have a sense that two different languages are in the environment, some mixing will continue for several years. It would seem that separate productive phonological and morphological systems are mastered first, and lexical and syntactic patterns are sorted out later. This approach, which treats the two languages as a unified system, is also revealed in the "leaps" reported for Hildegard and Stephen, where with a little exposure one language quickly reached the level of the other. Kessler (1971) and Tremaine (1973) demonstrated that a unified syntactic system develops in parallel, for both languages, insofar as possible. When they move from one language environment to another, children appear to have a great facility in attaining previous levels of the new language, and in losing the old one. This holds true especially for production skills, but may also hold true for comprehension (e.g., Stephen's Garo, in Burling, 1959).

It is important to note that contrary to the claims of some pedagogues, the children in all the cases cited here were completely normal in nonlinguistic development. In the Trites and Price (1976) study, it appeared that children who had difficulties in a French immersion program actually had higher IQs than those who succeeded.

Perceptual Judgments and Phonological Production

The psycholinguistic studies in this section focus on phonological aspects of bilingualism, those aspects that deal with sound segments and their permissible combinations. Since it is currently taught that the monolingual systematizes the acoustic (or articulatory) universe into discrete units (phonemes), we may ask how the bilingual deals with two such systems. The monolingual, in addition, internalizes a set of co-occurrence rules that govern phoneme sequencing in a given language. How does the bilingual deal with two potentially contradictory sets of such rules? Do different patterns arise in different individuals depending on the order of language acquisition? Can learning a second language affect perception or production skills in the first language? Clearly the interdependence versus independence paradigm will be relevant to these studies.

Anisfeld, Anisfeld, and Semogas (1969) tested the phonological intuitions of 24 Lithuanian–English bilinguals who had lived an average of 14 years in Montreal. An older group was Lithuanian dominant, whereas a younger group was highly proficient in both languages. Subjects were asked to judge the acceptability of consonant-initial sequences in either language. Four groups of CCə syllables were taped and presented sequences which occur in one or the other language or in both, and sequences which cannot occur in either. On a scale of 1 to 5, subjects rated the acceptability of calling a new product by a name beginning with the cluster in question. After this, subjects were asked whether or not words in the language actually began with the cluster. A good deal of interference was evidenced; the subjects' judgments did not dovetail with those of the phoneticians who prepared the stimuli. That is, all subjects found sequences that are in fact permissible in English to be more acceptable in both languages than sequences that are not acceptable in English. Thus all subjects evidenced the influence of English on their intuitions about Lithuanian. The older subjects also showed the opposite effect of Lithuanian on English judgments. Comparison with English monolinguals showed that even the younger group had interference with their English due to their bilingualism.

Another test with similar stimulus categories was performed by Cohen, Tucker, and Lambert (1967) on French–English bilinguals. Here the response required was repetition of the CCə syllables, and the results were recorded and transcribed by phoneticians. Error analysis showed that sequences not occurring in either language were likely to be mistaken for sequences in their own language by both English and French monolinguals. Thus an English speaker might simplify /#ps/ to /#s/. Bilinguals likewise changed sequences according to constraints in either of their two languages; unfortunately no figures on the direction or type of change were given to compare the more balanced bilinguals with those who were dominant in one or the other language.

A further interesting result was the error rate for repetition, which was significantly less under all four stimulus conditions for the English monolinguals and for the balanced bilinguals than for the monolingual French speakers or for either of the dominant groups. Academic level had been balanced for all subjects. Can we conclude that being a balanced bilingual sharpens one's receptive and/or productive capacities? Since the error rate was highest for French monolinguals (except for sequences obtaining only in French, and even in this case the errors were not significantly fewer than those of English monolingual speakers) we must assume either some test artifact, or perhaps some language-specific effect, related to the relative frequency or predictability of CCə syllables in the respective languages. Such an explanation would also account for French-dominant bilinguals making so many more errors than members of the other two bilingual groups. It remains difficult to explain why English monolinguals performed better than balanced bilinguals on all four test conditions. It is hard to imagine that the perception of the balanced bilinguals was somehow "tainted" by their knowledge of French.

Anisfeld and Gordon (1971) described judgment in highly dominant bilinguals; their subjects were English speakers who had one course in German. They asked their 13 subjects and 28 controls (who did not study German) to judge 48 nonsense words on a scale from "perfectly acceptable" as an English word to "impossible" as an English word. The nonsense words were chosen with respect to their phonological properties; they were either possible in both English and German, (e.g., /plor/), impossible in both languages (e.g., /fmit/), or possible in one but not the other (e.g., /skurn/ and /šlenit/). As a check of perceptual accuracy, subjects were asked to write what they had heard in Latin orthography on the second presentation of stimuli.

The experimental group, subjects who had studied German for one term, performed better than the control group in perception (as measured by writing) of those words acceptable in both English and German languages. Anisfeld and Gordon claimed that this result indicates that exposure to German sounds improves their perceptibility. Were that the case, however, greater accuracy should have been found with those words acceptable in German but not in English. Why should one course in German improve perceptibility of nonsense words sounding like English words? It seems unlikely that learning German per se aided the experimental group. Perhaps their recent learning of a new language helped them focus on perceiving phoneme sequences, or perhaps precisely those students with such perceptual skills elect to study a new language in college.

In the acceptability-judgment tasks the German learners again outperformed the controls only on those sequences acceptable in both English and German. This means they correctly labeled as potential English words nonsense words that could be phonologically acceptable in either English or German more often than did the control group. The authors interpreted this finding as lending support to the hypothesis that limited experience with a foreign language can affect the student's native language, or, more precisely, her judgments about the potentials of her native language.

Scholes (1968) tested categorical perception of synthetic vowel sounds in six nonnative speakers of English (one Russian, one Greek, one Persian, and three Korean). Subjects were presented with individual taped vowel sounds in an array which ranged in first formant frequency from 250 to 850 Hz, and in second formant frequency from 800 to 2600 Hz. In the first session the subjects were asked to categorize the sounds by associating each one with a word of the native language (if there were one) that has a similar sound, or else by indicating that there was no similar sound in the native language. In the second session, the words and sound judgments were given with respect to English.

Because the linguistic background of the subjects was so diverse, and because of the small number of subjects, no statistical correlations were attempted. The results, nevertheless, were consistent with the hypothesis that the cluster-distribution of allophones into phonemes in the native language influences assignment of allophones into phonemes in the second language.

Native speakers of English divide the matrix into:

i   u

ɪ

e ɛ   ʊ

o

æ

a

The Russian speaker heard this:

i   ɨ u

o

e

ɛ

a

for his native language, and the following pattern in English:

i   u

e   o

a

It is clear that his native /i/ corresponded to English /u/, while the native distinction between /e/ and /ɪ/ was not important to his English (even though the /ɪ/ occurred in the same position on his Russian matrix and the Americans' English one).

The Greek pattern,

i   u

   e   o

a

resulted in the Greek subject labeling English as follows:

i   u

(ɪ)

  e   o

a

The Persian subject gave the following English pattern:

when his native Persian was the same with the inclusion of an /u/. In the case of the Persian and of the Russian, it is interesting to note that fewer sounds in the matrix were labeled at all for English; the phonemes were more restricted in their range than they are in the native language.

Of the three Korean subjects, two thought they heard more different sounds in English than in Korean (which traditionally has 11 phonemic vowel distinctions. In normal speech, however, these distinctions may be seen to reduce to five.) Scholes found that the noncontinuous categories could be reduced, and thus the speaker who had seven categories in Korean had seven in English, the one with eight had eight; the third subject "had a good ear," and piled 11 piles for English and 10 for Korean, but the correspondences were not as well patterned as they had been with other subjects. This subject delimited an /a/ category in English, which is nonphonemic in Korean and distinguished /ɔ/ from /o/—a distinction possible in Korean, but not reported in the Korean trial by this subject.

This experiment provides a convincing demonstration of transfer of phonemic categories of perception from an earlier to a later language. At the same time it suggests that many dominant bilinguals will expect or permit a broader range per allophone in their native language than in their nonnative language.

The experiments discussed up to this point have focused on perceptual judgments. The remaining studies looked for correspondences between perception and production.

In 1973, Caramazza *et al.* tested stop consonant perception and production in French-Canadian bilinguals. Their 20 subjects had all learned English before the age of 7. Each subject was tested in two sessions: one in an English environment, the other in a French environment. The investigators first tested subjects reading a list of words beginning with a certain stop consonant pair (e.g., /p–b/). Ten subjects listened to a tape of synthesized stops which varied in voice onset time (VOT). They were instructed to judge whether each stimulus was a /p/ or a /b/. The taped consonants (although randomized) ranged along a continuum from VOT preceding the plosion, to VOT following it. Thus it was possible to determine the point at which each subject stopped labeling (i.e., perceiving) the voiced member of the pair and started hearing the unvoiced member. After the session, the initial consonants from the words which the subjects had read were analyzed by spectrograph, and VOT was determined.

Twenty monolingual subjects were tested as controls. On the production test, the bilinguals performed, in the French environment, almost exactly like the French monolingual speakers. In the English situation, when reading English words, the bilingual speakers were intermediate between the two monolingual groups. This may be attributable to the fact that their English was nonnative. We may assume that this spectrographic evidence of "accent" is not perceptible to the human ear. In any case, the average VOT for the same phoneme (e.g., /t/) differed for the bilingual depending on whether he was reading a French or an English word. We may infer that two output systems were operating in these bilinguals.

On the perception side, however, the results were different. The data for perception suggest that the bilinguals had a single system intermediate between those systems of the two monolingual groups. The average crossover points between the stops labeled as a voiced member of the pair and the stops labeled as unvoiced was different for the monolingual French and English speakers. The balanced bilinguals, in each environmental condition, demonstrated a crossover point intermediate to those of the monolinguals. In one respect, the balanced bilinguals performed like the English speakers; this was with regard to the variability of response. The French monolingual speakers evidenced a broad range of stops which they might label as the voiced member one time and the unvoiced member another time. That is, there was no clear crossover point between voiced and unvoiced stops for the monolingual French speakers. The authors suggested that this finding indicates that VOT is a less crucial distinctive feature in French than in English. The balanced bilinguals, while evidencing a crossover point intermediate between the average French one and the average English one, performed in the more clear-cut fashion of the English monolinguals. We may infer that these bilinguals processed VOT in either language, even though such processing might not be necessary in their native language, French.

In collaboration with Zurif and Caramazza, we performed a test similar to the preceding one, with Hebrew–English bilinguals. Our 12 bilingual subjects were balanced bilinguals who had learned both languages before the age of 6, continued to use both languages, and judged themselves equally proficient in each language.

At present, we have analysis only of the perception data. Performance of the monolingual Americans in our study did not differ from that of the English speakers of Caramazza et al. (1973). The monolingual Hebrew speakers, like the monolingual Canadian-French speakers, regularly switched to voiceless consonants at lower VOTs than did the monolingual Americans (e.g., although all English speakers would label as /g/ a particular sound for which the voicing started 5 msec after the plosion, some Hebrew speakers labeled this sound as /k/). Furthermore, the Hebrew curves had lower slope, implying a wider range of variation and less significance to the VOT cue. (see Figure 1).

The perceptual performance curves for the bilinguals fell between those of the monolingual groups. This means that whether the bilinguals were in the English or in the Hebrew testing environment, there was not much difference in their categorization decisions; these decisions fell between those of the monolingual groups. As with the French–English bilinguals, our Hebrew–English subjects showed an early entry into the crossover range.

The study of Garnes (1977) demonstrated results similar to those of Caramazza et al. (1973) and to our own data on Hebrew–English bilingual perception. Garnes tested two groups of Icelandic university students. Seventeen subjects were monolinguals who knew a second language only minimally. Nine subjects were Icelandic–English bilinguals who were fluent in their second language, English, and had resided abroad for at least 9 months. The stimuli were synthesized VC syllables, composed of the vowel /i/ and the consonant /s/. In Icelandic, but not in English, syllable quantity is phonemic, so Garnes's stimuli systematically varied the duration of the vowel and of the consonant. Subjects

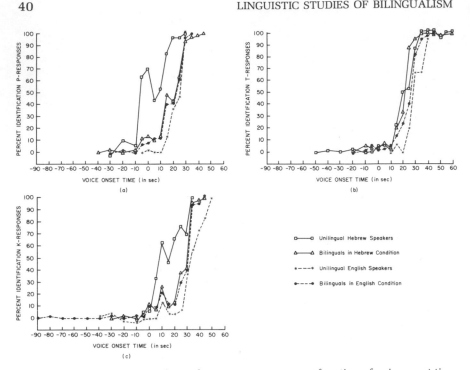

Figure 1. *Percentage of voiceless stop responses as a function of voice onset time (VOT).*

had to identify the syllable they heard as one of two words /iːs/ 'ice' or /iss/ 'of ice'. In one respect, both monolinguals and bilinguals performed similarly; for both groups it was the vowel length which provided the crucial cue to which word was being heard. The significant difference between the two groups arose with respect to perception of the consonant length. The bilinguals showed a much wider range of awareness, or guessing; that is, within the bilingual group there were more stimuli labeled both (iːs) and (iss). The monolinguals were in agreement on a larger set of stimuli; only a few of the intermediate stimuli were labeled as either word. Garnes suggested that her results support a "confusion" hypothesis, inasmuch as the bilinguals perceived the contrast in their native language "less accurately" than did the monolinguals. We tend to prefer her second conclusion, that mastery of a second language affects the perceptual system of the first language. In fact, it is not "confusion" that results, so much as a loosening of constraints, a new openness or flexibility.

    One additional study indicating a dissociation between phonological production and perceptive-judgment skills was that of Terry and

Cooper (1969). They analyzed the productive speech of 45 Spanish–English bilinguals in New York on the basis of three variables: fluency range in English, Spanish accent in English, and dominant language for reading. No correlation was found between these productive variables and the correctness of the subject's perceptual judgments. The perception test asked subjects to judge which of two minimally different taped words sounded closer to a third word. (Surprising to note, subjects made these judgments equally well whether the stimuli were in Spanish or English.)

The studies discussed in this section take their evidence for organization of phonological systems from the intuitions of bilinguals either about permissible consonant clusters, or about categorization of allophones into phonemes. All the studies treat the phonological input system, and it appears that the bilingual builds a unitary system for perception. In the Caramazza et al. (1973) studies, for example, the perception data for bilinguals were intermediate to those of respective monolinguals. Scholes's (1968) study showed the influence of L_1 phonemic categories on L_2. The studies of Anisfeld, Anisfeld, and Semogas (1969) and Cohen et al. (1967) showed the influence of L_2 structures on perceiving of L_1. The production system, however, may well be a dual system for the bilingual. The evidence of the studies of Caramazza and his colleagues strongly suggests that the bilingual maintains two systems for output.

Conclusion

The evidence from linguistic studies of bilingualism supports the theory that language production and language perception systems are to some degree independent of each other. It appears that for the bilinguals a more compound system exists for perception, while two coordinate systems may exist for production.

Interference can be treated synchronically, as part of the speaker's competence in a language, or diachronically, as a stage in her acquisition of the language. We have suggested that a model of bilingualism must account not only for interference phenomena when they occur; it must account for instances where interference does not occur, as well. Although more difficult to test, interference in comprehension must be considered, since interference in the production system may be qualitatively different from interference in the perception system.

In acquisition of a second language, particularly in young children, it would seem that, for production, the individual will start with a single system. He will essentially tend to fit the new language system that is being learned into the old system. Only over time will the bilingual develop a dual system for production. While the 3-year-old child may be aware of learning two languages, he is not likely to manage effective separation of the two until around age 7 (cf. C. Chomsky, 1969, on monolingual acquisition of complex structures after age 5). Learning patterns for the second language may be influenced, we have seen, by the age of learning the second language, and by differences in cognitive style. A linguistic factor that may influence the pattern of learning a new language is the "distance" between the structures of the new language and the structures of previously known languages.

3

Psychological Studies of Bilingualism

Introduction

The psychologist studying bilingualism is interested in the area of overlap between cognition and language. A number of earlier studies correlated IQ scores with parameters of bilingualism, while more recent studies have modified standard psychological instruments (such as list recall, semantic differential, and association tasks) to study the structure of the bilingual lexicon. Work has also been done on semantic processing of sentences in the two languages. In addition, psychologists have provided bilingualism research with description of and correlation among numerous parameters which contribute to language use by the individual bilingual. The first section of this chapter deals with these parameters, and those measures which have been suggested to define them.

Measurement Parameters

In this section we first sketch the parameters which psychologists have suggested as ones that may affect the language capabilities of the individual multilingual. Then we review several studies which have developed specific tests and standards for measuring some of the parameters involved in bilingual proficiency.

In his major treatise, *Pensée et Polyglossie* (1916), Epstein foreshadowed later studies. He discussed such factors as the mode of acquisition of a second language (direct or indirect method of instruction); the age of acquisition (children lose an unused language more readily; adults learn faster than children by the visual method); the place, conversation topic, and people associated with a given language; the recency of usage of a language (any modality); and the curious effects of pathology, anesthesia, and hypnosis (the latter is reported to rid one of accent, and restore lost languages).

Weinreich (1953) in his study, *Languages in Contact*, spoke of a range of proficiency and of attitudinal factors that interrelate with bilingual performance patterns. Among the former he pointed to language aptitude (whatever that consists of; we may still wonder why some people apparently learn languages more easily than others), switching facility, modes of use, and acquisition situation. When we search for underlying neurological mechanisms and organization patterns, it is important to account for the effect of affect and attitude on language proficiency.

Epstein and Weinreich provided descriptive taxonomies of factors likely to influence bilingual skills. Of these factors, only the age of acquisition may be easily measured. In the studies that follow, the authors have deliberately chosen quantifiable measures, and determined correlations between them.

An early example of such a study is that of Johnson (1953). He measured the relative proficiency of his Spanish–English pupils by comparing the number of Spanish and English words they could name in 5 min. The 30 boys, aged 9–12, were native speakers of Spanish in English-language schools. They were tested in Spanish in one session, and in English in the other. The mean number of English words produced was 71; the mean of Spanish words was 54. Individuals were then given scores that were the ratio of English to Spanish words. Johnson correlated these scores to results of the Hoffman measure of bilingual background, and to a measure of verbal–nonverbal IQ. The Hoffman measure of bilingual background showed no correlation to the verbal fluency measure. The nonverbal IQ measure he employed, the Goodenough Draw-a-Man Test, did, however. The children, moreover, performed near to the norm for their age on this test (98.77). On the Otis Self-Administering Test of Mental Ability, a test of verbal IQ, the pupils were below average (86.33). Subjects whose ratio of

English to Spanish words was highest (i.e., who produced few Spanish words in comparison to English words) had the closest correspondence between the Otis and Goodenough scores. It comes as no surprise that such students both showed dominant fluency for English, and also were able to perform at their IQ level (as measured by a nonverbal task) on an English-language test of mental ability.

Lambert (1955) found a high correlation among three measures of bilingual proficiency. One was the number of years of experience the subject had in the second language. A second measure was of productive fluency; subjects were instructed to give as many verbal association items as possible in 45 sec. The third task was a reaction time (RT) measure of comprehension. Subjects were to push one of eight colored buttons in response to color names. The instructions for the individual trials were written in abbreviated syntax. For example "Gauche, rouge" meant the subject was to press the red key among the four keys covered by the fingers of his left hand. Lambert compared the RT with French commands to that with English commands and developed a measure of relative language dominance by relating this score to the total RT of the individual.

It is of note that both Johnson and Lambert found a correlation between a production measure and a comprehension measure, since the two are not necessarily logically dependent. Comprehension of a second language, for example, often precedes production. Perhaps different subject populations would give different results. Lambert's subjects were from three groups: 14 undergraduates learning French, 14 more advanced graduate students of French, and 14 native French speakers who had lived in an English-speaking country for an average of 7 years.

Macnamara (1969) discussed a number of possible tests by which to measure the extent of a bilingual's dual proficiency. In the course of listing them, we can glean what factors are thought to contribute to the language organization of the bilingual. In a large study which he undertook in Montreal, regression analysis of various parameters was done, so we have some idea of the relative importance of the measures.

A language background questionnaire, asking questions about the subject's usage patterns and those of her family, did not prove highly predictive of other scores. Self-rating for the several language skills, however, proved highly predictive. Walters (personal communication, 1977) notes that self-rating skills may prove most accurately predictive in a well-educated population. In a second set of tests, Macnamara determined productive fluency. He found that word naming and word completion tests were weak predictors of overall language skill. A test of reading speed, on the other hand, was a good predictor for his Canadian population.

A third set of tests were labeled flexibility tests. Again, cultural factors of language, use, and style may enter into flexibility, which measures the ability to find near-synonymous paraphrasings. A multiple choice test that relied always on secondary meanings of a common verb proved only a moderately powerful measure in Macnamara's regression analysis. Lambert's test of word finding in a long nonsense word (e.g., how many words can you find in *Dansonodent*?) correlated with vocabulary scores in a Montreal population, and to grammar scores as well. A simple indirect test of language dominance was mentioned (that of Lambert, Havelka, & Gardner, 1959), which presented visually ambiguous stimuli (e.g., *pipe*) in English or French among a mixed list of words and asked subjects to read them aloud. The tendency to read in one or the other language was assumed to correspond to dominance in that language.

In the discussion that followed presentation of this paper, Macnamara supported the use of reaction time measures of bilingual dominance. He stated that one basic intelligence, one basic memory, and one basic reaction time are to be assumed for the individual bilingual. If this individual performs differently in language tests of cognition, memory, or reaction time, this must indicate different degrees of proficiency in the languages involved.

Fishman and Cooper (1969) tested 48 Spanish-English bilinguals and performed factor analysis on the intercorrelations of 124 proposed measures of bilingual proficiency. Among these were tests of **listening comprehension** given mixed speech (subjects were later asked questions on the information which they had heard in Spanish, and their answers were compared for accuracy with answers to questions on information given in English); **word naming** given a category; **word association** to noun stimuli; **word frequency**; **personal usage estimation**; **estimated usage of the language** with other bilinguals in the home, for reading, for writing, and for speaking; and **phonological variation** over different registers of speech. Subjects were also scored on the degree of **accent** in each language, the range of **registers** employed in each and judged appropriately in the speech of others, and their **reading** skills in each language. The authors found that the best predictors among the various bilingual criteria were self-reports on proficiency and usage.

Thus, for some reason, even the most careful questionnaires on personal language history are not good predictors of language skill, when compared to self-evaluation questionnaires. That is to say, the answer to the question "How good are you at speaking language X?" is more valuable in predicting experimental behavior than the answer to the questions "How old were you when you began to learn X?" or "How did you learn X?" Tests of specific skills (e.g., reading speed) or combinations of skills (e.g., IQ tests) may also provide comparative measures of proficiency in and between individuals.

The Nature of the Bilingual Lexicon

Numerous experiments employ single-word stimuli (out of grammatical context) in order to test the degree of independence and/or interdependence of the lexical storage systems of the bilingual. We have some reservations about these studies. Firstly, the results of these tests are often overgeneralized. Authors may imply that their results speak to interdependence of the language systems of the bilingual, when in fact they deal only with the lexicon and semantic fields. These subsystems may well be organized differently from subsystems for syntactic, phonological, and morphological decoding and production. Many of these studies are done with English-speaking bilinguals whose second language is French, Spanish, or German. Certain language-specific effects that may occur are ignored, as a rule, in discussion of the results. These languages, for example, share a number of cognate words, and an orthographic system as well. Such sharing may well encourage a more compound system of bilingualism than would other pairs of languages (e.g., Chinese and English). Many of the studies rely on written stimuli and oral response. Little consideration is given to the possibility that other combinations of stimulus and response mode might give different results. Recall of auditory stimuli, for example, might be subject to more interference under oral response than would recall of written stimuli. A final criticism is that a number of the studies involve tasks where practice in translation may be expected to influence results. Although language histories and self-evaluation measures of basic skills are taken, the amount of specific practice in translation often remains unmentioned.

In order to simplify presentation of the studies of bilingual lexical tasks, we have divided them into three groups. The first set of studies employs association tasks; the second set employs list-learning tasks. The final set is comprised of various studies of semantic measures.

ASSOCIATION TASKS

In association studies the subject is instructed to say the first word or words that come to mind upon reading or hearing a stimulus word.

In bilingual association studies, the stimuli in a set may be from only one language or from both languages. Subjects may be permitted to respond in either language or constrained to respond in one of the languages. The test may ask for free response or may restrict response to certain semantic categories (e.g., a place in which the stimulus object might be found). The stimuli may include items that are translation equivalents of other stimulus items. The responses may be judged to be syntagmatically related to the stimuli (e.g., *bird, sing*), or paradigmatically related (e.g., *bird, nest*). They may be stereotypic (e.g., *bird, sing*) or idiosyncratic (e.g., *bird, pen*).

In the monolingual, responses to the association task may be assumed to reflect lexical organization. In the bilingual, it follows, this task can provide a window on the degree of independence or interdependence of the two lexical systems. For example, we may ask how translation equivalents are stored, and how such storage compares to storage of synonyms in the same language of a given bilingual. Independent or interdependent production patterns can be observed as well, when association chains are the required task.

Qualitative analysis of association responses can answer other questions. Categorization of responses as syntagmatic or paradigmatic, for example, may provide evidence of the developmental process in bilingualism, since in monolinguals, syntagmatic responses are characteristic of young children, while paradigmatic responses outnumber syntagmatic ones in older children. Indeed, an association task in a second language learner may sort out for us if this monolingual finding depends more on cognitive development or on linguistic maturity.

Lambert (1956a,b,c) used association tests to evaluate certain hypotheses about language learning in adulthood. His subjects were undergraduate French students, graduate French students, and, as controls, native French speakers who had resided in English-speaking countries for approximately 7 years. There were 14 subjects in each group. The instructions (apparently in English) asked for 45 sec of association to the individual stimulus word. On the initial items subjects could associate in both languages; on the later items they were to restrict themselves to the language of the stimulus. The stimuli were high-frequency nouns and adjectives. Translation equivalents were avoided.

The expectation was that as subjects progressed from undergraduate to graduate French study, their performance on this task should better approximate that of the native French speakers. In some cases this proved true; graduate students gave more responses than did undergraduate students when the stimuli were in French. Graduate students also gave more associations in French than did the under- graduates when they were free to respond in either language. The more advanced students used more low-frequency words in listing their associations. In addition, the number of associations per French stimu- lus item matched better between the graduate and native-speaker groups than between the undergraduate and native groups.

Some expectations were not confirmed. It was assumed that the French word order for noun–adjective phrases would influence the word class of associations to nouns and adjectives, and it was hypothesized that graduate students would give more adjectives to noun stimuli, since that is the usual order of the noun–adjective phrase in French, whereas adjectives precede nouns in English. Instead it was found that the French subjects gave 17% adjective response to all noun stimuli, while the Americans averaged 11%; and there was no signifi- cant difference between the two American groups. In all three groups the trend was of greater adjective response to French stimuli than to English stimuli. Moreover, there was also an increase in percentage of adjectival responses to the English words from the undergraduate to the graduate to the native French subjects.

It is unclear whether these results may be attributed to the struc- tures of the languages involved (and thus imply a compound system at this lexicosyntactic level), or if the results may be explained in terms of age, education, or cognitive styles. It has been generally noted that older children and adults give more paradigmatic associations than do younger children, who give more syntagmatic ones (Entwistle, Forsyth, & Muus, 1964).

Lambert also hypothesized that stereotypy of associative response would decrease as the learners progressed in the language. This hypothesis was not supported by the results. The authors reported that the two languages provoked differing amounts of stereotypy, French provoking more stereotypical responses. (We must assume that this difference was not an artifact of the different words chosen as stimuli in each language.) At the same time he found that the Americans gave more stereotypical responses than did the French subjects. Lambert suggests that these differences may be due to the different load of "information" carried by different types of languages. We suggest, as an alternative, that these data can be explained by the greater body of shared French experience among the English learners than among the French speakers.

Lambert hypothesized that greater experience in a certain language would change the proportion of types of response (e.g., definitional,

exemplary, syntagmatic, and evaluational). While the American subjects gave more definitions and French subjects gave more personal
evaluational responses to stimuli in both languages, there was little
difference between the two English-speaking groups, the undergraduate and graduate learners. Again it is unclear whether this difference
between English and French speakers may be attributed to greater age
or education on the part of the French subjects, or to differing cognitive
style. If a culturally determined cognitive style accounts for the difference, then we must assume that all the subjects had a compound
linguistic system and/or that they had a single prelinguistic cognitive
system that could express itself through either of the two languages.

A native French speaker was asked to compare the pronunciation
of the American groups to that of the native French speakers. The
improvement of graduate students over undergraduates was not reli-
ably consistent, and there was a significant difference between both of
these groups and the French groups. We may take this finding as
experimental confirmation of the common observation that advanced
study of a second language does not necessarily result in native-like
accent.

Kolers (1963) performed word-association tests inter- and intralin-
gually on English-speaking bilinguals whose mother tongue was Thai,
Spanish, or German. Subjects were instructed as to the language of
response expected, and simple translation of the stimulus was forbid-
den. In the course of the experiment, association was obtained for a
given word and for its translated dictionary equivalent. One-third of
the responses to a word in one language were in fact translations of the
responses to its translation in the other language (e.g., a response of *dog*
to the stimulus *cat*, and also of *chien* to *chat*). These words most often
referred to concrete objects, whereas words referring to abstract states
(e.g., *truth*) or emotions (e.g., *love*) elicited more different responses in
the two languages (i.e., less stereotypy). Kolers interpreted the data on
differences for abstract stimuli as indicating that experiences and
memories are not stored in some supralinguistic form, but rather are
language tagged, depending on how the subject defined the experience
to himself. We suggest an explanation more closely linked to the task
tested; words in a language are likely to be linked contextually, through
experience in the language, with a network of other words in that
language. This network is not necessarily the same as (i.e., a literal
translation of) the one that experience in the other language builds up.
No striking differences between the Thai–English and the other bilinguals were reported.

In another study, Ervin and Landar (1963) tested word association in 37 adult Navaho subjects, of whom 8 were monolinguals, 16 knew some English, and 13 were bilinguals for whom English was the dominant language. Subjects were presented 114 stimulus items in Navaho, and were expected to repeat each and mention the first association that came to mind.

Analysis was made according to the syntagmatic and paradigmatic possibilities of the response word. The results showed that the level of commonality of responses was much lower than that seen by Russell and Jenkins (1954) for college English speakers (17% commonality in this group as compared to 45% in the English speakers). The authors attributed this difference to the fact that Navahos are spread over a wide geographical area. Paradigmatic and full sentence response items accounted for a smaller percentage of the responses than one would have expected in adults, a result that the authors attributed to lower educational level among Navahos, as compared to other United States samples. Indeed, those who had schooling or who were English dominant tended to give more paradigmatic responses. It is unclear to us, however, whether the tendency of Navahos to give few paradigmatic responses is an effect purely of Navaho education, of their bilingualism, or of biculturalism.

Davis and Wertheimer (1967) controlled for language set and degree of language competence in an association test, presenting stimuli in both French and English. The four university-age subject groups were 17 first-year audiolingual French students, 19 third-year students, 13 graduate students, and 10 native speakers. In order to encourage a set in one or the other language, fixation instructions were read to half of each group in French and to the other half in English. Then subjects filled out language history questionnaires in the same language. This was followed by the presentation of a booklet containing 24 individual stimulus words, of which 8 were in French, 8 in English, and 8 visually ambiguous (e.g., *coin*). Subjects were to write as many associative terms as they could in 15 sec.

The authors found confirmation of Lambert's (1956a) results, that the number of responses in L_2 increases with competence in the language. They further noted that the increase in French responses coincided with a reduction in English responses. They pointed out that this balancing procedure supports the Ervin and Osgood (1954a) model of compound and coordinate systems, inasmuch as the beginning learner, as a compound (or, perhaps better, subordinate) bilingual, was most likely to translate a stimulus item and then go on to associate to the item in English, while the more coordinate advanced learners could associate in either language. The decrease in English responses with increased proficiency in French, however, might also be taken to support a unified-system production model in which languages must compete for the limited processing and/or expression channel, and one language is used at the expense of the other.

The authors saw further evidence for the development from a compound to a coordinate state in the fact that the two less proficient groups gave more French responses to English stimuli than to French stimuli. This was interpreted as meaning that, despite the audiolingual method of language learning, beginning learners were compound bilinguals for whom translation was frequent. It is unclear whether the authors in fact analyzed the responses as to the proportion of translation equivalents given.

The influence of set, or language of instruction, was seen to yield significant differences in total responses per language only for the two lower proficiency groups. The number of French associations to the visually ambiguous words, however, was affected by the language of instruction as well as by proficiency in French. It was not affected by the language of the two stimulus items immediately preceding the ambiguous item. These facts taken together would indicate that the set phenomenon, as defined, determines perception of items more than production. Of course, the way the set fixation was realized primed the subjects to expect stimulation in one or the other language but left their responses relatively unchanneled (cf. Dalrymple-Alford, 1967, where reading words aloud was used to induce production set).

Half of the stimuli in this test were adjectives and half were nouns, and analysis was made of the word class of responses. Unlike Lambert (1956b), who found more adjectives associated with noun stimuli by people with greater fluency in French, Davis and Wertheimer saw no differences between groups. In their study, subjects were more likely to associate nouns with nouns, and adjectives with adjectives, even across languages. Such paradigmatic behavior indicates their students were behaving like older rather than younger children (Entwisle et al., 1964), and may also suggest that word form categories have some reality at a level higher than that of the language-specific lexicons.

Macnamara (1967b) instructed Gaelic–English and Latin–English bilinguals to say as many words as possible in a given time, upon being given a stimulus in one of the two languages they knew. They were four conditions for response. In two conditions, subjects were to respond in only one or the other language. In the third condition, subjects were to give alternate words in alternate languages, but to avoid translation (e.g., *chat, dog, lait, bowl*). The fourth condition consisted of associations and their translation equivalents (e.g., *chat–cat, chien–dog,* and *lait—milk*). There was a language effect seen in the first two, unilingual conditions. As one might have predicted, production of associations in Latin was low, since the subjects were clerical students who had probably focused their study on reading the language and were not used to producing it. The different alternating conditions also produced different results. The switching task decreased the number of response item totals significantly, while the translation task increased it somewhat, although the total number of "concepts" expressed was lower under this condition than under simple word naming. Macnamara took these results to demonstrate linguistic independence for storage and retrieval. It is also possible that these results suggest a model of modified interdependence. A good strategy for the fourth condition would be to select only those associations for which the translation word came quickly to mind. In any case, the unusual nature of the switching tasks, or even the word translating tasks, ought not to be taken as evidence for the natural language switch; in these tasks "conscious" labeling, or keeping track of each word as to which language it belonged to, was necessary.

Riegel, Ramsey, and Riegel (1967) proposed to describe differences in the first and second languages of American and Spanish students. Their instrument was a restricted association test. Subjects were asked, in Spanish in one session and in English in another, to give categorized single item responses, with no time limit, to 35 common nouns. They were asked for responses in the following categories: class name (e.g., *fork—utensil*), class member (e.g., *fork—spoon*), synonym (e.g., *fork—rake*), antonym (e.g., *fork—spoon*), usage (e.g., *fork—eat*), quality (e.g., *fork—pointed*), essential part or attribute (e.g., *fork—handle*). The subject groups were matched for size and median self-assessment (fair—good in the second language). The 24 native English speakers were undergraduates in the fifth semester of Spanish. Approximately one-half of the native Spanish speakers were graduate students in a university in the United States, and the other half were for the most part wives of these students.

Riegel *et al.* found that subjects left more items unanswered in their second language. The English speakers left more blanks in Spanish (22%) than the Spanish speakers did in English (7%). The results of speakers for their native language were parallel, however (Spanish speakers left 3% blank in Spanish, whereas English speakers left 1% blank); the authors suggest that the difference in L_2 performance may reflect differences between the two languages, rather than between the groups.

Analysis was made of the extent to which responses in the second language overlapped with the responses of native speakers to the same items. The native Spanish speakers approximated the results of the native English speakers in the English test better than the English speakers approximated the Spanish results of the Spanish speakers. This finding was most outstanding in the subtests for similar items and for qualities of items. The Spanish native speakers showed evidence of idiosyncrasy on the qualities test only. On the other hand, the native Spanish speakers repeated associations across English subtests to a greater degree than did the native English speakers in the Spanish tests. By this last measure, the English speakers approximated native Spanish better (68%) than the Spanish speakers approximated native English (52%). The English speakers had lower correlations (46%) than the Spanish speakers (79%) between the repetition configurations of their results on the two languages.

The authors pointed out that these results may be influenced by the different manner of acquistion of the L_2 by the two groups but did not mention the differing educational levels of the groups, nor the different demands of daily usage. They interpreted the data as showing that conceptual distinctions in second language speakers are less clear than those of native speakers. They also suggested that formal language training facilitates identification of the conceptual structure of the L_2, while informal live-in learning hastens vocabulary acquisition and verbal fluency.

In the association test presented to Spanish–English bilinguals by Massad, Yamamoto, and Davis (1970), both verbal and pictorial stimuli were flashed to subjects. Subjects were to respond, as instructed, to the words in the same language and to the pictures in one or the other language. Analysis of the responses was made as to percentage of sense impression words elicited, and the tendency was for verbal stimuli to suggest more sense impression words than did pictorial stimuli, and for Spanish to suggest more than English.

Gekoski (1970) employed an association test to look at the psychological usefulness of the compound–coordinate distinction. He selected compound and coordinate bilinguals on the basis of the cultural context of their language learning. By his definition, the compound subjects learned the second language in a classroom situation in the culture of their L_1. This might be expected to encourage finding translation equivalents. The coordinate subjects learned the second language in the second culture. All his subjects learned the second language (Spanish or English) after puberty. The four groups of 18 each (Spanish and English native speakers, compound and coordinate) were matched for socioeconomic level, education, fluency, and language experience factors.

Forty-eight English words and their Spanish translation equivalents were presented visually by means of a memory drum, and the subjects were informed in advance of each item, in which language to expect the stimulus, and the language and type expected for the written response. Response type was initially free, then restricted. For half of the restricted cases, subjects were asked to name an appropriate location for the object given. In the other half of the cases, they were instructed to give a superordinate response (e.g., "utensil" for the stimulus "knife"). Whatever the condition, whether the stimulus and response were in the same language (English–English or Spanish–Spanish) or opposite languages (English–Spanish, Spanish–English), the compound subjects gave more translation-equivalent responses than did the coordinate subjects. In the case of restricted association this was true to a significant degree. Gekoski explained his results on the basis of the alleged impossibility of becoming a true coordinate bilingual in adulthood.

Rüke-Dravina (1971) drew general conclusions about the process of association and also distinguished between her monolinguals (people who spoke only one language well, but who may have learned other languages in high school or university) and multilinguals (who knew more than one language from childhood). Subjects were given 5 min to write down all the words they could think of, regardless of what languages they were in, upon stimulus of a Swedish word. Both groups used foreign words, but for the monolinguals these were usually the translation equivalents of the stimulus. In the multilinguals, as a rule, the frequent language switching involved true chaining of association. This would imply a unified cognition system with output in any language possible when encouraged. The multilingual adults also produced considerably more associations than did the monolinguals, although the Latvian–Swedish bilingual adolescents produced fewest of all. This may be a result of greater education on the part of the multilinguals, or of greater verbal facility through practice.

Taylor (1971) clarified the results of the study by Macnamara (1967b) on category switching by asking English-dominant French speakers to free associate in writing to a written key word with various conditions of switch imposed. Translation was discouraged. When language change was permitted if and when the subject wanted, or even required on every fifth item, the resulting number of associations was not significantly different from that when subjects were required to use only one language. When the switch was obligatory after every three words or every other word, however, resultant word quantity dropped, especially in the latter condition. Clearly, obligatory frequent switch interferes with production of associations, perhaps by unnaturally requiring attention to the language of response. In the freer conditions, the probability of changing language after any given response was greater in French than in English. This implies that the subjects were more comfortable in English. For both languages, however, the probability of changing language was quite low. Subjects thus evidenced within-language clusters; it was easier for them to continue in either language than to switch languages. Nevertheless, given the freedom to change languages or not at will, use of the cross-language option did obtain. This spontaneous use of language changing implies some measure of interdependence and cross-language semantic clustering.

Riegel and Zivian (1972) required inter- or intralingual association from 24 English-dominant speakers of German. In a screening test of fluency, subjects were asked to write as many words as they could in 3 min; they gave an average of 66 in English and 31 in German. On the association tasks subjects were asked to write down the first word that came to mind upon reading a stimulus word. Their response was to be in the language noted at the top of the page. The free association tests preceded restricted association tests where subjects were asked to respond with the same semantic categories as in Riegel *et al.* (1967), in addition to a category for words likely to precede the given stimulus, and another category for words likely to follow it. A set of French words was to be responded to in English, but the data on these could not be interpreted as data for an unknown language since a number of the subjects had experience in French. (Twenty-four percent of the responses to French items by subjects with no French knowledge were translation equivalents!)

Subjects gave more stereotypical associations in English to English stimuli than in German to German stimuli. In this unrestricted condition most of the response words were syntagmatically connected with the stimuli (36% likely to follow, 30% likely to precede), while in the interlingual conditions these categories each accounted only for 11% of the totals, and paradigmatic associations (e.g., grammatically similar words; including translation equivalents, and superordinates) accounted for a greater proportion. This is probably because the translation strategy accounted for many responses.

Translation was a common response for the interlingual situations (56% of German responses to English stimuli were translation equivalents; 62% of English responses to German stimuli were). The other response type accounting for a significant number of associations in the interlingual tests was response by identical initial letters. These scores were highest for French stimuli in the subjects with no French knowledge (68% of total responses) and higher for French and German stimuli with English responses (38% and 39%, respectively) than for English stimuli with German responses (27%) or the intralingual conditions (German–German, 16%; English–English, 70%). This hierarchy suggests that, in the early stages of learning a language, lexical storage strategy (additional to that of translation equivalence or meaning), uses the initial letter (or sound) to associate words. Semantic associations later predominate. In any case it must be remembered that these subjects were postpubertal learners, and were learning under a school methodology; so translation equivalents and visual cues like initial letter were to be expected. Responses under the restricted condition did not modify the conclusions.

Several conclusions can be drawn from this series of association tests. As one would predict, greater proficiency in a language results in more associations in it (Lambert, 1956a; Davis & Wertheimer, 1967). The manner of acquisition of the second language will influence the type of words which are chosen; a person learning the new language in the new culture will give more of the same associations to a stimulus than will a person learning in a school in the native culture (Riegel et al., 1967). The strategy of giving translation equivalents as association items seems to be a common one, when it is permitted, especially for compound bilinguals or subjects who are not particularly fluent in a language (Rüke-Dravina, 1971; Riegel & Zivian, 1972). Giving translation equivalents is one way in which language switching may work "naturally" in an association task. Even when translation is prohibited, subjects will rarely "naturally" confine themselves to responses in one language; however, if they are obliged to change languages at certain times, this will slow down or inhibit their association process (Macnamara, 1967b; Taylor, 1971).

When subjects are free to alternate between their two languages in chain association, they will tend to produce clusters in each language (Taylor, 1971). Several factors will contribute to the quantity and quality of association responses. More proficient speakers will produce more responses, and these will be more stereotypic (Lambert, 1956b). Language-specific factors (or cultural ones underlying them) may also contribute to stereotypy of response, however (Riegel et al., 1967; Riegel & Zivian, 1972), as well as to other language linguistic-response-type parameters such as paradigmatic versus syntagmatic responses (Ervin & Landar, 1963). While the status of being bi- or multilingual may result in a somewhat greater number of responses than in monolingualism (Rüke-Dravina, 1971), there would nevertheless seem to be a cognitive limit to the number of responses given (Davis & Wertheimer, 1967).

LIST LEARNING AND RECALL TASKS

Patterns of list learning and list recall can speak to questions of lexical organization. On the basis of retrieval evidence, inferences can be made about lexical storage. Comparison of mixed-language lists to single-language lists may provide cues about the degree of independence or interdependence of the lexical systems of the bilingual. Manipulation of semantic relations between words within a list can increase both facilitation of list recall and interference in list recall, even in the monolingual. If one contrasts results on these tests between monolinguals and bilinguals, and between bilingual groups with different language histories, different patterns of lexical organization may become apparent.

In the studies to be reported, subjects were expected to recall as many items as possible from a list of words. The presentation mode was usually visual, although it was occasionally auditory. Lists could be mixed, or in only one or the other language. The items within a list, or across lists, were at times related semantically. Another variable in list recall tests was the interval between presentation of the items and their recall. This was long or short and filled (or not) with different potentially interfering tasks.

Lambert, Havelka, and Crosby (1958) set out to refine the notions of compound and coordinate bilingualism. They performed an experiment in which 32 balanced French–English subjects were divided into compound bilinguals, who had acquired the two languages in a fused situation (when both languages could be used interchangeably), and coordinate bilinguals, who had learned two languages with some distinct separation between appropriate usage situations. The latter group was further divided into unicultural separate learning (one parent used each language, or one language was used at home and one in school) and bicultural separate learning (the two languages were learned in two cultural contexts). A test of associative independence was administered to these subjects, in which either a list of nonsense words or a list of French words was interpolated in the interval between the learning and recall of a list of 20 English words. For the compound group, the French list was facilitative of recall; for both the coordinate groups it served as indifferently as a list of nonsense words.

As part of a series of studies on bilingualism, Ervin (1961b) tested learning and recall facility in two groups of Italian–English bilinguals in Boston. English was dominant for one group (16 subjects) composed of compound bilinguals who had arrived in the United States before age 6 and who were accustomed to using the two languages freely in their daily lives. Another group was composed of 16 subjects who were older and for whom Italian was dominant; they had arrived in the United States after age 9—thus they were more coordinate. Only this latter group showed significant differences in recall on the following test.

During an initial learning session, RT was measured for naming in one or the other language. Each of 18 pictures was shown twice. Subjects were told to learn the items for recall. After a 6-min interval filled by a task of assigning Italian adjectives to Italian nonsense items, subjects were instructed to recall as many items as they could in one or the other language. The results showed that for the Italian-dominant, or coordinate, subjects, pictures which were easier to name in the dominant language (Italian) were recalled best in that language, while pictures easier to name in the nondominant language (English), while learned better in that language (according to the RT measure), were recalled equally well in either language. This interchangeability points to a possible translation mechanism from the nondominant to the dominant language. Such a translation mechanism would operate automatically for the coordinate subjects only, prior to memory storage of an item.

Kolers (1965) tried to facilitate recall of long lists (70 words) by coding the items of one language in color, and by listing words of the same language contiguously. The 16 subjects were fluent speakers of English and French. Half of the group were native speakers of each language. The lists of monosyllabic words were presented visually by means of a memory drum. The color-coded words were either in monolingual lists or in mixed lists. The latter lists were either exclusive of translation or doubled lists, consisting of each word and its translation equivalent. After presentation of the list, subjects were asked to write all the words they remembered, either in the correct pen color, or in the correct language. Analysis was made only of the interior words, in positions 11–60, in order to avoid the memory effects of primacy and recency.

Mixing colors halved the number of words remembered (11.05 words on the black list, 11.5 in the red list, and 5.7 in the mixed color list), whereas mixing languages had no such effect (9.1 words on the English list, 13.8 on the French, and 12.6 on the mixed list). Kolers argued that learning on the mixed color list was clearly paired-associate learning; the subjects had to learn both the word and the

color. This additional task of marking for color hindered the learning of
words. In the bilingual lists, apparently, no inhibitory effort was involved. We might simply conclude that, for these subjects, the memory
for a language tag was a more practiced skill than memory for color of
print. It might be, however, that lexical storage for the two languages
was separate enough that the translation equivalent of an item provided
no more interference than did any other word. It may also be that the
written nature of the task encouraged use of certain language tags. Had
the stimuli been presented aurally, they might have been directly
processed for meaning, with a concomitant loss of language tag.

Kolers (1968) reviewed a number of his earlier studies and briefly
sketched a recall task which gave evidence for language interdependence in the bilingual. French–English subjects were presented visually with a mixed language list of words, some of which were repeated
more than once, and some of which were repeated inasmuch as their
translation equivalents were also included. These translation equivalents were picked so as to share no visual or phonetic element, but only
a semantic one (e.g., *pli–fold*). When it turned out that the two kinds of
repetition (literal, or by translation equivalent) facilitated recall
equally, Kolers concluded that subjects were storing items semantically, regardless of their language tag.

Lambert, Ignatow, and Krauthammer (1968) tested two groups of
bilinguals. Twenty-four subjects in a French–English group were balanced by age of learning and self-report of present skills. Twenty-four
subjects in a Russian–English group had attended parochial schools
since childhood, but considered themselves balanced bilinguals only
in audiolingual skills. Subjects were expected to recall words from
40-item visually presented lists that contained either stimuli from both
languages, or from only one language. Half of the lists contained 10
words each, from four different common categories (e.g., fruit). There
were two types of mixed language category lists; in the concordant lists
two categories were in one language and two in the other. In the
discordant lists, categories included items in both languages.

The English–French bilinguals recalled more words in French
than in English (12.65 words to 10.83, respectively). Lambert *et al.* took
these results to reinforce Kolers' (1965) suggestion that French may
have more lexical and phonemic distinction between words, especially
since the Russian–English bilinguals performed equally in both languages, as the authors, at least, would have expected. This was true for
the uncategorized lists, but the categorized lists revealed an opposite
trend. Here the English and French results were equivalent, while the
Russian–English bilinguals performed better with English words. This

latter condition might have been predicted from the different language histories of the two groups. Mixed lists were not recalled more poorly than unilingual lists for either group of subjects. Categorized lists gave better scores than random lists, and concordant lists, better scores than discordant ones. In the latter condition (discordant lists) the highest number of translation errors were made, which implied semantic processing instead of language tag processing. The Russian–English group made twice as many translation errors of this sort, as the French–English group (34 to 17 errors, respectively), while their total correct recall was slightly higher across all conditions.

Lambert et al. concluded that bilingual capacity is expressed differently according to task requirements. We would add that with these data it is unclear whether the manner in which a language was learned or language-specific features (Russian versus French) brought about the opposing trends of greater language dominance for categorized or uncategorized lists.

Young and Navar (1968) looked at retroactive inhibition under list-learning conditions in Spanish–English bilinguals. Half of the 40 subjects were dominant in each language, as determined by self-evaluation, self-judgment of language preference for thinking, and experimenter judgment of speaking ability. Each subject learned a paired-associate list first in one language and then in the other, order of list-learning being counterbalanced across the groups. Finally, subjects relearned the first list. Items in the two lists were translation equivalents of each other, but they were paired differently. The results of trials to relearn the first list were analyzed for both experimental and control groups (although it was never explicitly stated what the differences were between these two groups), and it was seen that no matter which language was dominant for the individual subjects, associations formed in one language would bring about forgetting in the other. Perhaps any time-filling task might have had the same effect. The authors considered their experiment to have provided support for a theory of bilingual language interdependence.

Nott and Lambert (1968) confirmed earlier free recall results (Lambert et al., 1968; Kolers, 1965) which showed no difference in oral recall, whether a printed list was in one language or the other, or mixed, when the lists contained semantically unrelated items. When the items in a mixed list could be grouped according to category, however, worse recall resulted. This discrepancy may be taken to reinforce the linguistic experience hypothesis proposed earlier; words are more closely associated with words in their language than with semantically related words in the other language; thus, when the task is monolingual, memory for the entire group of words is facilitated. The confusion caused by mixed lists, however, when words of a similar semantic field are in the list, shows that there is involuntary association of words with their translation equivalents. Furthermore, the French–English balanced bilinguals recalled significantly more words on any given list than those subjects dominant in one of the two languages. In this task, balanced bilinguals had some across-the-board skill that the nonbalanced did not have. Their more frequent translation errors, moreover, supported the hypothesis of involuntary deep semantic processing of input.

Evers' (1970) dissertation dealt with recall of German and English words presented aurally. Subjects were 40 bilingual college students in the United States, half of whom were native speakers of each language. The subjects were exposed to tapes of common monosyllabic and disyllabic nouns and asked to recall orally as many as possible. In some tapes translation equivalent pairs were included; in others they were not. Those series with translation items were found to facilitate recall. On the basis of this finding, and that of a large number of wrong-language recall errors, Evers concluded that, at least in unconnected discourse, the bilingual stores items which are presented auditorily in terms of their underlying semantic concepts and has difficulty noting the language tag of the item, even when specifically instructed to do so. It must be noted that in this study words were chosen for their high degree of translatability. It may be the case that Evers' rule holds for such items, but that the lexicon as a whole is not so compounded. In that case, we would expect different pairs of languages to encourage mutual compound storage to a greater or lesser extent.

A second variable entered into recall on this test: that of language set. Half the subjects were treated in a condition of separate language presentation, the other half in a mixed language presentation. The second group made almost twice as many recall errors as the first group, perhaps implying that sets separating or restricting expectations facilitate language recall tasks.

Tulving and Colotla (1970) extended previous studies on free recall to show that uncategorized multilingual lists (English, French, and Spanish) are harder to recall than unilingual lists. Their six subjects were proficient in at least the three languages mentioned. (A test of reading speed did not correlate with the results but a similar free-recall test on English–Estonian bilinguals was mentioned as having given similar results.) Subjects were exposed to unilingual, bilingual, and trilingual lists, presented visually, the instructions being to recall orally at the conclusion of each list.

Analysis of recall divided the responses into those from what was called primary memory (seven or fewer items of presentation and/or recall between the item and its recall) and secondary memory (more than seven items between the two events). For primary memory items, no differences were found across the parameters checked by the authors. With secondary memory, however, unilingual lists were best recalled, and trilingual lists worst recalled. The total recall results of the unilingual lists were compared for each subject in order to determine his relative proficiency.

Tulving and Colotla found that the most proficient language was most impaired in the bilingual and trilingual lists, while the least proficient language resulted in similar number of recalled items under all three conditions. They suggested that the impaired performance on bi- and trilingual lists resulted not from impaired storage, but from impaired accessibility, due to the difficulty of forming higher-level organizational units for the members of the list. This interpretation assumed a fair degree of coordinateness or independence between the several lexical systems.

Kintsch (1970) exposed 19 nonbalanced German–English bilinguals to a continuous list. They were instructed to read each item and judge whether or not the word had appeared before. If it had appeared previously, they were to judge if it had been in the same or the other language. (Note that this instruction primed subjects to expect translation items.) All subjects performed better in response to English stimuli (perhaps because of their current dominant usage of it, as Kintsch suggests, or perhaps because of their response set being English words "yes," "no," "same," "other"). For the group who had to consider translation equivalents as repetitions, there was a significant difference between treatment of untranslated, simple recurrences and that of translated recurrences, the former being more likely to be correctly identified (95% versus 87%), implying nonimmediate equivalence of translation items, whatever the storage system might be. For the group which was to treat translation equivalents as new words, however, there was a high percentage of false recognition, implying again the impossibility of ignoring semantic cues.

Goggin and Wickens (1971) tested the language independence of bilinguals to see if a shift in language was equivalent to a switch in semantic category. Their vehicle was the test of release from proactive interference wherein a control group is exposed to four trials of four words to remember; after each exposure the group is prevented from rehearsing the words, and then asked to recall them. The standard pattern of recall across the four trials is one of decreased proficiency, unless some change in semantic category (i.e., words to numbers) is made, in which case recall for that trial improves. The experimental group can be given various sets of words on the fourth trial, and, on the basis of subjects' percentage of improved recall over the deterioration of the controls, one can judge the strength of associative independence between each set and that of the previous three trials.

In this experiment Goggin and Wickens changed either semantic category (foodstuff versus body parts) or language (Spanish versus English) or both. Across their 384 subjects, changing of both language and category resulted in the highest increase of recall or recovery percentage (90.2%). Changing category but not language resulted in the next highest recovery percentage (79.4%), and changing language but not category resulted in the least release (68.0%) but was still significantly different ($p < .01$) from the control group.

The subjects for this experiment were 384 college students in Texas. They were asked to rate their bilingual knowledge on a scale from 1 (know Spanish only) to 9 (know English only). Subjects who graded themselves 1 or 9 were excluded, and the remaining subjects were divided into a group of balanced bilinguals (scoring in the 4–6 range) and dominant bilinguals (scoring 2,3,7,8). The authors point out that this division was made only after the data were collected; so equal numbers of balanced and unbalanced subjects were not assigned to the different experimental and control conditions.

Nevertheless, when the findings are reviewed from this perspective, we can summarize the Goggin and Wickens data as shown in Table 1.

Table 1
Percentage of Release from Interference[a]

	Category changed	Language changed	Category and language changed
Balanced bilinguals	72.4	97.7	114.9
Dominant bilinguals	85.0	43.9	70.1

[a] Data summarized from Goggin and Wickens (1971).

Under the condition in which only the category changed in the final trial, the dominant bilinguals recovered somewhat more than did balanced bilinguals. No explanation was given for this. When the category remained constant (a condition that usually results in decreased performance) but the language changed, both groups of subjects evidenced recovery, strongly suggesting some degree of independence or "psychological distinctness" between the two languages in the individual bilinguals. The balanced group evidenced greater independence than did the dominant group, who, Goggin and Wickens suggested, may have had to translate stimuli to their dominant language for this task. Such translation would result in less independence.

Palmer (1972) ran correlated list recall tests with other measures of bilingualism. His subjects were elementary school children from the fifth through the eighth grades. They were divided into four groups (English monolingual, balanced bilingual, English-dominant bilingual and Spanish-dominant bilingual) on the basis of two measures, which, it should be noted, yielded identical results. One was self-report; the second was RT for naming pictures from the picture-identification subtest of the Stanford-Binet Form L-M. Subjects were told before each picture in which language they were to respond, and mean differences of less than 25% between languages were considered indicative of balanced bilingualism. Six lists of three sorts, and instructions in both languages, were tape-recorded. The lists were either categorized or noncategorized, and either in Spanish, in English, or mixed. Categorized lists were composed of 40 frequent words from 4 semantic categories (colors, etc.); noncategorized lists were composed of 40 words from 40 semantic categories. Subjects were instructed to remember as many words as they could, and their responses were tape-recorded.

Results were analyzed for extent of clustering by category and by language, and for total recall. The covariates incorporated were socioeconomic status (on the basis of education and occupation of head of household), vocabulary level (by Wechsler subtest, essentially in English), and age in months. By an analysis of the intercorrelations of covariate control and dependent variables, it was not seen that age, vocabulary, or socioeconomic standing interacted significantly with either total recall per language condition, or with the strategy factors of clustering. It was calculated that there was no significant difference between groups for total recall, but that for English recall, the monolingual English children were the poorest and those speakers who were Spanish dominant did best! Over the total tests, balanced bilinguals recalled most words (see Table 2).

Palmer believed that bilingualism creates problems. Therefore he argued that one must remember that all the students tested were in an educational system conducted in English. He noted that all groups performed better in English than in Spanish, and said that this was

Table 2
Average Words Recalled[a]

Subjects	English lists	Spanish lists	Mixed lists	Total average
Monolingual English	11.3	1.7	6.3	6.4
English-dominant	13.2	7.0	6.8	9.0
Spanish-dominant	16.7	12.7	10.9	13.4
Balanced	15.4	14.4	11.2	13.7

[a]Data summarized from Palmer (1972).

because English "is a more highly structured language, whose categorizations are more accessible." Furthermore, he checked the raw data and discovered that the higher the socioeconomic status of the groups, the poorer the performance. The monolingual English speakers were of a higher socioeconomic status, and this, he suggested, explained their poor results.

Although Palmer's results cannot be taken to prove that bilinguals per se have better all-around language skills than monolinguals, the trend of the results to support this statement is certainly striking.

Saegert, Kazarian, and Young (1973) used a free-recall task, through a part–whole list transfer-expectation paradigm. They compared the results of 64 native Spanish, English usage-dominant bilinguals, and 64 native Arabic, English speakers, with results of monolinguals. Unilingual part–whole transfer was positive for initial trials, then negative in later trials for all the unilingual conditions in the present experiments. In bilingual conditions, the effect of dominance was important; learning the partial list in the dominant language and the whole list in the nondominant language produced negative transfer, whereas in the opposite condition, positive transfer occurred. The authors explained this on the basis of interdependent (lexical) systems within which subjective groupings are more easily formable and less easily modifiable in the dominant than in the nondominant language.

Champagnol (1973) presented 24-item lists to be learned by French students of English. His 56 subjects were divided equally into four groups according to the number of years they had studied English; they ranged from beginners to advanced students. Four different lists were composed: two unilingual and two mixed. In each list the words fell equally into four semantic categories, such as body parts. Subjects were given 12 presentations of each written list and were asked to recall the items in any order by writing. After 1 week they were asked what items they still recalled.

Except for performance by the youngest group, with whom the mixed lists were better recalled than the English lists, Champagnol's results with respect to recall showed that French lists were better recalled than English lists, and that the unilingual lists were better recalled than mixed ones. Although advanced students performed better on the unilingual lists than did the less advanced students, their performance on the mixed lists was no better. Nor was there any difference on the mixed lists between the number of French words recalled and the number of English words recalled.

As to remembering by semantic clustering, this was seen to improve with age. It was stronger in French than in English, but this superiority decreased with age (i.e., learning of the second language increased the facility for semantic clustering in it). For the mixed lists, words were more likely to be remembered by semantic categorization grouping than by language-tag grouping. Nevertheless, translation errors were rare, increasing somewhat across the three high school groups, while being insignificant for the more advanced students. Champagnol attributed this latter fact to greater effort put to tagging for language by the oldest students, or else to the tendency not to respond to items about which the subjects were unsure.

Champagnol postulated (cognitive) semantic categories superordinate to the language-specific semantic categories in order to account for the developing semantic interdependence seen in his tests. These cognitive categories, however, of necessity brought into play with the mixed lists, were weaker than the intralanguage categories, and as a result, the mixed lists were harder to recall. We feel that it is unclear whether language-specific semantic structures have to do with semantic notions or if they might rather be explained by frequency of associative usage.

In any case these results show a development toward reliance on deep semantic categorization in the oldest group. In the light of the additional factor of decreased translation errors, we may see support of Riegel's (1968) hypothesis that development in second language learning is from a compound system to a coordinate one.

Positive transfer across language was reconfirmed in the study by Lopez and Young (1974). Subjects were Mexican Americans who had learned both English and Spanish at the same time, but were usage-dominant in English at the time of the testing, as determined by self-judgment of which language was used for thinking. The subjects were asked to read a list of common adjectives aloud six times, then to learn a second list which was to be free-recalled in response to taped stimuli. When the second list contained items translated from the first list, recall was facilitated more than when the two lists were unrelated. This was seen more often when the language of the initial familiarization was Spanish and the second list was in English. This imbalance suggests that subjects had greater facility in translation from Spanish to English than from English to Spanish.

Lopez, Hicks, and Young (1974) further supported the language interdependence hypothesis by a measure of retroactive inhibition in bilingual paired-associate learning. Thirty-two Mexican Americans who had learned Spanish earlier but were currently English usage-dominant were the subjects. Four combinations of lists were taught auditorily: Only the language of paired items was changed, or items but not the language were changed, or both were changed, or entirely different items were given. Translation errors were more frequent in the two conditions where the language of the new list was changed. Again we see involuntary processing at the semantic level with apparent disregard for the language label of items concerned, resulting in encoding confusion. Whether or not the results are due to the compound bilingual history of the subjects, leading to interdependent storage, is debatable.

The situation of involuntary processing is evident in the study by Liepmann and Saegert (1974), who used native Arabic speakers in an English-speaking university, and presented unilingual English lists and bilingual lists visually for free-recall response of the exact words given (and not their translation equivalents). Initially the two sorts of lists resulted in equal numbers of words recalled, but on subsequent trials of lists drawn from the same word pool, the bilingual listing resulted in significantly fewer words recalled. Whether this is due entirely to translation errors is not made clear. In any case, in this instance where the script and the different morphological system might have been expected to render language labeling easier, subjects were again seen to confuse items by some sort of semantic process.

Yadrick and Kausler (1974) tested the effects of bilingual lists on a verbal discrimination learning task. The 60 subjects were second-year students of German in a university in the United States. They were exposed to lists of 12 pairs, composed either of German words as the "right" items paired with English ones as the "wrong" items, or vice versa, or to a mixed list where half of the right and wrong words were in each language. A control condition replaced the words of either language by other words in the pool. For the intrapair condition, words were paired with their translation equivalents, while for the interpair condition these translation equivalents were paired randomly within the list. Each subject was given 10 trials to learn each list by the anticipation method. Analysis was made of the errors, and it was found that, as one would expect, verbal discrimination learning decreased for those lists containing interpair relationships, but did so less for lists containing intrapair relationships (see Table 3).

Table 3
Mean Errors[a]

Interpair condition	16.6
Intrapair condition	15.6
Control condition	13.1

[a] Data summarized from Yadrick and Kausler (1974).

Contrary to expectation, however, this discrepancy occurred only when the "right" words were in English and the "wrong" ones in German, and not vice versa. The authors suggested that semantic, phonemic, and orthographic features come into play differently for learning the "right" and "wrong" words.

The list-learning studies we have reviewed speak particularly to the issue of compound versus independent lexical storage in the bilingual. There is no doubt that a word and its translation equivalent are connected in a nonrandom way. This is evidenced by the fact that translation equivalents often facilitated recall on list-recall tests (e.g., Evers, 1970). The connection may be on some nonlinguistic semantic level, since in a number of studies we have seen that language tag was forgotten while a concept was remembered (Kolers, 1968; Nott & Lambert, 1968; Evers, 1970; Lopez et al., 1974). Additional evidence for this notion is that mixed lists were sometimes recalled as well as unilingual lists (Kolers, 1965; Lambert et al., 1968; Nott & Lambert, 1968). Some separation of the two languages or lack of full translation equivalence can occur, however. Evidence is in the study by Kintsch (1970), in which translation equivalents were recognized somewhat less frequently than exact repetition of list items. Further evidence comes from the studies which employed mixed and unilingual lists. In these tests unilingual lists were best recalled (much as categorized lists usually are), while fewer items on mixed lists were recalled (Tulving & Colotla, 1970; Champagnol, 1973; Liepmann & Saegert, 1974).

LEXICOSEMANTIC TESTS

In contrast to the association and list-learning tasks, which give free rein to semantic processing, the set of studies discussed in this section attempt to manipulate semantic processing, either by diminishing it (e.g., by semantic satiation) or by focusing on it (e.g., by requiring subjects to abstract core concepts from word lists). The relative difficulty of divorcing lexical form from lexical content in each language of a bilingual may reflect language proficiency and other usage parameters. Likewise, if different semantic-processing skills are apparent in the two languages of a bilingual, one might speculate that linguistic or cognitive differences exist for the subject in the two languages.

Among the tests performed on compound and coordinate bilinguals by Lambert et al. (1958) was a test of semantic satiation. In this test, the subject was presented with a word (e.g., house) and asked to rate the word along a semantic scale (e.g., good—bad). When a comparison was made of responses to a word and to its translation equivalent, coordinate subjects evidenced greater semantic differential than did compound subjects (e.g., the word house might be rated fairly "good" whereas its equivalent maison might be more "mauvais"). Actually, only coordinate subjects with bicultural experience showed different responses to translation equivalence items. Coordinate subjects without real experience in two cultures performed like the compounds; they noted a word and its translation equivalent in the same way.

In a subsequent study, Jacobovits and Lambert (1961) tested lexical interference by means of a semantic satiation test. After rating a visually presented word (e.g., house) on a number of semantic scales (e.g., good—bad), subjects repeated the word rapidly for 15 sec and then were asked to rate either the same word, its translated equivalent, or an unrelated word. The subjects were 62 balanced French—English bilinguals, divided into compound and coordinate groups on the basis of language acquisition and usage histories. The compound bilinguals performed as expected; under satiation conditions, the same word resulted in decreased semantic weight, and under cross-satiation (response to translated equivalent), the decrease was only slightly less. Thus, the meaningfulness of a word was affected through the repetition of its translation, which the authors took to confirm an "interdependent language system." Another explanation is possible: A single deep cognitive level might connect to lexical stores; meaningful incoming stimuli would obligatorily be processed in this semantic level, whereas information pertinent to surface lexical features would normally not be retained.

Two further results of this study remain to be explained. One is curious at first glance. The coordinate bilinguals showed greater decrease in semantic differential through repetition in the cross-satiation condition than they did in the satiation condition (i.e., the translation equivalent evinced more semantic satiation than did the repeated word itself. The authors suggested an explanation revolving around the bilingual switch. They assumed that the experimental procedure, with its constant switching of languages, enhanced the switch mechanism, and that coordinate bilinguals must be particularly facile at using this switch to alternate effectively between the two language systems. Compound bilinguals, on the other hand, must have had to develop strong inhibitory mechanisms in place of a true switch in order to keep from confusing the two languages. As a result, the experimental condition was inhibitory for them. (An alternate explanation, however, may be that the coordinates, by virtue of the language use history that was employed to define them, had less practice in translation.)

Second, the bilinguals as a group manifested significantly less semantic satiation than did monolinguals. Among the bilinguals, coordinates evidenced less satiation than did compounds. The authors suggested that the efficient language learning necessary to become a balanced bilingual may call for the ability to avoid the semantic satiation effect. Perhaps bilinguals develop a more abstract notion of language to begin with and are not susceptible to the inducement of meaninglessness that the semantic satiation test wreaks in monolinguals.

The hypothesis that bilingualism results in people who treat language more abstractly is supported by two studies on children. Ianco-Worrall (1972) tested Leopold's (1939–1949) observation that bilingual children achieve linguistic relativity at an earlier age than do monolingual children. Linguistic relativity in this instance means the separation of semantic elements from the phonetic elements of a word. Her subjects were 30 Afrikaans–English bilinguals in two age groups, 4–6 (nursery school) and 7–9 (Grades 2 and 3). Each subject was matched with two monolinguals, one a speaker of each language, for age, sex, school grade, and social class. Bilingualism was defined as dual-language acquisition in a social situation where the usage separation according to language of the listener was fairly rigid.

Two experiments were run in each session, and bilinguals were called back for a second session in the other language. In the first experiment, subjects were asked to judge which of two words was more like the verbally presented stimulus word (e.g., *cap: can* or *hat*). In each of the eight instances, the stimulus word was a common monosyllabic word; one of the choice words was chosen for its initial phonetic similarity to the stimulus item, and the other for its semantic similarity. All eight sets were presented three times, and the order of phonetic and semantic choice words was balanced.

A subject was judged to be using semantic criteria if at least 66% of her or his choices were of the semantic item, and to be using phonetic criteria if 66% of his or her choices were of the phonetic item. The other subjects were deemed likely to have chosen by irrelevant position criteria. In the younger group 54% of the bilingual subjects were operating on the semantic basis, while 8% were operating on a phonetic basis. Of the monolingual subjects, only one, an English speaker, consistently chose semantically similar items. Ianco-Worrall took these results to be a confirmation of Leopold's assertion of the earlier division of semantic and phonological properties in bilinguals as compared to monolinguals.

The second experiment required subjects to explain names (e.g., "Why is a dog called a dog?"), to consider the arbitrariness of names (e.g., "Could you call a dog 'cow' and a cow 'dog'?"), and to deal with applications of information (e.g., "Let us play a game. Let us call a dog a 'cow'. Does this cow have horns?"). Differences between the monolinguals and bilinguals were to be found only on the second task; while all subjects could deal equally well with the game, in the younger age groups the bilinguals were more willing to admit to the possibility of reassigning names.

Note that two other tests of cognitive functioning were run on the same subjects. These tests evidenced no developmental differences between the bilingual and monolingual subjects. They were tests of intended and actual classification of objects, and of optional shift behavior. Thus, bilingualism does not necessarily change cognitive abilities across the board. Rather, it may induce earlier or better abilities to deal with language abstractly.

Ben-Zeev (1972, as discussed in Segalowitz, 1977) tested Hebrew–English bilingual children between the ages of 5 and 8 on verbal and nonverbal tests. On an auditory-transformation task, in which a recorded word was repeated over and over, bilinguals experienced more transformations and experienced them sooner than did monolinguals. This result was taken as an indication of greater cognitive flexibility on the part of the bilinguals. In a similar vein, when asked to substitute words into a sentence where they did not fit syntactically (e.g., clean for into), bilinguals were more successful than monolinguals. Finally, in a task of transposing a remembered matrix array of varying cylinders and then explaining why they performed as they did, the bilingual children performed as the monolinguals in the nonverbal part of the task but were superior in explaining why they did what they did. From this we may conclude that nonverbal skills are not impaired in these young bilinguals, while verbal skills matured earlier.

A naming test by Hickey (1972) might be taken as an indication that bilingual children are not necessarily better at all kinds of cognitive abstraction. In an attempt to modify the Peabody Picture Vocabulary Test in order to make it fairer to Mexican-American children, Hickey (1972) discovered that the English verbal noun caused severe difficulties to the Spanish–English bilingual preschooler. He first ran an unmodified version of the test on 100 monolingual English children and 100 bilingual children in the Los Angeles Head Start program. The measure of bilingualism was family history and usage in social activities. The test was presented to subjects individually, in English, by a speaker of English. Each item consisted of a stimulus word that must be matched to one of four pictures. One-fifth of the items were verbal nouns ending in -ing (e.g., singing). Only these items resulted in a clear-cut difference between the two groups; the bilinguals gave more incorrect or no-response answers. In the second phase of the experiment these items were deleted from the test, and the modified version was run on 60 different children in each group. There was then no difference between the two groups. Hickey argued that these results could be explained by the differential usage of verbal nouns between the two languages. In Spanish, verbal nouns are used unequivocally or with modification; in English they can be more abstract. He maintained that it is this syntactic difference which accounted for the poorer results in Spanish-speaking children, not that Spanish was more developed in or used more by these bilingual children.

A different test of semantic categorization was run by Segalowitz and Lambert (1969). Subjects were trained in either French or English to generalize a concept from a mixed language list which was flashed to them visually, item by item. After the training, subjects were asked to press a button when they saw one of the original category items. They were confronted with a series of words that contained original category words, same-language synonyms for these, other-language translations of the original words, other-language synonyms, and unrelated words in both languages. An RT measure was taken of all responses.

Neutral words were responded to fastest, then other-language synonyms, and then same-language synonyms. In this test, where attention to the semantic nature of the stimulus was required, subjects did generalize across the languages but were compelled to pay some attention to the language label of the words, too. It is hard to determine how much of this attention was consciously controlled. Although no significant differences were found between coordinate and compound bilinguals, if we consider synonyms or neutral words separately, we see that compound bilinguals showed less difference in RT between these two word categories than did coordinates.

The authors took this difference between compounds and coordinates as an indication that the two groups were processing the words differently; coordinates relied more on the meaning in processing the words, whereas compounds relied more on the nonmeaning parameters like language label or physical features. Significant differences were also found between those whose training words had been in French and those for whom the training words had been in English; the former had an easier time excluding other-language synonyms (i.e., English synonyms). The authors explained this on the basis of the imbalance between original language of the subjects; for 12 it was French, for 4 it was English, and for an additional 4 it was both. It must be kept in mind, however, that the subjects had been deemed balanced bilinguals on reliable measures (self-rating and the visual Stroop test). The data showed that English synonyms were disqualified faster than French synonyms for both compound and coordinate groups. Thus this French effect was due to neither manner nor chronology of acquisition.

In a related study, Lambert and Rawlings (1969) tested the ability of bilinguals to label "core concepts" after being given unilingual and mixed English–French associational networks. Balanced bilinguals were divided into coordinate and compound groups on the basis of the language acquisition history, especially the age of learning, 6 years of age being the dividing point. Compound bilinguals did significantly better on the mixed-language tasks, as was predicted, but also on both monolingual tasks. The authors suggested that the language-switching procedure across subsections of the experiment may have confused the coordinates, while leaving the compounds unruffled.

Another method for testing lexical organization in the bilingual is the Stroop test (Stroop, 1935). In this test, subjects are asked to label ink colors as fast as possible. In the control condition, they label colors on a card containing rows and columns of meaningless designs. Then they are asked to label ink colors of words. The time needed to label ink colors when the card has words on it is greater than the time to label ink colors when the card has designs on it. The interference (i.e., more time needed to label items) is greatest when the words are color words written in an ink color that is different from their meaning (e.g., the word red in blue ink).

Preston and Lambert (1969) demonstrated cross-language semantic processing of visual verbal material with their bilingual presentation of the Stroop Color-Word Interference Test. Presumably balanced

French–English, Hungarian–English, and German–English subjects were asked to label the ink color of printed words bearing conflicting semantic value (e.g., the word red in green ink). Subjects displayed a fair amount of interference whatever the language of response, although the interference (as measured by reading time) was greater when the words and the responses were in the same language. Moreover, the most errors were on items visually and phonologically similar between the two languages (e.g., blue, bleu).

Using the Stroop test, we studied a group of 20 balanced Hebrew–English bilinguals who had learned both languages before puberty and judged themselves to be equally proficient in both, presently (6 or 7 on scales ranging from 1 to 7). A second group of 20 English-dominant subjects were also tested; a third group contained 16 Hebrew-dominant subjects. Each subject was first asked to label as quickly as possible the ink color of wavy lines on a card containing 10 columns of 20 stimuli. Five colors of ink were used randomly: green, blue, red, black, and brown. Then subjects were asked to label as quickly as possible the ink colors of printed color words on one of two cards in one of the two languages. (Order of presentation was counterbalanced across subjects). The results are displayed in Table 4.

Table 4
Stroop Response Time (in sec)

| Test condition | Subjects | | | | | |
| | Balanced (N = 20) | | Native English (N = 20) | | Native Hebrew (N = 16) | |
	Hebrew labels	English labels	Hebrew labels	English labels	Hebrew labels	English labels
Designs	57.2	56.8	67.3	52.4	56.9	67.5
English print	82.4	91.4	86.8	88.5	74.7	91.9
Hebrew print	87.4	81.6	92.2	73.4	82.2	88.2

As in the Preston and Lambert (1969) experiment, we found the longest RTs for both groups when the language of print and the language of response were the same. For the balanced bilinguals this result may be considered an effect of intralanguage interference, since their scores for cards with wavy lines were nearly equal for the two languages. With the nondominant groups, however, the relative slowness of labeling colors at all (as evidenced in the wavy-lines condition) was added to the print interference when the L_2 stimuli were labeled in L_2.

It is of interest to note that the balanced bilinguals performed slower on labeling wavy lines in English than did the English-dominant group, although they had considered themselves fluent in the language. Interesting to note, also, is that the most frequent error (except hesitation) in the cross-language conditions was that subjects would offer the translation of the written word and never the written word itself, as they would do for the same-language situation condition.

Hamers and Lambert (1972) ran an auditory version of the Stroop test on 16 balanced French–English bilinguals. Subjects were presented four stimulus words: *high–haut, low–bas*. These four words were produced at high and low pitches, and the subject had to judge whether they were pronounced at a high or at a low pitch. Two response modalities were tested, verbal labeling and key press. The results evidenced the expected interference, and the key responses invariably took less time than the verbal responses, indicating that perception and production were not entirely independent. The necessity to respond verbally to verbal stimuli may have caused additional interference on this task.

The speed in translating words was tested by Lambert et al. (1958), on the assumption that it would indicate switching facility. No differences were found between compound and coordinate French–English speakers. This may mean that switching is equally facile in both groups (contra Jacobovits and Lambert, 1961, previously discussed), or it may mean that translation is an "unnatural" language skill, independent of other language skills.

Two studies focused on both phonological and semantic material. Slobin (1968) tested appreciation of nonobvious phonetic symbolism in 91 American university students with no experience in the experimental languages in question. The stimuli were antonym pairs (e.g., *sweet–sour, sharp–dull*) in Thai, Kanarese, and Yoruba, which were to be matched by guessing to their English equivalents. Half of the subjects only read the stimuli in Latin transcription; the other half heard tape-recorded stimuli. Subjects were instructed to pair the foreign sets with English sets. Since the groups from both conditions performed similarly, analysis of the group that both heard and read stimuli is considered.

The results of interest to us are those which related performance to number and years of foreign language study. Of the subjects who had studied two or more foreign languages, 80% (16 of 20 subjects) performed above the mean of 34 correct pairs out of 56, whereas, of those who had studied one or no foreign languages, less than 50% did so (12 of 26 subjects). Of those who had studied foreign language more than 3 years, 75% were above average (15 out of 20 subjects), whereas, of those who had studied less than 4 years, only 35% performed above the mean. This would seem to imply that experience in study of foreign language expands the individual's sensitivity to universals of phonetic symbolism. Such a skill may be considered a device of compounding at some phonological analytic level.

Lerea and LaPorta (1971) studied the vocabulary and phonological learning skills of bilinguals and monolinguals. Their subjects were young adult university students. The monolingual group consisted of 17 subjects, the bilinguals were divided into two groups, each of 17 subjects. Coordinate subjects were those who had learned both languages as children, one at home and one in school, while the compound group were taught their second language after age 13. Although the compound group learned the second language at an average age of 17, their scores on the Hoffman Assessment of Bilingual Background averaged 3.47, while those of the coordinate group averaged 3.22. The languages known by the bilinguals were Indo-European ones, exclusive of those containing /x/ as a phoneme.

The task in each condition was to learn a list of nine Hebrew words containing the phoneme /x/ (initially, medially, or finally) and their English translation equivalents. In one condition the words were presented visually on a memory drum, and subjects were instructed to write the Hebrew words in Latin transcription. In the second condition the presentation was auditory, by means of a tape recorder, and the subjects were to pronounce the words accurately. Analysis was done of the number of trials necessary to correct reproduction of the vocabulary items. In the auditory condition a measure of the pronunciation of the /x/ was made after the final trial (but correct pronunciation was not necessary to terminate the task).

In the visual mode the monolinguals took significantly fewer trials to learn the task than did the compound bilinguals. In the auditory mode the compounds took significantly fewer trials than the monolinguals. (The coordinate bilinguals were intermediate in both conditions.) In the auditory mode the bilingual groups together took significantly fewer trials than did the monolinguals. For the monolinguals it would appear that the auditory learning task was harder than the visual, but for the bilingual groups it was not significantly harder. The number of words in which the /x/ was accurately pronounced was judged by three fluent Hebrew speakers. By the ninth trial the compound groups produced the consonant more accurately than either of the other two groups. All three groups continued to improve until their final trial, but the compounds were still significantly better, and there was no difference between the coordinate and the monolingual groups. Within the coordinate group, however, a significant inverse correlation was found between the number of words correctly pronounced and the number of trials necessary to achieve learning.

The authors explained their results on the basis of learning set: The compound bilinguals had most recently been involved in learning a new language, and by aural–oral means; so they had acquired the necessary learning strategy for this test. Monolinguals probably chose to remain monolinguals because they knew themselves to prefer the visual modality, and therefore considered themselves poor language learners.

It must be pointed out that this experiment may contradict the notion that people who become bilingual at an early age will later have more facility in picking up a third language. Were that the case, the coordinate bilinguals would have been expected to outperform the compound subjects, at least on the phonological task, since phonological imitation must be involved in second language learning. (One might argue that paired-associate vocabulary learning is anathema to the supposed separate systems language style of coordinate bilinguals.)

CONCLUSION

The studies discussed in this section made several points. The series of bilingual Stroop tests, both visual and auditory, suggested that linguistic input is processed for meaning in each language, regardless of the language it is in (e.g., Preston & Lambert, 1969). In these studies some differences are seen between compound and coordinate bilinguals. Lambert *et al.* (1958) and Jacobovits and Lambert (1961) found that compounds and coordinates performed differently on semantic satiation tests; as predicted, the compound bilinguals responded in similar fashion to a word and its translation equivalent, while the coordinate subjects did not. A second difference between the two groups was evidenced in their ability to learn new language items. Lerea and LaPorta (1971) showed that coordinate bilinguals took less time to learn by the visual modality, whereas the compounds learned auditorily presented material better. A final theme in these studies was the superior linguistic sensitivity of bilinguals. This was seen in earlier development of an abstract attitude toward language in children (Ianco-Worrall, 1972; Ben-Zeev, 1972). In adults, language learning in the auditory mode was better in bilinguals (Lerea & LaPorta, 1971), and intuition about sound–meaning correspondences in unknown languages was higher in bilinguals (Slobin, 1968).

Syntax and Sentence Semantics

Three groups of studies deal with language processing and response at the sentential level. One focuses on factors influencing facility in processing sentences, a second on forced switching from one language to the other, and a third on simultaneous translation.

SENTENCE PROCESSING

The lexical studies discussed in the previous sections account for only one linguistic subsystem: the lexicon. One may view this system as subordinate to the syntactic component of the grammar, into which lexical items must be plugged. Yet perhaps because lexical units are easy to define and test, the greatest body of psychological literature on bilingualism has focused on them. Some questions we might ask with respect to syntax, and in particular with respect to bilingual sentence processing are: How closely is sentence processing tied to language-specific features? How closely is it tied to cognition? Can some syntactic "rules" be represented in compound manner, and others in coordinate manner? What constitutes interference at the sentence level? Does language tagging obtain at the sentence level? The studies which follow speak to some of these issues.

Doob (1957) studied recall of propositions by testing four sample populations whose active language was not English (Gandans, Luos, Zulus, and Afrikaaners). In each group more than 100 male high school students were tested. Subjects were given a written questionnaire and told, in English, that they were to agree or disagree with the statements on its two pages. The first page of 10 statements was in either English or the native language, and the second page was in the other language. A typical statement was "Brothers can never be friends." When subjects had finished the task, the examiner replaced the questionnaires with blank sheets and asked for content recall of as many of the statements as possible. Finally, the Zulu group was asked to recall and label the language the original statement had been in.

Although as a rule subjects tended to agree more with statements in their own language, memory for language of presentation was imperfect. When subjects were asked to label the language the original statement had been in, they made errors or left blanks. From this we may conclude that when the instruction was to focus on the content of visually presented sentences, the meaning would be processed beyond the language-specific level and reproduced in the other language without awareness on the part of the subject.

When analysis was made of the number of items recalled, different relationships were found for the different groups. For the Afrikaans group, there was no relation between the language of exposure and the ease of recall of statements. For the Zulus, English was facilitative of recall. The Luos and Gandans were intermediate with respect to the influence of linguistic parameters on ease of recall.

Forster and Clyne (1968) tested sentence construction (or actually reconstruction) in balanced German–English bilinguals and in English-dominant bilinguals. Their task involved exposure to a sentence of which either the initial or the final half of the words had been deleted and replaced by blanks. German half-sentences were alternated with English half-sentences. Subjects were to complete the sentences as quickly as possible. Reaction time was measured to the nearest second.

The original sentences were constructed with respect to their surface complexity. In half of the sentences deletion of either one of the halves damaged a high number of constituents; these will be referred to as the complex sentences. In the other half of the sentences, deletion damaged relatively fewer constituents; these are the simple sentences. Forster (in press) had seen previously that this measure of complexity correlated with difficulty for monolingual English speakers only in instances when the first half of a sentence was deleted. For German monolinguals, on the other hand, greater complexity by this measure correlated with difficulty on both words of half-sentences. This finding was interpreted as reflecting on the different linguistic structures of the two languages. English is typically a right-branching language (with phrasal modifiers following the elements they modify), while German behaves like a left-branching language (with modifiers preceding the elements they modify). The question posited in this study was whether balanced bilinguals would perform like each monolingual group when dealing with sentences in the respective languages, or whether they would have a single strategy or skill which was intermediate to those of the two monolingual populations.

The balanced bilingual subjects were chosen on the basis of their estimation that their English was at least as good as their German (most were native speakers of German) and their report that they had been using the languages equally for at least the preceding 5 years. The nonbalanced group were Australian students who had learned some German but did not use it frequently.

In discussion of the results, we refer only to those for sentences of high surface complexity, since a previous study showed simple sentences to manifest little difference across languages. For the balanced bilinguals, the results were consistent with those of the previous study in monolingual subjects. With the German sentences, there was less difference than with the English sentences, between the time required to complete initial sentence halves and the time required to complete final sentence halves (13.91 sec for German, 24.85 sec for English). It would appear that even in the mixed-language experimental condition opted for here, the bilingual subjects were able to switch strategies of processing for sentence reconstruction in the two different languages, and perform like the respective monolinguals.

The results for the German learners were not parallel to those of the bilinguals. For the English-dominant group, German was even more difficult to treat than English when the sentence beginnings were deleted. That is to say, the difference in RT between sentences without beginnings and sentences without ends was greater in German than in English (24.54 sec and 10.88 sec, respectively, cf. for the balanced bilinguals, 2.94 sec difference for German and 17.16 sec for English). Since this finding held true for these subjects regardless of the complexity of the sentences, in contradiction to predictions for the simpler sentences on the basis of intralanguage monolingual testing, we may wonder if these language learners were not operating on their L_2 task in an exaggeration of the strategies they used for L_1, not having learned yet that this strategy was inappropriate for the language in question. It may be also that language learning proceeds from memorization of linear structures as units, to the mastery of enough of these to induce the abstraction of rules (not taught "grammar rules") necessary for true creation of sentences. For people with control only over the preliminary linear skill, it would make sense that completing an initial half-sentence would be easier than initiating an appropriate sentence beginning.

Stafford (1968) predicted that compound bilingualism involved a greater amount of interference between the languages, which would result in a reduced efficiency of cognitive behavior. He attempted to prove this by a problem-solving task that involved pressing one of four buttons which were beside each box of a 2 × 2 matrix, displaying various combinations of a square, a triangle, and two blanks. The subject had to discover the correct configuration (or rule), from a simple task (to press the button by the square) through three progressively more difficult ones (the hardest being to press the button by the square when the square and triangle were contiguous, but the button by the triangle when they were diagonals). After the test, subjects were asked which language(s) they had used in answering. Measure was made of trials to learning and of percentage of problems correctly answered.

The subjects were Navaho Indian pupils of Grade 8 (aged approximately 15). The criterion of compound bilingualism was learning both English and Navaho in the preschool period; and that of coordinate bilingualism, learning English after starting school. Monolinguals spoke only English. The compound group had 41 subjects; the coordinate, 44 subjects; and the monolinguals, 20 subjects. On the nonlanguage section of the California Test of Mental Maturity, the compound subjects performed slightly higher than the coordinate subjects (81 ± 10.7 to 78 ± 10.0 in one school, 90.6 ± 10.3 to 85.9 ± 10.3 in the other). The monolinguals averaged significantly higher (98 ± 17.2). The instructions were given in English.

While many of the correlation statistics approached significance, two comparisons achieved it. The compound group took significantly more trials to solve the problems than did the monolinguals ($p < .01$), and they solved fewer of the problems than did the coordinate bilinguals ($p = .05$). Yet the coordinate and monolingual groups did not perform significantly differently, even though the latter manifested higher IQ. Among the coordinate group from one school the ratio of pupils who used both languages in solving the problems to those who used only one was 1.5:1. Among the compound subjects it was 3.6:1.

Stafford concluded that encouragement of coordinate bilingualism would be pedagogically sound, since compound bilingualism correlates with poor cognitive performance. We suggest that socioeconomic variables (uncontrolled in this experiment) could explain the poor performance of the compound bilinguals on this task and the good performance of the coordinate bilinguals. Or perhaps the fact that the language of the instructions was English accounts for the results. Another possibility, however, is that the different language capacities of the different groups made different strategies (verbal versus nonverbal) available in the solving of such tasks. It may also be that different styles of bilingualism (compound or coordinate) make different use of the cerebral hemispheres.

MacKay and Bowman (1969) noted that unilingual practice in repeating a sentence increased the speed at which it was produced, and they tested whether this phenomenon was due primarily to the semantic, syntactic, or phonological structure. Subjects were 12 German–English college students. Half the group were dominant in each language. They were given various literary sentences and translations of these to read as fast as possible. As expected, the time necessary to produce the sentences decreased with practice. After 12 practice repetitions, subjects were given a second sentence to read. When it was a translation of the first sentence bearing similar word order, the speed of production was almost that which had been reached in the final four trials. When the second sentence was a translation with a different word order, the speed to produce it was close to that of the second four trials of the original set. Thus both semantic and syntactic facilitation obtained. Further proof of the contribution of obligatory semantic processing of the syntax came from comparing the results of the same test when the sentences were scrambled strings and their literal translations; facilitation did not obtain. Finally, nonsense strings of items obeying the phonological rules of one or the other of the languages were repeated, with the expected speedup in later trials, but no transference occurred between nonsense strings "in" the other language. Under delayed auditory feedback, which MacKay (1970) found to produce fewer stuttering errors in the bilingual's dominant language, the effect of syntactic–semantic processing was again seen; repetition decreased stuttering errors in the translation conditions.

Macnamara (1970) reviewed a number of his studies pertaining to reading in a fairly fluent second language. The first study measured the accuracy in solving verbal problems when the individual words and structures of the problems were all understood. His subjects for the first test were Irish sixth graders who were native speakers of English, but who had studied Gaelic for at least 6 years. Half of the approximately 400 subjects were given the English form of the test; the other half were given the Gaelic form. Each problem was presented once as a unit (e.g., If May is the sixth month of the year and if a pound is not more than an ounce divide 81 by 9. Otherwise subtract 3 from 7.), and once divided into its component commands so that Macnamara could analyze only those problems for which the words and syntactic relationships were clearly understood (e.g., May is the sixth month of the year. Right, wrong, I don't know; Divide 81 by 9, If a crow is white, write 8, otherwise write 9, etc.).

In about half of the complex problems whose parts were all understood, a significantly larger proportion of students answered correctly to the English presentation than to the Gaelic presentation. This suggested that complex syntactic processing could be imperfect even after 6 years of language instruction. We are not told how much instruction the children had had, and how fluent they were, but Macnamara felt that differential "grasp of language" was responsible for the different results.

There was no time limit in the preceding study, but time had been seen to be a factor in a previous study in which fifth- and sixth-grade children had solved problems with equal accuracy in both languages but had taken more time in the L_2; so Macnamara timed reading aloud in 40 of the subjects of the present study. They were asked to read verbal arithmetical problems three times, and it was seen that although the Gaelic versions took longer, the subjects sped up more in Gaelic over the course of the three readings. Macnamara assumed that there was a cognitive system beyond the language-specific ones and so suggested that a difficulty in the language "input process" accounted for the initially slow, but then improved, reading problems in the L_2.

Also reported in this article was another set of related studies carried out by Macnamara on 24 French–English college-student bilinguals (whose L_1 was English) in Montreal. These studies compared the times required for various sorts of language processing. For example, RT was measured in response to tachistoscopically presented nouns. No difference was seen between the languages. Reaction time was measured for true–false judgments to sentences composed of the nouns used previously. They were all of the form *A hen has a door*, in an attempt to minimize the demands of syntactic processing. No difference obtained between the languages. In a third test words and a picture were presented simultaneously, and the subjects had to judge if the word named the picture. This task took significantly longer if the word was in French than if it was in English. (These times were corrected for the perceptual thresholds measured in the first experiments.) On the parallel test with sentence stimuli, however, no difference obtained between the two languages. Subjects were then asked to read, both silently and aloud, two sorts of passages. One passage was composed of the sentences previously constructed. The other was formed by scrambling the words of such a text. The subjects took longer to read words aloud in French, and they made less use of transitional probabilities in French. That is, the syntax of the unscrambled French text helped them less in comparison to the scrambled text in reading English than did that of the unscrambled English text. The difference in times required to read the scrambled and unscrambled texts in English was greater than that in French.

In conclusion, Macnamara posed the question of why time differences in processing the two languages might necessitate differences in cognitive capacity. He pointed out that performance constraints such as short-term memory are probably involved, and that the slower reading rate in the L_2 prohibits the subject from thinking about what he has read. Numerous other linguistic factors may be reflected in the time differential, which might also account for lesser facility in dealing with L_2 verbal problems. Among them is the ability to deal with redundant information. In perceiving input, the native speaker has command over many levels of cue, so that he can correctly interpret speech which is masked to a fair extent, probably more easily than the nonnative speaker can. In producing speech, the native speaker should have better control over the rules of permissible phonological reduction and thus should read aloud more rapidly. A factor increasing time in silent reading may be that the L_2 reader has not overcome phonological reading to the extent that he has in his native reading, where he may grasp full words, clauses, or sentences and immediately process semantically without necessity for a subvocal phonological mediator.

Heras and Nelson (1972) tested language tagging in conjunction with semantic or syntactic memory storage in 5-year-old Spanish–English bilinguals. Subjects had stories that consisted of three sentences read to them, and were instructed in advance that they would be given a sentence to judge if it had occurred in the story and also asked in what language the final sentence had been. Although the subjects spoke and comprehended English well, Spanish was their dominant language. It would appear that the test instructions were in English. The question about the final sentence, however, was asked in the language of the test sentence, which subjects had to judge for occurrence in the story. The stories were composed of two sentences in one language and one in the other. The test statement was either changed in meaning (by changing subject N and V), syntax (by changing position of a prepositional phrase), or language (by translating).

While the children made significantly more correct judgments that a sentence was not in the story when meaning had been changed than when syntactic order had been changed, there was no significant difference if a translation of the sentence was provided (presumably subjects were to say "yes" when a translation equivalent was given). Finally, subjects were asked, half the time in English and half in Spanish, as to the language identity of the third sentence of the story. They were able to answer this question best when all the material between the end of the story and their answer to this question had been in the same language. Thus the demands of switching may encourage remembering by meaning with loss of language-tag information.

As with single-word stimuli, so with sentence stimuli; we again see evidence that semantic encoding is the usual procedure for dealing with language input, whereas language tagging is not (Doob, 1957; Heras & Nelson, 1972). Surface, or linear, syntax does play some role in language processing, however, as MacKay and Bowman (1969) showed. The extent to which surface syntax can be utilized in a sentence completion or repetition task, however, depends on the degree of one's proficiency in a given language (Forster & Clyne, 1968; Macnamara, 1970).

LANGUAGE SWITCHING

For many bilinguals, spontaneous switching from one language to another, even in the middle of a sentence (although usually at a major constituent boundary), is a comfortable, natural, unconscious language act. For others, a separation must be rigorously maintained between usage of the two languages. We may ask what "switching" mechanism or system is responsible for controlling the "switch" or inhibition of "switch." How is this "switch" related to the linguistic systems? Is the "switch" which is involved in producing mixed-language speech the same one that must process mixed-language speech or writing? Is the notion of "switch" an appropriate one at all, or does the notion "monitor system" provide a better working hypothesis?

Kolers (1966) tested French-dominant and English-dominant bilinguals in a reading comprehension test. The linguistic form of the passages was either unilingual, with alternation of languages at sentence boundaries, or with mixed languages within sentences. Subjects' written responses were best in the unilingual situation of their mother tongue and worst in the unilingual situation of the other language. Alternating passages produced results close to those of the native tongue, whereas mixed-language passages gave results closer to those of the monolingual nonnative passage. This was taken by Kolers to imply that the weightier factor in distracting or confusing the subjects was the lack of proficiency in the nondominant language, and not the unusual nature of the language switch task. The evidence supports the notion of semantic processing at the discourse level. We cannot argue that syntactic rules were entirely ignored in the mixed passages, since French and English share many rules; the opposite order of adjectives and nouns, for example, did not figure prominently in the passages.

Subjects were timed for reading aloud the same passages. The alternating passages took times intermediate between those of the native and the second language; reading the mixed passages took the longest. In the light of the preceding experiment, these data may be taken as evidence for some additional effort involved in switching languages within sentences. Note that one of the cues a bilingual may deliberately employ in speech, to indicate to his listener that he is using a word from another language, is to set it off by a preceding pause.

The total difference in reading times was divided by the number of switches entailed. The result showed that output switching operated at an average of from .3 to .5 sec. Error analysis on this reading task showed phonological and translation interference in both directions for each bilingual. Beyond pronouncing graphemes as if they were of the other language, Kolers reports, subjects would use a new "accent," involving features not noticeably present in their unilingual productions, when reading the mixed texts rapidly. Furthermore, subjects did some reordering of structurally ambiguous forms into more common ones. Next, when subjects were encouraged to generate alternating and mixed speech, the switch time calculated was 1.01–1.44 sec. We can ask whether these lengthy switch times are effects purely of the output switch; or of the highly unusual, unpracticed nature of the task; or of some underlying difference between the passive process of reading aloud and the active one of speech production, or of all three.

Error analysis revealed a tendency to increase redundancy in the alternating and mixed production conditions (e.g., *Il n'en a pas eu any of them*). This may reflect the noncompatibility of the two grammatical systems, and perhaps the disassociated, independent brain mechanisms producing them. Error analysis of parts of speech showed no significant differences. When subjects were given unilingual or interlinearly mixed texts and asked to base their mixed speech on them, the interlinear text facilitated frequent switching (average string/language was 1.5 words). The entire practice of generation of mixed speech based on mixed texts did not facilitate a free generation task afterwards. In this free-generation task, strings reverted to 3.9 words in any given language. The greater length of the strings probably indicated automacity of phrases. Such automacity may have resulted from some kind of buildup of syntagmatic associative strength, through long syntactic practice in speaking only one language. It would be interesting to do further linguistic analysis of the patterns and history of bilinguals who switch from one language to the other within sentences. Diebold (1963) and Weinreich (1953) mentioned that such bilinguals switch with more frequency at syntactic boundaries than within such boundaries.

Macnamara, Krauthammer, and Bolgar (1968) studied output switching time in French–English bilingual subjects. One group of subjects was balanced; the other two groups were dominant in one of the languages. In an attempt to ensure that the production switch was being tested, the stimuli were "linguistically neutral," that is, digits. Subjects were to respond verbally to the digits according to a task that involved either reading in one language or changing language, and either reading the number presented or manipulating the number by adding one to it. Within the switching condition, both regular (i.e., predictable) and irregular patterns were employed. The task to be performed was indicated by use of four geometrical symbols. Reaction time was measured by a voice key.

The results were that predictable, regular switching was significantly faster than irregular, unpredictable switching. The combined results of both the language change and the number manipulation task showed time per switch to be .21 sec when the switches were regular and .39 sec when they were not. There was no significant difference between the time required for subjects to change languages and the time required to add one to the number, so the authors interpreted their results in the light of a general set-switching model. They argued that the bilingual can be considered to have a set for responding in each language, with an automatic and hard-to-consciously-control switch mechanism governing change. They observed that there are apparently greater difficulties in operating the output switch than the input one. This assertion should probably be modified to read "consciously manipulating" instead of "operating," since in normal conversational situations the expectations put on the input and the output switches are different; it is as important to have an input processor that encourages switching by scanning or searching incoming messages and testing for the correct language of input among the various possible ones, as it is to have an output mechanism that inhibits switching during speaking.

Macnamara and Kushnir (1971) divorced input processing from verbal output, using the same reading passages as Kolers (1966). They took 30 fluent bilinguals of whom half were native in French and half in English. Subjects were instructed to read carefully in order to prepare for comprehension questions. Analysis of their reading times showed that in the mixed-language condition, subjects took longer by a measure of .17 sec per switch. Macnamara suggested that Kolers' .3– .5-sec times involved both input and output switching. A second experiment asked subjects to judge true or false, visually and auditorily presented sentences with more or fewer switches (e.g., from *Horses smoke pommes de terre*, to *Les oiseaux have deux wings*). Measure of key-press choice RT revealed differences in both conditions, increasing with the number of switches necessitated for processing the sentences. The mean time for one switch was .21 in the visual presentation and .26 in the auditory mode.

In an effort to reduce the switch effect by making it predictable, sentences were printed with the intruding items in red, and such sentences were distributed randomly with unilingual sentences in one condition and alternated with them in a second condition. Curiously, the random set produced faster RTs than the alternating set, indicating that the strategy used by subjects given these particular explicit color cues was inferior to whatever their natural one would have been.

We may conclude that the unnatural language switching described in the series of experiments in this section takes a measurable amount of time. This switching time may combine a certain interval for switching at the input end, and a certain interval at the output end. Nevertheless, when forced to produce mixed speech, facilitating strategies may be elicited. Kolers (1966) reported that his subjects read mixed speech with an unfamiliar "accent." This suggests that they may have unconsciously made an effort to reduce the dual production system to a single intermediate system.

SIMULTANEOUS TRANSLATION

In the literature reviewed in the preceding sections, we have seen evidence of separation between production and perception systems. A crucial task in testing the interaction between these systems is simultaneous translation. Translators are obliged to listen to and process a stream of incoming speech in one language, and to translate it aloud as soon and as accurately as possible. What precisely is involved in this linguistic skill?

Treisman (1965) tested the relative difficulty of shadowing (orally following an auditory stimulus) and of simultaneous translating. Thirty subjects were divided equally into French-dominant, English-dominant, and balanced bilinguals. They were trained in both tasks until no further improvement was seen, then given the experimental passages. Analysis of responses showed translation to be a more difficult task than shadowing. Each nonbalanced group did better shadowing in the native language. When input was distorted to produce various orders of approximation to the two languages, the difference between the two languages increased. The explanation suggests itself that even for such a task as shadowing, which might theoretically be done by thoughtless repetition, language input processing involuntarily takes place. In the more difficult situation of dealing with distorted language, where less redundancy is perceived, the processing system with less experience, with fewer varied strategies, that is, that of the nondominant language, evidences confusion or inefficiency.

Ear–voice span (the time between learning an item and pronouncing the response), however, was greater for translation (four to five words) than for shadowing (three words), perhaps implying that less thorough syntactic processing was going on in the shadowing task. The span was longer in the translation of English passages than of French for all subjects; however, all subjects did better (i.e., translated more words) when translating from French into English. Again we see unidirectional effects; perhaps they are explainable by test artifact, or perhaps by the more frequent practice or greater necessity for all these Oxford subjects to translate from French to English.

Gerver (1974a) purported to deal with the degree of comprehension involved in simultaneous translation. He presented three recorded French texts to nine subjects who were finishing a course in French-to-English translation. Each text was followed by 10 written questions in English on the content. Subjects were instructed in advance either to listen to the passage, to shadow it, or to translate simultaneously (i.e., interpret). Shadowing resulted in significantly fewer performance errors (6%) than did interpreting (18%), indicating that interpreting is a harder task. It is interesting to note that training in simultaneous translation included considerable practice in shadowing; so shadowing may be assumed to contribute to translation, perhaps only so far as to accustom the translator to the peculiar task of long-term simultaneous speaking and listening. The responses to the content questions showed listening to give the best results (58% correct), then interpreting (51%), and lastly shadowing (43%). The differences between the tasks were significant.

It is unclear whether these results must be interpreted, as they were by Gerver, on the basis of complex versus simple information processing. The complex task, simultaneous translation, by this analysis, would facilitate memory more than does the relatively simpler task of shadowing. It may be that the correctness differences result from the fact that the questions were in English and the subjects had been producing English in the translation condition, while producing French in the shadowing condition. Gerver also suggested that something about the shadowing task could inhibit recall (or perhaps absorption) of the information. Shadowing may produce a masking effect, similar to that reported by Rabbitt (1968), who found that levels of noise which interfere with recall and understanding of material might nevertheless permit perception. There are two differences between the shadowing task and the translation task. In shadowing, one must continuously produce speech, while in translation, one can wait for a pause in the incoming speech. Shadowing also does not demand semantic and syntactic processing, whereas translation does.

Goldman-Eisler (1972) further evaluated factors involved in simultaneous translation by testing six professional English–French and English–German translators. Analysis of the linguistic structure of the ear–voice span showed that in 90–95% of all cases, the lag encompassed at least a complete predicative expression, implying at least an anticipated lack of lexical and phrase-syntactic compatibility across languages. Significant differences were found in ear–voice span length from German to English, and these differences were clearly attributable to the verb-final pattern in German, which renders predication incomplete until clause end. The greatest lags occurred at the end of input clauses, which the author attributed to the increase in predictability of meaning at sentence ends, and the more critical (i.e., less predictable) meaning at the beginning of the next sentence. This difference in predictability would cause these professionals to withhold potentially interfering speech while processing sentence beginnings. It is clear that subjects cannot rely on waiting for pauses in order to produce their translations; they must prejudge how crucial an upcoming sequence of words will be. Goldman-Eisler mentioned that informal inquiry revealed that a purely alternating pattern of listening and then translating would not be to her subjects' liking. We might conclude that some input processing must go on while the translator is speaking, although perhaps some of the redundancies are lost.

The question can be posed as to the process of short-term storage during the ear–voice lag. Although there is no proof, a solution would be storage in the language of input, then translation at the time of output. This solution would allow opportunity for later input to influence earlier estimations of probability, without necessitating a second translation stage. Further experimentation remains to be done to determine who make good simultaneous translators, and what changes occur during the course of their professional education. Also interesting would be investigation of the implications of using several language skills simultaneously (i.e., comprehension of one item and production of another).[1]

Barik (1974) analyzed simultaneous interpretation by six French–English interpreters for errors and for such temporal aspects of the interpreter's speech as synchronization, rate, and rhythm. Of the six

---

[1]A relevant work on this point is that of Goldman-Eisler and Cohen (1974), which is misleadingly entitled "An Experimental Study of Interference between Receptive and Productive Processes Relating to Simultaneous Translation," since in fact it has nothing to do with translation, but rather with a task the authors think may be related to translation. Moreover, the subjects are not bilinguals and so cannot evidence the difference in brain structure that bilingualism may entail. It is of interest to note, however, that production of automatic language tasks (counting aloud from 1 to 100) did not interfere with a listening comprehension task, while the more complex cognitive task (subtracting 1,2,3, etc., respectively, from 100 aloud) did.

subjects two were professional simultaneous interpreters, two had just completed a course in the field, and two were fluent bilinguals with no experience in simultaneous translation. Of each pair, one subject was dominant in French, one in English.

The findings that are of relevance to our study are the following: The amateurs made more errors and were more literal in translation than were the other four subjects. Unlike the trained subjects who performed equally in either direction, the amateurs made more errors in interpreting from their weak to their dominant language. Trained subjects may gain some mechanism for overcoming the interference that speaking a strong language causes to simultaneous understanding of a weaker language.

The results on the temporal factors for amateurs were no different, however, from those of trained subjects. Nor were differences found between translation from the dominant to the nondominant language and translation in the other direction. This finding implies that the temporal strategies used by trained interpreters are natural strategies. All subjects tended to speak during pauses in the speaker's speech; they avoided, insofar as possible, having to produce and listen to speech at the same time. The greater the time lag between the interpreter and the speaker, the more omissions were made. On the other hand, better translation was done by waiting for full phrases rather than translating, word by word, literally. Thus, factors of memory span may conflict with factors of processing to the meaning level in simultaneous translation.

Causing special difficulty were two sorts of words with no direct translation equivalents: function words, and abstract words or concepts. Barik observed that unnecessary order reversals obtained occasionally; for example, *the classroom and the laboratory* was rendered *the laboratory and the classroom*. These observations reveal that a tendency to lexemic translation co-occurs with deep semantic processing during a simultaneous interpretation task.

Skillful simultaneous translation would appear to necessitate several abilities:

1. Avoidance of literal or word-by-word translation.
2. Registration of units (up to the clause level) in short-term memory, even while speaking.
3. Semantic processing.
4. Anticipation of input.

It must be noted that Treisman (1965) reported translation to be a more difficult task than shadowing, whereas Gerver (1974a) saw shadowing to be the more difficult task. The contradiction can be resolved if we consider that Treisman was judging adequacy of speech production, whereas Gerver was testing comprehension.

Conclusion

The psychological studies discussed in this chapter provide us with a number of points which any model of bilingualism must explain. Subjects seem to process language input (both words and sentences) at some semantic level beyond the language-specific. The lexicons of the two languages seem to be more or less compounded, depending in part on the manner and/or age of second language acquisition. Both association and list-learning tasks suggest that a word in one language and its translation equivalent, when there is one in the second language, are related, much as a word and its synonym in the same language may be connected in an associational network. As to language production, there is certainly some prohibition against mixing languages, which manifests itself by language clustering in the chain-association tasks, and by a measurable time increment in the reading aloud of mixed speech. An input switch may prime the language processor(s) to expect one or the other language. That the input and output switches may operate independently is suggested most strikingly by the existence of simultaneous translators. The skill they practice may be an extension of the increased "linguistic sensitivity" of the bilingual.

4

Neuropsychological Studies of Bilingualism

Introduction

This chapter will evaluate both clinical and experimental neuro-psychological studies of polyglots (in neuropsychology, bilinguals are often included in the term **polyglot**). The clinical studies are of four types: in-depth individual case studies of polyglot aphasics, group studies of polyglot aphasics, anatomic studies on brains of nonaphasic polyglots, and reviews of the preceding. Each of these four types of research contributes a different point. The bulk of the case studies on individual polyglot aphasics documents different types of aphasia in each language, or different recovery patterns in aphasia, for each of the several languages known to the patient. The group studies of polyglot aphasics, on the other hand, suggest that cases of different patterns in the several languages are in fact rare; the average polyglot will lose and recover both languages with the same deficits, and to the extent that she previously knew them. The articles reviewing these case studies often summarize a number of cases of differential recovery in polyglot aphasics. Postmortem studies of polyglot brains, as a rule, give evidence that knowledge of multiple languages has anatomical consequences.

In the section on experimental neuropsychology, we shall review lateralization studies on healthy bilingual speakers of several different languages. In that section we also present our own series of experiments on Hebrew–English bilinguals.

Polyglot Aphasia—Case Studies

Before presenting the various statistical arguments as to factors influencing impairment and recovery patterns in polyglot aphasics, we want to sketch some of the case studies which illustrate the various issues. First, we discuss cases which suggest various explanations of recovery patterns (namely, Pitres's rule, Ribot's rule, and affect), then we look at cases exemplifying some of the aphasic deficits that could only occur in polyglot subjects (different types of aphasia in different languages, inability to switch to a second language, inappropriate mixing of the languages, and regression of one language as a second begins to recover).

The rule of Ribot states that the first learned language should be less impaired and should recover first in aphasia. Dreifuss's (1961) case of aphasia in a young polyglot poet exemplifies the primacy of the earliest tongue. His first language was German. At age 16 he had an attack of migraine with aphasia in which he interpreted English newspaper headlines in German. From this time on the patient felt his previous fluency of expression was somewhat impaired; he could no longer write poetry, nor learn foreign languages with his former excellence. His second attack at age 16 again caused aphasia. A third attack, at age 19, paralleled the second. The next attack, at age 28, combined agrammatism and amnestic dysphasia with a right homonymous hemianopia. An electroencephalogram performed 5 hours after the attack showed only some high voltage 4-cycle-per-sec activity from both occipital regions, especially the left. Dreifuss interpreted this case to be an indication of the irreversibility of migraine when sensitive evaluation measures, like the ability to produce poetry, are employed. This patient, who was seen at age 34, was a right-hander who had immigrated from Germany to the United States at age 10. After that time he had no exposure to German. His first migraine attack at age 15 was right frontal. During a second attack at age 16, to his surprise, he thought in German and could only produce German curses. His orientation and comprehension of English were preserved and after 10 min his English speech returned, although for half an hour he continued to misuse and circumlocute words. During the next attack, 6 months later, while reading, he realized he could not understand the words. He could speak, but function words were omitted or misused. Within a few minutes he could only produce German curses, although this time he was thinking in English. He wrote what he believed to be "I am ill" to a friend, but this note was unintelligible. The recovery was as before, with writing preceding reading.

The rule of Pitres states that the most "familiar," or most recently used, language returns first in polyglot aphasia. Halpern (1941) presented two cases of immigrants to Israel in whom Hebrew was the first language to return. Both cases were young men who had learned to read and write Hebrew as children, but had immigrated to Palestine only about 5 years before their injuries. The 20-year-old was a Russian-born left-hander who suffered a right temporal wound. His speech in Hebrew recovered within a month, whereas his Russian speech had not returned 3 months posttrauma. His comprehension of Russian was poor, and he answered Russian questions in Hebrew. Agraphia and alexia were soon the only remaining impairments in Hebrew. The second case was of a 24-year-old German who had gone to Israel at age 20. A bullet wound to the left temporal region resulted in sensory aphasia. Although the first words he spoke were in German, his Hebrew speech was soon better than the German. His comprehension of Hebrew returned before comprehension of German. Additionally, his reading was better in Hebrew than in German.

When neither the rule of Pitres nor that of Ribot applies, affective factors have been cited to explain the order of recovery of languages. One such case is that of Krapf (1957). An Englishman who had learned to speak Spanish fluently suffered cranial trauma, resulting in a sensory aphasia. His comprehension of English was most impaired when his English-speaking mother visited him.

A modification on the affect theory is that the language environment aids a person to recover a certain language. Minkowski (1963) referred to several cases in the Russian literature on polyglot aphasics in which young men from Central Asia whose native languages were Turkmenian, Kazakh, or Georgian were inducted into the Russian army. There they learned to speak Russian. When wounded, these men found themselves in Russian hospitals, with Russian speakers around them. Their Russian recovered first and best.

Bychowski (1919) described the case of an unschooled, bullet-injured Pole with resultant right hemiplegia, whose Polish hardly returned, and the German of his youth not at all; his Russian, learned at age 24 in the Russian army, recovered best in the Russian hospital. Bychowski suggested, as we will discuss, the participation of the right hemisphere in recovery, and possible different initial hemispheric division for the two languages. He emphasized the effects of language exercises and the influence of the post-accident affective environment. Hoff and Poetzl (1932) reported the case of a 58-year-old left-handed German male whose wife was Italian. In the 4-day interval between his left-sided seizures and his death, he spoke paraphasic Italian with his wife and would produce stereotypic German utterances with his German doctor.

In polyglot aphasia, it is theoretically possible that each language might suffer a different aphasic syndrome. We have described such a case (Albert & Obler, 1975). This was a right-handed Hungarian-born woman who spent some of her later childhood in France, then went to England and America, before immigrating to Israel at age 16. The earliest symptoms giving cause for suspicion of her tumor included disturbance in English but not Hebrew. After partial ablation of a large left posterior temporal glioma at age 35, she was tested over the course of 10 days in a Hebrew-speaking environment, and found to display a pattern consistent with the clinical diagnosis of Wernicke's aphasia in English, and a Broca's aphasia in Hebrew, with her Hungarian and French sharing elements of both. This striking cooccurrence of two different kinds of aphasia in different languages, in one and the same person, led to the hypothesis of a neurological dissociation between the coresiding language systems in her brain. Silverberg and Gordon (forthcoming) have described two further cases. One is that of a 26-year-old right-handed nurse whose stroke caused a nonfluent aphasia in her native language, Spanish (which she continued to use up to and after the stroke), and a fluent aphasia in the Hebrew she had learned 3 years previously. In the second case, a 54-year-old physician who had studied and used Hebrew in the 2 years prior to his stroke, a mild anomia was evident in his native Russian, whereas his Hebrew was globally affected shortly after the stroke. Two months post-onset, his Hebrew was recovering in a nonfluent pattern, while he evidenced only mild (i.e., sophisticated) comprehension errors in Russian.

A variant on the theme of different aphasic syndromes in different languages comes from cases of differential impairment in specific language modalities. The fact that some people learn a language by written means is sometimes called on to explain their differential impairment. A classic case is that of Hinshelwood (1902). He reported that a highly educated man suffered a stroke at age 34. The patient had difficulties with comprehension and naming, but his most striking deficit was an alexia in English. His reading in Greek, on the other hand, was perfect. Even French and Latin, which, unlike Greek, are written in the same alphabet as is English, were easier to read than English.

A similar case was reported by Wechsler (1977). His patient, a 57-year-old right-handed male, suffered an infarction in the left occipital lobe. This lesion resulted in alexia (without agraphia) which was much more severe in the patient's native English than in the French he had learned in high school and college. Wechsler speculated that "as far as reading is concerned, later acquisitions may be more bilaterally represented in the brain."

Another such case is that of Lyman, Kwan, and Chao (1938). They described a patient with alexia and agraphia which were much more severe in his native Chinese than in English. The functional deficits resulted from a left occipital tumor, clearly pushing on the right hemisphere. The defects were also evident postoperatively, although both languages improved. The patient used a system of spelling out English words. This is impossible with Chinese characters. In Chinese, he would attempt to trace out characters with his finger. In English he would make spelling errors (especially on silent letters); in Chinese he would often write homonyms, synonyms, or characters which were partially correct. The authors pointed to parallel cases in the literature on monolingual Japanese aphasics who may lose one or the other of the two writing systems, a phonological and a character system. Although the Lyman *et al.* report is excellent from the point of view of its documentation of pre- and postoperative abilities, it unfortunately omits mention of the patient's handedness and, furthermore, consistently confuses the difference between English and Chinese orthographic systems for a difference of language structure. This case suggests that various strategies for reading may result in differential impairment in aphasia.

The case of Peuser and Leischner (1974) indicates that different decoding strategies, namely, lexical versus phonological, may result in differential impairment in writing. They described a 39-year-old linguist with sensory-anomic aphasia after encephalitis. They did not tell us his native language, although we may guess that it was German. Also we must assume that he learned the international phonetic alphabet (IPA) tertiarily. Upon dictation, his orthography was best for either language in phonetic transcription, although some errors did obtain even in phonetic transcription. His spelling was worst in English, and his spelling in German was intermediate. Peuser and Leischer attributed his surprising agraphic pattern to the intactness of the phonetic decoding system, independent of the semantic one. This theory is supported by Luria (1960, as reported in Critchley, 1974), who suggested that differential agraphia may result from different degrees of correspondence between the sound systems and the orthographic systems of the different languages. Thus, Luria reported a case of a French journalist equally alexic in his four languages (French, Russian, German, and Polish) but agraphic most pronouncedly in French and least in Russian, which is written in a different script, Cyrillic. (The sound–grapheme correspondence in Russian is much greater than in French, where numerous letters may remain unpronounced.) He would often mistakenly write homophonic words, much like the Chinese patient reported in Lyman *et al.* (1938).

To this point we have been considering the possibly discrepant nature of aphasic syndromes in the polyglot aphasic. If we turn to recovery patterns, we see that while parallel recovery may be the most common pattern in polyglot aphasics, some cases clearly do not recover in parallel. Of the cases which do not recover in parallel, some recover only one language, whereas others evidence regression of the first-returned language as the second-returned language improves.

Goldstein (1948) suggested that recovery of only one language resulted from an impairment of the switching mechanism. He reported a case in which the switching mechanism, instead of becoming entirely inoperative, operated too readily in spontaneous speech but could not be activated on command. His case was that of an intelligent Swedish woman who would shift from English into Swedish for more emotional statements. She could not translate from either language upon command.

If there is a bilingual switch, it may fail to operate, with aphasia, in a number of ways. It may operate inappropriately, as in Goldstein's case just described. It may be "closed down," and as a result it may restrict all output to one language. Or it may not operate, and both languages may be mixed within sentences and words. To distinguish this aphasic mixing of languages from the interference which can occur in healthy nonaphasics may be difficult. We must rely on the reports of family and colleagues as to the nature of the premorbid language.

One case of mixing is reported by L'Hermitte *et al.* (1966). The case in point is that of a 46-year-old right-handed English businessman who lived for about 10 years in Paris, with much practice in translation, both oral and written, and in reading. When his anterior left temporal lobe glioma was ablated, the result was a sensory aphasia, characterized by a "peculiar" influence of his English on his French, in both oral and written production.

A case of lexical mixing reported by Mossner and Pilch (1971) is that of a woman with motor aphasia that resulted from removal of a left temporal tumor. Although the woman's native language was German, she had immigrated to Australia at the age of 20. There, she had married and spoken only English with her daughters. When she was 32, the family returned to Germany. At age 36 she was operated on, and then for 2 months she was given speech therapy in German. Both her English and her German exhibited phonological impairment, such as reduction of consonant clusters and devoicing of voiced stops. The patient made syntactic errors in both languages, misusing functional words or morphs. For example, she might delete an article or use the wrong preposition (e.g., replace *kaufen* by *verkaufen*). Her spontaneous speech was restricted to the sentence type. It is interesting to note that she freely borrowed English words of all sorts into German. For example,

V: *ich kann nicht remember.*

Prep: *von Sydney to Singapore*

N: *Krieg und peace*

Adj: *Was ist in first Fernsehen?*

N, prep phrase: *Einhalb year seit zwansig of September.*

Jakobson (in DeReuck & O'Connor, 1964) reported an instance when he could not inhibit language switch. After an auto accident, he was aphasic for 2 hours, and "without any need . . . automatically" translated each sentence he spoke into four or five languages.

By regression, we mean cases in which one language first starts to return and then becomes less proficient when the second language starts to return. Chlenov (1948) reported the case of an educated German printer and salesman who had learned English and Spanish in school and who spoke French and Russian as well. In his early twenties, this man had worked as an English interpreter, but he had not spoken the language since. A left parieto-occipital wound at the age of 40 reportedly resulted in right hemiparesis and aphasia. The patient spoke only English at first, but then some Spanish and German returned. As they returned, his English got worse: He experienced anomic difficulties in English, and his accent deteriorated. By the time of his evaluation 3 years posttrauma, his German was better than his English.

REVIEW STUDIES OF INDIVIDUAL CASES OF POLYGLOT APHASIA

A number of authors have collected previously published case studies in order to extract patterns of impairment on recovery.

Freud (1953, 1891) integrated his comments on polyglot aphasia into his essay which was critical of simple localizationist theory in aphasia. He maintained that newly acquired languages must be organized in the same areas known to be the centers for the first-learned language, since otherwise we would expect to see cases in which organic lesions would cause impairment of the mother tongue while the other language would remain untouched. This, he claimed, never happens. He attributed the character of speech disorders in polyglots to two functional factors: age of acquisition and practice. It would seem that Freud was not aware of those cases which had been reported in which the mother tongue was impaired markedly in contrast to a later-learned language. Freud's two factors also did not account for those cases in which two languages were learned natively and then efficiently kept apart in usage. He gave no hint as to what might be the neuropsychological or neuroanatomical correlates of his functional factors.

Pitres (1895) referred to previous reports and added his own more detailed case studies. He observed that, although one might expect all languages of a multilingual aphasic to be lost in equal measure and regained simultaneously, or else one might expect by Ribot's rule that the more recently acquired language would be lost more completely, neither of these rules always holds. Nevertheless, he said, it would be wrong to assume that there are different centers for each language because:

1. Often enough, one language is lost in all modalities and another is not, and in the light of our knowledge of the existence of four speech areas, it would be unlikely that exactly that part of each belonging to the lost language had been damaged.
2. Sufficient explanation can be made on the basis of hierarchical return of association systems.

He went on to argue that in the case of partial damage to the speech areas (and not complete destruction) a temporary inactivity (inertia) of the cortical language centers results in most solidly established associations being recovered first. Whence Pitres's rule: The most familiar language recovers first. This may often be the first learned language but may also be that in use at the time of the accident. If, on the other hand, speech centers are totally damaged, then all languages will exhibit the same effects to equal degrees.

Leischner (1948) tabulated cases from earlier western European literature, with the exception of those in Pitres's article, and categorized them (according to explanations given) for the recovery pattern. Thus, anatomical location was offered as a factor in 13 cases, the language of the accident situation in 8 cases, affective factors in 10, visual influence of writing in 6, with one case each for "form of speech," influence of visual imagery, and different locations of different languages.

Goldstein (1948) argued that the writing system is an important factor in determining which language will return first. He noted that dialect often returned before a formal school language, but that in two of Minkowski's cases, the literary languages returned first. Minkowski had attributed this pattern to affective factors, and the additional reinforcement provided by the visual images of written words. Goldstein proposed that it was the fact that a literary language had always been used more consciously that aided in its recovery.

Minkowski (1963) drew on the European literature and on his own numerous published cases to discuss the issues of polyglot aphasia. He supported Pitres's assertion of the unlikelihood of a lesion harming selectively the centers and pathways of only one or another language. He preferred to assume a common cortical substratum, within which functional and biodynamic relations between different languages operate. He pointed out clearly the obvious but highly significant point of the extreme variability of various systematic features in the individual case and in its development. He concluded that deviations from Pitres's rule may come about through affective needs, when "the most current language of a polyglot presents particular difficulties in reactivation and restoration because of the mode of its acquisition and its special linguistic structure in view of the specific localization, extension, neuropathological dynamics of a brain lesion in the dominant hemisphere or both [p. 155]." (We must criticize this use of the term *because*, implicit in so many of the papers, since the causality implied is untested.) Minkowski spoke of a "natural synergy" between languages, which may work for or against their parallel restoration, often resulting in transitory or even permanent intermixing of the two languages (although, as Vildomec, 1963, pp. 64–65 pointed out, it is hard to say that the patient did not do this before the injury). Minkowski found the idea of a localized switching center attractive, although unproven.

Gloning and Gloning (1965) reviewed 11 published cases of polyglot aphasia in which precise details on localization of the lesion were given, and added four cases of their own. They drew up a table displaying lesion site (third frontal convolution, inferior parietal lobe, first temporal convolution, and second and third temporal convolutions) and the polyglot behavior resulting from the lesion (mixed-language speech, fixing on only one language, and differential impairment between the two languages). They concluded that no specific brain area is necessarily tied to the phenomenon of polyglot aphasia, in contradiction to Poetzl's (1925) rule that the angular and supramarginal gyri must be involved. Rather, they believed, polyglot aphasia is an overlay to any aphasia, resulting from any lesion in the speech region.

Gloning and Gloning also correlated handedness and side of lesion (they seem to have assumed that cases in which handedness was not mentioned were right-handers), and found that in the four left-handed patients, three had only a right-hemispheric lesion. In monolingual left-handed aphasics, 60% have unilateral lesions in the left hemisphere (Goodglass & Quadfasel, 1954). On this basis, the authors concluded that fluent bilinguals are less strongly lateralized than monolinguals, and that their nondominant hemisphere is involved in their language skills. This ambilaterality is also seen, though less strikingly, in the 11 right-handers of whom 8 had unilateral left hemispheric lesions; 1, a unilateral right hemispheric lesion; and 2, bilateral lesions.

Paradis (1977) has provided the most comprehensive review to date. His article on "Bilingualism and Aphasia" is particularly valuable because it provides, in tabular form, a summary of each of 138 cases of polyglot aphasia. The bulk of the chapter treats recovery patterns. Paradis abstracted five basic patterns of recovery. In **synergistic recovery**, both languages progress simultaneously. This progress may be **parallel**, if both languages are equally impaired, and if they return at the same rate. Synergistic recovery is **differential** if the languages are not equally impaired, or if they recover at different rates. Parallel synergistic recovery is the most common pattern among the cases Paradis reviewed. A rarer form of recovery is **antagonistic**, or regressive, recovery, where the return of one language appears to be at the expense of a previously recovered language. Paradis reported a number of cases of **successive** recovery in which one language returns only after another one has been completely restored. In **selective** recovery, a patient does not regain some of his languages at all. Finally, in **mixed** recovery, interference obtains between two languages, of a type which has not been evidenced premorbidly.

Paradis went on to review the inadequacies of the various rules and explanatory factors which have been proposed to account for recovery patterns. He seemed to feel most comfortable with the "multiple factors view," which holds that the following may influence the order of recovery of two languages: order of learning the languages, degree of proficiency in them, affective attitudes toward the languages, site and size of the lesion, the role of physiological factors, and the general biological condition of the patient.

Paradis also reviewed the contradictory evidence on a switch mechanism and concluded that localization of the switch mechanism is impossible. Loss of switching ability (i.e., selective restitution) and inappropriate switching (i.e., mixed restitution) "occur irrespective of the locus of the lesion." As to hemispheric lateralization, Paradis concluded that the right hemisphere of the bilingual seems to play no greater role in the language of bilinguals than it does in monolinguals.

Whitaker (forthcoming) discussed the data of Paradis (1977) on polyglot aphasic cases. Of the four possible sequences of recovery, two were deemed so rare that exploration was pointless. These two were regression of the language first recovered upon progress in the second one, and improvement in a language recovered second, only after fairly complete recovery had occurred in a first one. The common recovery patterns were either comparable progress in both languages, or selective improvement of one language while the other remained severely impaired. The latter case, selective improvement, was most interesting, since the former could be explained by a neural substrate for language shared by both languages. The only difference might be in terms of the relative degree of pretrauma proficiency in the various languages. Selective impairment could be explained, according to Paradis's review, by psychosocial factors, by the reinforcement of written skills in one or another language, and by the possibility of differential lateralization of the different languages. Whitaker added the possibility that language substrate may be shared to a greater degree if the languages in question are "linguistically comparable." Whitaker adjudged the experimental evidence of extra right hemisphere participation in early (prepubertal) acquisition to be weak. He concluded, however, that it is reasonable to assume different representations of the different languages in the brain of the bilingual. The patterns of language recovery in polyglot aphasics, Whitaker pointed out, cannot be taken as support for or against the manner of classifying bilinguals as compound or coordinate. Nevertheless, he did speculate that the earlier the introduction of a second language within childhood, "the more likely the neural substrate for it will parallel that of the native or first language."

We object to the observation that, because mixing or interlanguage interference has been reported to obtain as an aphasic problem in only a small percentage (7%) of polyglot cases, it is not worth speculating about. Such a position also ignores the importance of explaining the preponderance of cases in which language switching problems do not obtain, regardless of what other aphasic impairments may obtain. The fact that switching capacity can be retained may imply that the "language switch" of the bilingual is represented at a cognitive level somewhat divorced from the cognitive level of other language skills.

Several neurologists comment on bilingualism in aphasia without citing specific cases. In their 1959 book, Penfield and Roberts asserted that a lesion must affect all languages equally; or if it does not appear to do so, that is only because of psychological factors.

Critchley (1974) posed the following:

1. The further apart two languages are structurally, the greater the hypothetical likelihood of rivalry between the two systems (contra Vildomec), and the more likely are symptoms in aphasia to be different. Critchley was claiming that this divergence is attributable not to neuroanatomical realities, but rather to language-specific structures.
2. No bilingual has ever achieved fame as a poet or prose writer in both languages (although such authors as Conrad and Nabokov have adopted a second language). (On this point, Critchley is wrong, since his argument is contradicted in other cultures, for example, Islamic.)
3. Perhaps it is only the person being talked to who influences the language chosen, as this would narrow the set of topics discussed.
4. There is the potential for diglossic effects even in English, given the real discrepancies between written language conventions and speech.
5. Perhaps one should look for differential loss of exotic phonetic items like tone, clicks, and implosives in the appropriate bilinguals.

GROUP STUDIES OF POLYGLOT APHASIA

The individual case studies on polyglot aphasics are published because they are "interesting"; they usually discuss some discrepancy between the two languages, either in impairment or recovery process, which cannot be attributed to premorbid proficiency in the languages. If, as our review of the studies found, no single rule can yet predict language recovery patterns in all the individual cases of prolonged aphasia, perhaps the answer is to be found in the polyglot aphasics who have not been described in case studies.

The coordinate–compound dichotomy was brought to bear on this subject by Lambert and Fillenbaum (1959), who compared Leischner's (1948) 14 cases with 14 of their own in Montreal, and then to Pitres's (1912) cases. The authors judged whether an individual case supported or negated Ribot's rule of chronological primacy, or Pitres's of habit strength; and whether it supported an affective hypothesis, which they attributed to Minkowski (1963). The European cases were seen to be 17 to 5 against Ribot, and 14 to 6 against Pitres, with 7 cases explainable by affective factors. The Montreal cases, on the contrary, were 8 to 2 in favor of Ribot, and 9 to 2 in favor of Pitres, with only 1 case of affective interference. The authors did admit that the striking differences may be due to the emphasis in the European literature on unusual cases, whereas Lambert and Fillenbaum tested every case available to them. They explained their data on the basis of sociological differences between the European experience and that of Montreal; multilingualism in the former situation was considered likely to be caused by physical change of place, conducive to the coordinate state, whereas living in bilingual Montreal, they argued, was likely to bring about compound bilingualism. No reason was given why a coordinate should conform neither to Pitres's nor to Ribot's rule, beyond the contention that affective factors are more likely to come into play in the case of the migrant.

Charlton (1964) suggested that the literature on polyglot aphasics is dominated by the "interesting" cases where the languages are lost or recover unequally. He sketched 9 out of 10 consecutive testable cases who entered the Neurological Institute of New York over a 3-month period. Of these cases, 3 were amnestic aphasics, 2, motor aphasics, and 4, central aphasics. Only two patients, both central aphasics (one severe and one not) had any differential productive abilities. The less severe case conversed a little in English, but claimed to have entirely forgotten Italian. He could, however, choose the correct Italian name for objects from multiple choice lists. Charlton thus concluded that the typical case of polyglot aphasia is a case in which all languages are lost to an equal degree, and in like manner.

L'Hermitte *et al.* (1966) and Hécaen, Mazars, Ramier, Goldblum, and Merienne (1971) together described nine case observations, of which eight were classed as coordinate bilinguals on the basis of age of acquisition. Each of them showed an identical deficit in all the languages she or he spoke; furthermore, this identical deficit held throughout the period of recovery. The impairments included amnestic, expressive, receptive, and global aphasia. In one sensory aphasic the authors observed a heavy interference of an earlier language on a once-fluent second language; such interference did not obtain in the expressive aphasics.

Nair and Virmani (1973) conducted a large-scale study on 78 Indian unilateral hemiplegics. Although it is difficult to ascertain the precise definition of aphasia that was employed, the authors reported that 70% of the right hemiplegics and 55% of the left hemiplegics evidenced aphasia. If we exclude as aphasics the 2 cases of dysarthria, then of the total 12 right-handed left hemiplegics, 10 had some expressive sign of aphasia. The authors noted that selection of patients was random and suggested that their results may be attributable to the high incidence of polyglotism in India; 33 of the 50, or 66%, of the aphasic hemiplegics were at least bilingual.

Of these 33 polyglot aphasics, 31 were deemed to have uniform impairment in all languages. Of the 2 cases in which language deficit was not the same in both languages, one was a patient who lost all verbal and graphic skills in Persian, while English and Hindi were better spared. The second patient was alexic and agraphic in Urdu (written with Arabic script, read right to left), while retaining all his English skills.

It may be of interest to note the male:female ratio of the Indian aphasic population, 35:15. Thus 30% of this hemiplegic population was female, whereas 22% of our European sample (p. 140) was female, and 25% of McGlone's (1976) Canadian sample. Since McGlone's data were likely to include a high percentage of monolinguals, we may deduce that the bilingualism does not override whatever factors result in decreased incidence of aphasia in women.

Fredman (1975) selected 40 coordinate polyglot aphasics who were within 6 weeks of the onset of their illness. Of the subjects 28 were male and 12 were female. Thirty-four subjects had suffered stroke, 4 an embolism, and 1 each, trauma and benign tumor. The study was conducted in Israel, so all the patients knew some Hebrew (the minimum time each subject had been in Israel premorbidly was 6 years). The subjects all spoke at least one of seven other languages: Arabic, Yiddish, German, Russian, Polish, French, and Hungarian. At the beginning and end of the study, subjects were scored on a version of the Wepman and Jones (1961) Language Modality Test of Aphasia, which had been adapted and translated into Hebrew. Subjects were also tested and retested in their home language, with the aid of a family member. In the interim between the two tests, all subjects were given 3 months of speech therapy, for 1 hour three times a week. Almost all subjects showed improvement in both languages despite the fact that they were being given therapy only in Hebrew. Fredman argued that spontaneous recovery alone could not account for the improvement measured in Hebrew, since several patients with little premorbid knowledge of Hebrew improved in Hebrew, with therapy, and learned words they had not previously known.

One other fact of interest emerges from her study. She indicated that mixing of words from the native language to Hebrew was much more frequent in older subjects, and in subjects whose native language was not Arabic. One might have predicted that, since Arabic and Hebrew are structurally close languages, Arabic would provide most interference, instead of least. We might explain this pattern simply by a sociolinguistic or affective argument, since Arabic has low prestige in Israel, and negative affective connotations. On the other hand, there may have been a language-specific effect operating, whereby Hebrew–Arabic bilinguals were obliged premorbidly to make more "effort" to keep the two languages separate.

TABULAR SUMMARY OF CASES OF POLYGLOT APHASIA

In this section we present, in outline form, summaries of anatomical and neurolinguistic information of 108 polyglot aphasics. Of these cases, 105 have been culled from the literature of the last century. Three are cases we have studied ourselves.

Cases are listed in alphabetical order, according to the author who first reported the case. In parentheses, following the primary bibliographic citation, are references to other articles that refer to the case. The excellent and comprehensive article of Paradis (1977) has not been cited, however, since it refers to many of the same cases. The subject or patient is then identified, by name or initials or number, when possible. Note is made of the sex of the subjects, and their handedness, when this is explicitly mentioned in the case reports. The mother tongue and then the other tongues are listed, with mention of age and place or manner of learning nonnative tongues, when that information is available. The listing includes the age of cerebral insult for the aphasic cases, and the type of lesion. For the type of aphasia, we have regularized the various terminologies used by the many authors. In our table, Broca's aphasia refers to a nonfluent, agrammatic speech, with minimal comprehension difficulties. Wernicke's aphasia refers to a fluent but empty, paraphasic speech, with comprehension difficulties. Expressive disorders and receptive disorders are not syndromes, like Broca's or Wernicke's aphasia; they refer respectively to nonfluent production and to clinically obvious comprehension deficits. In the section on aphasia type, abbreviation is made of the languages referred to. If the subject knew only Hungarian, then H will refer to Hungarian. If she or he knew both Hungarian and Hebrew, then the abbreviations will be respectively Hu and He.

Finally we summarize the authors' comments on their cases and list our coding results for information known or deducible about the case. Cases have been coded for certain personal factors: sex, handedness, education, etiology of lesion, polyglotism versus bilingualism, and type of bilingualism (coordinate versus compound). Note is then made of aphasic type and recovery pattern, whether there was parallel or differential recovery. If recovery was different in the languages, we noted whether it followed the rule of Pitres and/or that of Ribot. In those cases where recovery included regression of one language as a second improved, this is mentioned. Two problems peculiar to polyglot aphasia are mentioned when they occur, apparent loss of switching, and apparent mixing of languages in people who had not mixed them premorbidly. Finally, note is made if patients received language therapy. Coding is also done of two types of common explanations for recovery patterns: cases in which an orthographic system, or special reading knowledge, may have influenced the recovery pattern, and cases in which affective factors were specified.

KEY TO SYMBOLS

R:	Reference(s)
P/P:	Patient, profession
H:	Handedness
MT:	Mother tongue(s)
OL:	Other languages
N:	Neurological findings
A:	Aphasia
AC:	Comments of author of case report
C:	Our coding system
?:	Questionable classification
+female:	All cases are male unless marked.
+educated:	At least high school education, either mentioned, or deduced from professional status or linguistic knowledge
+left:	Patient was not right-handed in childhood.
+young:	Below 35
+trauma:	The aphasia resulted from cerebral trauma.
+polyglot:	Patient knew more than two languages.
+discrepancy:	There was some differential impairment or recovery, either in degree or in type.
+Pitres:	Followed rule of Pitres, that the language used most in the extended period preceding the insult recovers first
+Ribot:	Followed rule of Ribot, that earliest language recovers first
+coordinate:	Two languages learned and/or used in separate circumstances (e.g., immigration, one parent strictly each language)
+compound:	Two languages learned and/or used in circumstances facilitating a unified language system (e.g., in school, in a bilingual culture)
+expressive:	Motor impairment evidenced
+receptive:	Sensory impairment evidenced
+amnestic:	Anomia, word-finding difficulties evidenced, also called *nominal*

+repetition:	Repetition difficulties evidenced
+central:	Central aphasia
+automatic:	Only automatic speech remained (e.g., curses, liturgy).
−translation:	Translation impossible
−switch:	Patient spoke a certain language inappropriately.
+mixing:	Patient mixed elements of two languages.
+regression:	A language that improved initially deteriorated as a second language improved.
+parallel:	Recovery of both languages followed the same course at the same pace.
+therapy:	Therapy was given the patient.
+writing:	The writing system could be seen to be a factor in differential language abilities.
+affective:	No better explanation could be found than psychological attitudes associated with the languages.
+environment:	The language spoken in one recovery environment is held to account for that one returning first.

1

R:	Alajouanine, Pichot & Durand, 1949
P/P:	
H:	
MT:	English
OL:	French, recently
N:	
A:	Pure anarthria, much worse in French; same phoneme might be correctly pronounced in English, incorrectly in French.
AC:	Not a purely motor problem, but a high-level articulatory one
C:	+? coordinate +expressive +discrepancy +Pitres

2

R:	Albert & Obler, 1975
P/P:	Woman
H:	Right
MT:	Hungarian
OL:	French residence in childhood, English residence in adolescence, Hebrew immigrant age 19
N:	Age 34, left posterior temporal low-grade astrocytoma, postoperative evaluation
A:	Broca's in E, Wernicke's in He, others intermediate
AC:	Possible different brain organization for each language
C:	+female +young +polyglot +educated +coordinate +compound +receptive +expressive (less in L_3 than in L_1 or L_2) +discrepancy + Pitres − Ribot

3

R:	Anastasopoulos, 1959
P/P:	
H:	
MT:	Greek (dialect)
OL:	Greek (standard), Russian, Turkish

N: Age 45, cerebrovascular attack (CVA)
A: Amnestic, alexia and agraphia in all languages, good comprehension in all
AC: Age 7, accident with damage to left side of head resulted in right hemisphere learning of all later skills (especially writing).
C: +polyglot   +expressive   −discrepancy

4
R: Asayama, 1914 (Lyman et al., 1938)
P/P: Professionally educated
H:
MT: Japanese
OL: Two scripts for Japanese
N: Right hemiplegia
A: Expressive, conduction, receptive, could read silently sentences in Chinese characters, but not in phonetic Kana, agraphia in Kana, only mild impairment in Chinese characters.
AC: This is true for all Japanese aphasics, sound connection not important, but only direct relation to concept.
C: +educated   +compound   +expressive   +receptive   +discrepancy
       +writing

5
R: Balint, 1923 (Leischner, 1948)
P/P: Political scientist and politician
H:
MT: Greek
OL: Russian, French. Age 40 learned German, also to write Greek
N: Age 60, accident, fissure of left half of cranium
A: Transcortical, later amnestic, good repetition Ge and Gr returned simultaneously; could write letters upon demand, but then read them in the opposite language; no mixing of alphabets within words; translation of Ge political writing to Gr was uncooperative, errors and word search.
AC: Political activity had been in German
C: −young   +educated   +polyglot   +coordinate   +trauma
       −discrepancy   −switch   + writing

6
R: Banks (Pitres 1895)
P/P: Educated
H:
MT: English
OL: Greek, Latin
N: Age 54, right hemiplegia
A: Soon spoke E, but G and L entirely lost until relearned after 6 years
AC:
C: +educated   +polyglot   +compound   +receptive
       +discrepancy   +Pitres   +Ribot   +writing

7
R: Bastian, 1875 (Pitres, 1895)
P/P:

H:
MT: German
OL: Long residence in England
N: Right hemiplegia
A: Began with only G words, later E recovered, but in word search G word would
      come to him.
AC:
C: +coordinate   +expressive   +discrepancy   +Pitres   +Ribot   +mixing

8
R: Bastian, 1875 (Leischner, 1948)
P/P: Scholar
H:
MT: German?
OL: Greek and Latin
N: Age 54, right hemiplegia
A: Had to relearn Gr and L, over 6 years; could then read favorite authors.
AC:
C: +educated   +polyglot   +compound   +receptive   +discrepancy
      +Pitres   +Ribot   +writing   +therapy

9
R: Beattie (Pitres, 1895)
P/P:
H:
MT:
OL: Greek
N:
A: Could use MT, lost G
AC:
C: +educated   +compound   +receptive   +discrepancy   +Pitres
      +Ribot   +writing

10
R: Bernard, 1885 (Pitres, 1895)
P/P: Woman
H:
MT: Italian birth
OL: Long French residence, Spanish
N: Age 39, hemiplegia, tested at age 57
A: Global, with agraphia and alexia; F recovered slowly, to reasonable speech; I and S
      remained expressive aphasic; agraphia and alexia remained for all three.
AC:
C: +female   +educated   +polyglot   +coordinate   +expressive
      +discrepancy   +Pitres   −Ribot   +environment

11
R: Bianchi, 1886 (Pitres, 1895)
P/P: Educated
H:
MT: Italian

OL: French, English
N: Age 24, emotional shock, right hemiplegia
A: Sensory, expressive, spontaneous writing impaired with work, I recovered somewhat, F and E not (4 months after accident).
AC:
C: +young   +educated   +polyglot   +expressive   +receptive
      +discrepancy   +Pitres   +Ribot

12
R: Bourdin, 1877 (Pitres, 1895)
P/P: Nun
H:
MT: French
OL: English, childhood
N:
A: Severe expressive in F
AC:
C: +female   +expressive   +discrepancy   +Pitres   −Ribot

13
R: Bychowski, 1919 (Minkowski, 1963; Leischner, 1948; Goldstein, 1948)
P/P: Garment worker
H:
MT: Polish
OL: German factory work, then Russian in army, age 24, although P usage maintained
N: Age 27, left shrapnel wound, frontal and parietal damage, right hemiplegia
A: R, slow but correct, improved with work; P little spontaneous speech and naming, repetition good; G entirely "lost," except repetition, understanding diminished.
AC: Bychowski: different form of aphasia in each language, speech therapy activated right hemisphere; Minkowski: affective factor of Russian environment.
C: −educated   +polyglot   +coordinate   +trauma   +expressive
      −repetition   +discrepancy   +Pitres   −Ribot   +environment
      +therapy

14
R: Charcot, 1884 (Pitres, 1895; Straussler, 1912; Leischner, 1948)
P/P: Russian officer
H:
MT: Russian
OL: French and German
N:
A: Sudden restriction to expression in R, F later partially regained, comprehension fine in all languages
AC:
C: +educated   +polyglot   +?compound   +trauma   +expressive
      +discrepancy   +Pitres   +Ribot

15
R: Charcot, 1887 (Lyman et al., 1938; Hinshelwood, 1902)
P/P:
H:

MT:
OL: German, Spanish, Latin, Greek, French.
N:
A: Literal writing problems in Ge and Gr, and reading problems in Gr
AC: Nonnative language recovered first.
C: +educated   +polyglot   +compound   +discrepancy   −Ribot
      +writing

16
R: Charlton, 1964
P/P: Case 1
H:
MT: Hungarian
OL: French, German in school, professionally English since age 28 as immigrant
N: Age 75, hypertensive, generalized cerebrovascular disease
A: Mild nominal aphasia, equal in all four languages
AC: Most polyglot aphasia affects all languages equally, especially when minimal.
C: −young   +polyglot   +compound   +coordinate   +amnestic
      −discrepancy

17
R: Charlton, 1964
P/P: Case 2, female with primary education
H:
MT: Russian and Yiddish
OL: Age 22, immigrated, English
N: Age 60, cerebral atrophy
A: Nominal aphasia equally in all three languages (same word would fail in all three)
AC: Follows rule of equal impairment
C: +female   −young   −educated   +polyglot   +coordinate
      +amnestic   −discrepancy

18
R: Charlton, 1964
P/P: Case 4
H:
MT: Spanish till age 34
OL: Since immigration at 34, English used equally with S.
N: Age 54, presumed CVA
A: Complete motor aphasia in both languages, later disappeared in both
AC: Follows rule of equal impairment
C: +coordinate   +expressive   −discrepancy

19
R: Charlton, 1964
P/P: Case 5
H:
MT: German until age 36
OL: Immigrating, German and English used equally
N: Age 45, left hemispheric abscess
A: Nominal aphasia became complete in both languages.

AC: Follows rule of equal impairment
C: +coordinate   +amnestic   −discrepancy

20
R: Charlton, 1964
P/P: Case 6, male actor and musician
H:
MT: English
OL: Two years in Italy age 35, claimed fluency in Italian due to acting.
N: Age 41, total intraclinoid occlusion of left carotid artery
A: Central aphasia in E, I claimed forgotten, though could pick visually multiple choice names.
AC: Must be affective, even though patient denied, possibly due to insufficient fluency previously, though others have less and are not impaired differentially.
C: +coordinate   +central   +discrepancy   +Pitres   +Ribot

21
R: Charlton, 1964
P/P: Case 7, male restaurant worker
H:
MT: Spanish (parents) and English (environment) until age 55 when only S
OL:
N: Age 60, left-sided glioblastoma
A: Central aphasia with dementia; throughout progressive deterioration, no observable difference between languages.
AC: Follows rule of equal impairment
C: −young   +coordinate   +central   −discrepancy

22
R: Charlton, 1964
P/P: Case 8, undereducated successful businessman
H:
MT: German until age 49
OL: Immigrating, equal use of G and English.
N: Age 76, stenosis at origin of left internal carotid artery, later complete occlusion
A: Jargonized G, developed to severe central aphasia with only stereotypic E phrases
AC: Exception to equal impairment rule, either to economize on what little language he knew he had, or because E was the language of the environment.
C: −young   −educated   +coordinate   +central   +discrepancy
      +Pitres   +Ribot   +automatic

23
R: Charlton, 1964
P/P: Case 9, well-educated female
H:
MT: Spanish
OL: English since age 10, socially and professionally
N: Age 40, cerebral atrophy
A: Nominal aphasia, equal in both languages
AC: Follows rule of equal impairment
C: +female   +educated   +compound   +amnestic   −discrepancy

24
R: Charlton, 1964
P/P: Case 10, well-educated male executive
H:
MT: Danish
OL: English in school, then immigrated around age 42, used both languages equally
N: Age 66, subdural hematoma
A: Marked central aphasia in both languages, disappeared equally after evacuation of
       hematoma
AC: Follows rule of equal impairment
C: −young   +educated   +?coordinate   +?compound   +central
       −discrepancy

25
R: Chlenov, 1948
P/P: Case 1, T
H:
MT: Kazakh to age 13
OL: From age 13 some Russian and Turkmenian, from age 17 mainly T
N: Age 23, wound right temporoparietal area, left hemiparesis
A: Motor and some amnestic and sensory element; R recovered faster than K or T.
AC:
C: +young   +coordinate   +trauma   +expressive   +receptive
       +amnestic   +discrepancies   −Ribot   +environment

26
R: Chlenov, 1948
P/P: Case 2, X
H:
MT: To age 19, only Turkmenian, but understood Kazakh and Uzbek.
OL: Age 20, began Russian.
N: Age 26, left temporoparietal area, right hemiplegia
A: Motor and sensory; R returned better and faster than T; responded to T questions
       in R, naming better in R.
AC:
C: +young   +polyglot   +coordinate   +expressive   +receptive
       +amnestic   +discrepancy   −Ribot   +environment

27
R: Chlenov, 1948
P/P: Case 3, A
H:
MT: Turkmenian
OL: Russian
N: Age 21, wound in left carotid artery, right hemiparesis
A: Motor aphasia, some amnestic, R better than T; one and a half years later, motor
       and amnestic aphasia remained significant, but no differences between R and T.
AC:
C: +?coordinate   +trauma   +expressive   +amnestic   +discrepancy
       −Ribot   +environment

28
R: Chlenov, 1948 (Minkowski, 1963)
P/P: Salesman, printer
H:
MT: German
OL: Spoke, read, wrote French, school English, and Spanish, spoke and wrote Russian.
       E not spoken since interpretation work 20 years previously.
N: Age 40, wounded left parieto-occipital area, right hemiparesis, evaluated age 43
A: Spoke only E initially, then S and G; E regressed; word finding difficulties, accent
       changed. G best at evaluation, though E quite good.
AC: Minkowski: antagonism between G and E
C: +educated   +polyglot   +compound   +expressive   +amnestic
       +discrepancy   +Pitres   −Ribot   +regression

29
R: Chlenov, 1948
P/P: Translator, teacher of English
H:
MT: Russian
OL: German, French, Latin, Old Gothic
N: Age 34, meningoencephalitis, loss of consciousness
A: Sensory, alexia, agraphia, some agrammatism; E speech more impaired than R; G, F,
       L, OG impossible.
AC: Pitres's rule
C: +young   +educated   +polyglot   +compound   +expressive
       +receptive   +discrepancy   +Pitres   +Ribot   +writing

30
R: Cros, 1857 (Pitres, 1895)
P/P: Brisson, physician
H:
MT: Patois
OL: French
N:
A: Lost all F, a few words of P remained
AC:
C: +educated   +compound   +expressive   +discrepancy   +Pitres
       +Ribot   +writing

31
R: Dedić, 1926
P/P: Officer
H:
MT: Russian
OL: Serbian for business in recent years, French
N: Age 33, syphilitic collapse
A: Motor aphasia, then amnestic; first comprehension returned; first spoke words in
       S, then mixed S and R, then only R; finally F returned; little spontaneous writing;
       dictation best in R, could write F best in Cyrillic alphabet; alexia; reading of
       syllables best in R, then S.
AC:

C: +young   +educated   +polyglot   +?compound   +expressive
        +amnestic   +discrepancy   +?regression   +writing

32
R: Dimitrijevic, 1940
P/P:
H:
MT: Yiddish and Bulgarian
OL: Age 34, immigrated to Serbia, used all three languages
N: Age 60, fell down, consciousness lost, mild right hemiparesis
A: Expressive dysarthria, good comprehension, answered B to questions in S
AC:
C: −young   +polygot   +compound   +coordinate   +expressive
        +discrepancy   +Pitres   +Ribot

33
R: Dimitrajevic, 1940
P/P: Woman
H:
MT: Yiddish and Bulgarian
OL: Immigrated to Belgrade, Serbian replaced B
N: A good deal older(!), CVAs
A: Y and B speech returned, no S
AC:
C: +female   −young   +polyglot   +coordinate   +compound
        +expressive   +discrepancy   −Pitres   +Ribot

34
R: Dreifuss, 1961
P/P: Intelligent male
H:
MT: German
OL: English exclusively by immigration, age 10, other(s) in high school
N: Migraine attacks (right frontal, age 15, with right homonymous hemianopia, age 28)
A: Expressive, only G curses possible, writing unintelligible; poetry and language learning skills henceforth diminished.
AC: Migraine can cause subtle language impairment.
C: +young   +educated   +coordinate   +expressive   +discrepancy
        −Pitres   +Ribot   +automatic

35
R: Eskridge, 1896
P/P: Miner
H:
MT: Bohemian
OL: Age 13, immigrated to United States, almost as fluent English as B
N: 1. Age 23, left cranial accident; 2. Removal of depressed bone in middle of second and third temporal; 3. Convulsions led to draining of subcortical hemorrhage beneath posterior first and second temporal convolutions.
A: 1. Initial slow E speech developed in delirium to only random B—no

comprehension in either language; 2. A few words in B, "yes" in E, no comprehension; 3. E recovered to some degree expressively and comprehension, more than B.

AC: "In his delirious state the brain cells reproduced from the memories made upon them when they were most impressionable"; otherwise, most-used E prevailed.

C: +young   −educated   +coordinate   +trauma   +expressive
    +receptive   +discrepancy   +Pitres   −Ribot   +automatic

36
R: Florenskaja, 1940
P/P:
H:
MT: (Russian)
OL: French
N: Korsakov syndrome
A: Amnestic; mixed languages within words in writing
AC:
C: +?compound   +amnestic   +mixing   +writing

37
R: Gloning & Gloning, 1965
P/P: 1, female cook
H: Right
MT: Slovak
OL: German school, Spanish in school (not used in last 10 years)—both fluent
N: Age 57, left frontal meningioma
A: Motor-amnestic, S least impaired
AC: Good feelings about Buenos Aires
C: +female   +polyglot   +expressive   +amnestic   +discrepancy
    +Ribot   +affective

38
R: Gloning & Gloning, 1965
P/P: 2, travel agent
H: Right
MT: Italian
OL: Dalmatian, fluent German, and Serbo-Croatian from childhood at home, and Spanish
N: 1. Age 56, insult; 2. Age 60, second insult, damage to inferior parietal lobe and first, second, and third temporal convolutions.
A: 1. Alexia, Gerstmann's syndrome, amnestic; G returned first, then I and Se simultaneously; 2. Sensory-amnestic, with mixing of I, D, and Se; some spoken D possible, no Sp.
AC:
C: +polyglot   +compound   +receptive   +amnestic   +discrepancy
    −Ribot   +Pitres   +mixing

39
R: Gloning & Gloning, 1965
P/P: 3, gardener
H: Left

MT: Bulgarian
OL: Age 36 immigrated to Germany, fluent predominantly spoken usage thereafter—minimal reading learned in German
N: Age 55, right-sided parieto-temporal—occipital glioblastoma
A: Spoke only B; amnestic aphasia developed to sensory, more severe in B; in the later period mixed paraphasic words of both languages together; alexia, with mixed alphabet paragraphias.
AC:
C: +left +coordinate +discrepancy +Ribot −Pitres +mixing −writing

40
R: Gloning & Gloning, 1965
P/P: 4, female worker
H: Left
MT: Hungarian
OL: Fluent German in community and school, with husband
N: Right parieto-temporal—occipital tumor
A: Global receded to sensory with alexia and agraphia; mixing of words and paraphasias in the two languages; then to amnestic aphasia, equal in both languages; lost sense of language appropriateness, and would speak only one or other language with individuals, no matter how addressed by them.
AC:
C: +female +coordinate +compound +receptive +amnestic −discrepancy −switch +mixing

41
R: Goldblum, 1928 (Gloning & Gloning, 1965)
P/P:
H: Right
MT: German
OL: Swiss German most used in environment
N: Age 53, tumor destroying third frontal convolution and anterior section of inferior parietal lobe of left hemisphere
A: Broca's, some amnestic, agraphia and alexia; with therapy only G returned, though both languages understood.
AC:
C: +coordinate +expressive +amnestic +discrepancy +therapy −Pitres +Ribot

42
R: Goldstein, 1948
P/P: Intelligent woman
H:
MT: Swedish
OL: English by immigration
N: Defect in abstraction
A: Could not translate upon command, though did shift otherwise, using E for exams and conversations, S for more emotional situations
AC: Act of voluntary shifting lost
C: +female +educated +coordinate −switch +affective

43
R: Gorlitzer, 1959
P/P: Illiterate
H: Ambidextrous
MT: Slovak until age 30
OL: German in military age 30; 54–94, G environment
N: Age 94, left embolism
A: Only spoke S
AC: Ambidextrous meant S in both hemispheres, G only left, however, since associated
       with right-handed use of military arms; so all G lost, but only half of S.
C: −young   +left   −educated   +coordinate   +expressive
       +discrepancy   −Pitres   +Ribot

44
R: Grasset, 1884
P/P: Religious woman, assistant in Catholic ceremonies
H:
MT: French
OL: Study of Latin
N: Age 60, suddenly
A: Spoke only L words
AC:
C: +female   +compound   +expressive   +discrepancy   −Pitres
       −Ribot   +automatic   +?writing

45
R: Halpern, 1941 (Minkowski, 1963)
P/P:
H:
MT: German, Hebrew read and written as child, spoken somewhat in Palestine after 20
OL:
N: Age 24, bullet wound, left temporal area
A: Sensory, first words G, but understanding of H regained first; H speech and
       reading more fluent and correct, too, for 8 months after accident.
AC: Minkowski: affective attitude towards the languages
C: +young   +coordinate   +trauma   +expressive   +receptive
       +discrepancy   +writing

46
R: Halpern, 1941 (Minkowski, 1963)
P/P:
H: Left
MT: Russian
OL: Age 8, Hebrew writing and reading, age 14, immigrated to Palestine
N: Age 20, right temporal wound, transient paresis left oculomotor nerve
A: H speech recovered in a month, though somewhat agraphic and alexic; R remained
       poorly comprehended, no spontaneous speech, through 3 months after accident;
       answered R questions in H.
AC: Minkowski: Pitres's rule
C: +young   +left   +coordinate   +trauma   +discrepancy   +Pitres
       −Ribot   −switch   +writing

47
R: Halpern, 1949, 1950 (Minkowski, 1963; Gloning & Gloning, 1965)
P/P: Educated farmer
H: Left, forced right-hand writing
MT: English
OL: Religious Hebrew, age 7; immigrated, age 20 to Palestine
N: Age 42, craniocerebral injury left parieto-temporal region
A: Sensory, alexia, agraphia, acalculia; only E returned first, no H comprehension or production the first two months; then with much work, H recovered, especially written; E comprehension remained better than H.
AC: Halpern: Left-handedness and visual learning of H resulted in H being more dependent on bilateral functioning.
C: +left   +educated   +coordinate   +expressive   +receptive
      +discrepancy   +Ribot   +writing

48
R: Hécaen et al., 1971
P/P:
H: Right, no familial left
MT: Vietnamese only
OL: Age 18, went to France, coordinate
N: Age 28, meningitis, resulting posterior right-temporal aneurysm removed
A: Severe global, regressed after 2 months to dysarthria, conduction, agraphia, some acalculia; comprehension, reading, and naming returned to normal; the impairments and recovery were similar in both languages; never any tonal problems in Vietnamese.
AC:
C: +young   +coordinate   +right lesion   +expressive   +receptive
      −discrepancy   +parallel

49
R: Hegler, 1931 (Leischner, 1948)
P/P: Merchant
H:
MT: French
OL: German residence last half-year to finish education, English
N: Age 18, cerebral embolism mild right hemiparesis, Babinski, pulmonary infarction, death
A: Good comprehension, G first, even to monolingual F-speaking brother; could, however, write F words but not speak them
AC: Affective
C: +young   +educated   +polyglot   +discrepancy   +Pitres   −Ribot
      −switch   +environment

50
R: Herschmann & Poetzl, 1920 (Minkowski, 1963; Leischner, 1948; Poetzl,1925, 1930; Gloning & Gloning, 1965)
P/P:
H:
MT: Czech
OL: Then German almost exclusively (since age 14?)

N: CVA, age 60, inferior parietal lobe destroyed, and adjacent part of angular gyrus
A: Initial comprehension loss recovered equally in C and G; spontaneous speech,
     word finding, repeating, reading, and writing disturbed. C dominant the first 2
     months, still mixed C syllables into G words
AC: Poetzl: earlier transient attack while visiting Czech relatives then perseverated in
     later stroke; lesions of inferior parietal region disturb the switching mechanism.
C: −young   +coordinate   +expressive   +repetition   +discrepancy
     −Pitres   +Ribot   +mixing

51
R: Hinshelwood, 1902 (Minkowski, 1963; Leischner, 1948; Goldstein, 1948)
P/P: Highly educated man, Case 1
H:
MT: English
OL: French, Latin, Greek
N: Age 34, CVA
A: Some anomia, comprehension problems, alexia for words (letters fluent), but far
      worse in E, F and L intermediate, whereas in G correct and reading facile (as with
      musical notes)
AC: Hinshelwood: separate location within center for words of each language;
      Minkowski: mode of acquisition influenced.
C: +young   +educated   +polyglot   +compound   +receptive
      +amnestic   +discrepancy   −Pitres   −Ribot   −environment
      +writing

52
R: Hoff & Poetzl, 1932 (Leischner, 1948; Gloning & Gloning, 1965)
P/P:
H: Left
MT: German
OL: Italian, with wife
N: Age 58, left-sided seizures, left hemiparesis, death in 4 days
A: Sensory, paraphasias, alexia, agraphia, could repeat, paraphasic I with wife,
      "Besser, besser" to G doctor
AC: Situation-bound response
C: +left   +?coordinate   +expressive   +receptive   −repetition
      +environment

53
R: Hofman, Shapira, & Streifler, 1975
P/P: Business woman
H: Converted left-hander?
MT: Polish
OL: German, Hebrew: written in childhood, before P
N: Auto accident with no findings, slight spatial and temporal confusion
A: Partial dyscalculia, only mirror writing and reading, only in H
AC: Hysteric? ambilateral cerebrality?
C: +female   +left   +polyglot   +?coordinate   +?compound
      +trauma   +discrepancy   +Ribot   +writing

54
R: Kauders, 1929 (Leischner, 1948; Krapf, 1957)
P/P: Hotel porter
H:
MT: German
OL: English, French both by immigration age 16, good accent, traveled to colonies of both, spoke E with son
N: Age 62   1. Transitory left hemiplegia; 2. CVA, right hemiparesis
A: 1. Motor aphasia, still read F and G papers; 2. Sensory aphasia, poor repetition, dysgraphia alexia; with therapy, F and some E returned, less paraphasia in F than G; mixed F words and G in speech, not writing, F with hospital staff, G with wife.
C: −young   +polyglot   +coordinate   +expressive   +receptive
       +repetition   +discrepancy   +Pitres   −Ribot   +mixing   +therapy

55
R: Krapf, 1957
P/P: Male
H:
MT: English
OL: Spanish spoken equally to E
N: Age 35, cranial trauma
A: Understood E worst when mother visited
AC: Affective factors, symptoms dependent on interlocutor
C: +young   +?compound   +?coordinate   +trauma   +receptive
       +discrepancy   +affective

56
R: Krapf, 1957
P/P:
H:
MT: German
OL: Spanish by immigration at age 50, but G at home
N: Sylvian area infarction
A: Mild receptive aphasia, under stress the syntax in G was Latinate but the vocabulary mixed
AC: Affective factors
C: −young   +coordinate   +receptive   +discrepancy   +affective

57
R: Leischner, 1948
P/P: JPs, physician
H:
MT: German
OL: Fluent Czech in childhood, not used recently
N: Age 49, right hemiplegia, multiple embolism of cerebral vessels
A: Sensory; spoke only C with no external cause
AC:
C: +educated   +receptive   +discrepancy   −Pitres   −Ribot   −switch
       −environment

58
R: Leischner, 1948 (Minkowski, 1963)
P/P: PS, lawyer
H:
MT: German (?)
OL: Latin, Greek, French, English in school
N: Age 64, right hemiparesis; age 71, slight softening of outstretched tongue on the
        right, rise in level of tonus
A: Spontaneous speech only sentence fragments, mild anomia, paragraphia
        sometimes, word alexia, discalculia, visual agnosia, amnesia and disturbance of
        memory for colors, disturbance of inner speech and abstraction; understood L but
        could not translate words nor phrases, asked if they were F; could write part of Gr
        alphabet, but asked to write words, wrote in script; alexic in Gr, slightly less in F;
        comprehension in F and E apparently nil.
AC: Leischner: minimal previous command of all except German; Minkowski: Pitres
C: −young   +educated   +polyglot   +compound   +expressive
        +receptive   +discrepancy   +Pitres   +Ribot   −switch   +writing

59
R: Leischner, 1948 (Gloning & Gloning, 1965)
P/P: OS
H: Sign language, Czech, latter accompanying former for emphasis
MT: German, like Czech, learned in school for deaf and dumb
OL:
N: Age 64, two apoplectic insults, right hemiplegia
A: Disturbance with SL, both productive and receptive; impaired coordination of
        gestures and speech; no G speech returned.
AC: Parasymbolia
C: −young   +polyglot   +compound   +expressive   +receptive
        +discrepancy   +Ribot

60
R: L'Hermitte *et al.*, 1966
P/P: 1, MK, hotel manager
H: Right
MT: Russian
OL: French and German studied in childhood; studies in the Caucasus, Turkey,
        Yugoslavia; learned English age 25; lived in France and Germany, married French
        speaker.
N: Age 62, right hemiparesis
A: Expressive aphasia
AC:
C: −young   +polyglot   +coordinate   +expressive   −discrepancy

61
R: L'Hermitte *et al.*, 1966
P/P: 2, PM, hotel manager−owner
H: Right
MT: Ukranian, Russian
OL: Russian, German, Polish, French; left Russia for France, age 19; French wife.

N: Age 66, CVA, left EEG slowing alterations 11 months later
A: Motor, and mild dysgraphia
AC: Equal impairment is the rule.
C: −young   +polyglot   +coordinate   +expressive   −discrepancy

62
R: L'Hermitte *et al.,* 1966
P/P: 3, RP, technical director of a French–German firm
H: Right
MT: German
OL: French wife, work, and residence
N: Age 34, left glioma angular gyrus
A: Mild anomia, and dysgraphia equal in G and F, true both pre- and postoperatively;
     oral translation possible, but from written texts was poor.
AC: Equal impairment is the rule.
C: +young   +educated   +coordinate   +amnestic   −discrepancy
     −translation   +parallel

63
R: L'Hermitte *et al.,* 1966
P/P: 4, GS, director of French–American firm
H: Right
MT: English
OL: German residence as adult, knew German fairly well, then 12 years in Paris; French
     in school, then speaking regularly since age 25; much translation and
     interpretation necessary to work; English with family
N: Age 46, ablation of anterior temporal glioma
A: Severe anomia in both tested languages, F and G; impossible in E, but E words
     given in F; equal problem repeating sentences in both F and E; persisting problems
     of interference of E or F, both syntactic and lexical.
AC: Sensory aphasics, unlike motor, are susceptible to interference.
C: +educated   +coordinate   +compound   +receptive   +amnestic
     +repetition   −discrepancy

64
R: L'Hermitte *et al.,* 1966
P/P: 5, FF, hygiene inspector
H:
MT: Spanish, with wife and relatives now
OL: French school, age 8, now at job and with children
N: Age 48, ablation of left Heschl gyri
A: Sensory, mild paraphasias, anomia, both S and F, improvement till language
     normal 4 years postoperatively
AC: Equal impairment is the rule.
C: +coordinate   +compound   +receptive   +amnestic   −discrepancy

65
R: L'Hermitte *et al.,* 1966
P/P: 6, MX, factory director
H: Right
MT: Judaeo-Spanish (Egyptian)

OL: Hebrew spoken and written from mother; Arabic school, age 4, then French; age 18
     learned Italian which he spoke with customers, Arabic with his employees; French
     with family.
N: Age 40, right hemiplegia, EEG activity left anteriorly, then temporally
A: Broca's, evolved towards expressive, verbal comprehension equally impaired in F,
     S, and E, naming equally impaired in F and S; true even 4 years after.
AC: Equal impairment is the rule.
C: +educated   +polyglot   +coordinate   +expressive   +receptive
     −discrepancy   +parallel   +writing

66
R: L'Hermitte *et al.*, 1966
P/P: 7, EG, physician
H: Right
MT: Alsatian
OL: Early schooling in German, then French through university; used mostly French,
      read in German too; must consciously translate to achieve language switch.
N: Age 30, cranial trauma, left inferior parietal lesion, right hemiplegia
A: Motor aphasia, agraphia−spelling problems in F and G
AC: Equal impairment is the rule.
C: +young   +educated   +compound   +trauma   +expressive
      −discrepancy   −switch

67
R: L'Hermitte *et al.*, 1966
P/P: 8, SI, baker, then drycleaner
H: Right
MT: Hungarian, German with mother
OL: In France since age 17, used the language predominantly but no written skills
N: Age 37, Rolandic meningioma, right hemiplegia
A: Severe Broca's repetition difficulties in both languages tested, H and F
AC: Equal impairment is the rule.
C: +polyglot   +coordinate   +expressive   −discrepancy   +writing

68
R: Lordat, 1843 (Pitres, 1895)
P/P: Priest
H:
MT: Patois
OL: French
N:
A: All F lost; he communicated in P
AC:
C: +compound   +discrepancy   +Ribot   +writing

69
R: Lyman *et al.*, 1938 (Gloning & Gloning, 1965)
P/P: Professional financier
H:
MT: Chinese
OL: English childhood, then studied abroad

N: Age 42, left parieto-occipital tumor
A: Alexia and agraphia, much worse in C than in E, acalculia
AC: E can be, and was, spelled out.
C: +educated   +coordinate   +compound   +discrepancy   −Ribot
    +writing

70
R: Michel, 1892 (Hinshelwood, 1902)
P/P:
H:
MT:
OL:
N:
A: Could read Gothic but not Latin characters
AC:
C: +discrepancy   +receptive   +writing

71
R: Minkowski, 1927 (Minkowski, 1963; Leischner, 1948)
P/P: Mechanic
H:
MT: Swiss German
OL: Since childhood used standard German (reading and speech), some French and Italian
N: Age 32, motor accident, possible bilateral lesions
A: Broca's agraphia, alexia; initially used only impaired literary G, though understood SG; continued interference of G in SG later; no production of comprehension of F or I possible during 16 months' observation.
AC: Visual imagery employed with G words, affective factors, participation of right hemisphere in recovery
C: +young   +polyglot   +trauma   +expressive   +receptive
    +discrepancy   +Pitres   −Ribot   +writing   +affective

72
R: Minkowski, 1927 (Minkowski, 1963; Leischner, 1948)
P/P: Math professor
H:
MT: Swiss German
OL: Literary German (childhood), French, Italian; since age 30, used more F in work, with family.
N: Age 44 or 54, CVA
A: Expressive, F and LG returned with work, some I; SG never returned, even after 5 years in Zurich.
AC: Affective necessity of F and LG
C: +educated   +polyglot   +compound   +expressive   +discrepancy
    +Pitres   −Ribot   +writing

73
R: Minkowski, 1928 (Minkowski, 1963; Chlenov, 1948)
P/P:
H:

MT: Swiss German
OL: Literary German in school, a little French, age 19 to France for 6 years, then returned and married a Swiss German.
N: Age 44, CVA—probably destroying left Broca speech areas and possibly Penfield arc
A: Comprehension fine, expression only possible in F; then after 3 weeks, in LG; only after 4 months, hesitant SG; in home, SG became fluent, F regressed.
AC: First-love French
C: +polyglot   +coordinate   +compound   +expressive   +discrepancy
      −Pitres   −Ribot   +regression   +affective

74
R: Minkowski, 1933 (Minkowski, 1963)
P/P: Joiner
H:
MT: Swiss German
OL: Early literary German; then French 20 years in Lausanne, and with wife
N: Age 46, accident, fracture of right parietal bone, paresis of right facial nerve and diminished hearing on right side; probably a temporal lobe contusion too
A: Initially word finding easiest in F; then SG, then G improved, F regressed
AC: Subject's preference for French
C: +polyglot   +coordinate   +compound   +trauma   +amnestic
      +discrepancy   +Pitres   +Ribot   +regression   +writing   +affective

75
R: Minkowski, 1949 (Minkowski, 1963)
P/P: Electrician
H:
MT: Swiss German, currently too
OL: Literary German, some French and Italian
N: Age 45, craniocerebral trauma, extensive injury
A: Anomic with some paraphasia, agrammatism, agraphia, hypolexia, agnosia; literary German speech returned first, SG after 3 months and exercises; no speech or comprehension of F or I; yet in Jacksonian epileptic attacks a year later, cried out in F.
AC: Use of visual image of word to help recall it
C: +polyglot   +trauma   +expressive   +receptive   +amnestic
      +discrepancy   +Pitres   −Ribot   +automatic   +writing   +therapy

76
R: Mossner & Pilch, 1971
P/P: Educated female
H:
MT: German
OL: Age 20, immigrated to English, returned to Germany age 32
N: Age 36, left temporal tumor operated on
A: Motor aphasia, originally responded in G to daughters with whom E had been spoken, E returned more syntactically impaired than G; some mixing of words.
AC:
C: +female   +educated   +expressive   +discrepancy   +Ribot
      +mixing   −switch

77
R: Nielsen & Raney, 1939 (Nielsen, 1962; Gloning & Gloning, 1965)
P/P: Sailor
H:
MT: German
OL: Danish, Swedish, Norwegian, Dutch, English
N: Right temporal tumor
A: Some aphasic symptoms before removal, and for only 5 weeks after; acalculia in E
       and S, but could at least count in other languages
AC: The left hemisphere took over the function.
C: +polyglot   +right lesion   +discrepancy

78
R: Obler & Albert, this monograph
P/P: AF—factory administrator
H: Right
MT: Czech
OL: German, English, Yiddish, French, age 20, immigrated, Hebrew
N: Age 55, car accident preceded CVA, right hemiparesis; EEG revealed general
       disturbance with emphasis in left frontal area.
A: Expressive and amnestic, with no comprehension difficulties; at initial evaluation
       several months after CVA and after H therapy, H production was superior to E, but
       there was no mixing of H forms or vocabulary into E, except automatisms like
       "yes" or "right" or "I don't know"; reading G and E was superior to H as it always
       was; H evidenced no mixing whereas F necessitated H and E vocabulary.
AC: Therapy, once daily in E and in H, over 2 months, resulted in no more mixing and
       in parallel recovery of E to H.
C: +educated   +polyglot   +coordinate   +compound   +?trauma
       +expressive   +amnestic   +mild receptive   ±discrepancy   +Pitres
       −Ribot   +automatic   +parallel   +writing   +therapy

79
R: Obler & Albert, this monograph
P/P: SK—intelligent female
H: Left
MT: Hebrew
OL: Fluent English by adolescent immigration, return to H age 18
N: Age 20, auto accident, bilateral frontal destruction removed
A: Three weeks after accident, understood E and H equally, writing E from right to
       left, by left–right reversing individual letters for name, or simply order for
       alphabet; further confusion in E alphabet, both phonetic and visual (F and B for P,
       K then B for R); no mixing of H letters into E words, some mixing of E letters into H
       words, especially for |r| and only during these mixed-language sessions.
AC:
C: +female   +young   +educated   +coordinate   −discrepancy
       +mixing   +switch

80
R: Ore, 1878 (Pitres, 1895)
P/P: Laborer
H:

MT: Patois
OL: French
N: Age 26, left cranial trauma
A: Comprehension and speech lost in F, not in P
AC:
C: +young   −educated   +compound   +trauma   +expressive
   +receptive   +discrepancy   +Pitres   +Ribot   +writing

81
R: Peuser & Leischner, 1974
P/P: Philologist
H:
MT: (German?)
OL: German, English, phonetic transcription
N: Age 39, encephalitis
A: Sensory-amnesic aphasia; dysgraphia worse in English than German, mild in
   phonetic transcription.
AC: Faulty semantic decoding, intact phonological decoding
C: +educated   +receptive   +amnestic   +discrepancy   −Ribot
   +writing

82
R: Pick, 1909 (Leischner, 1948)
P/P:
H:
MT: German
OL: Fluent Czech
N: Accident—lesion in posterior left temporal first and second convolutions.
A: Sensory agnosia, agraphia, repetition difficulties, answered all questions only in
   C, with some inappropriate words
AC:
C: +trauma   +receptive   +repetition   +discrepancy   −Ribot   −switch

83
R: Pick, 1913 (Leischner, 1948)
P/P:
H:
MT: Czech
OL: German
N: Age 35, meningitis
A: Temporary speech and writing disorders; written G displayed agrammatism;
   grammatical categories of C interfered.
AC:
C: +young   +expressive   +discrepancy   +Ribot   +mixing

84
R: Pick, 1909 (Gloning & Gloning, 1965)
P/P: KZ, maid
H:
MT: German

OL: Fluent Czech
N: Age 86, entire left hemisphere somewhat atrophied, softening of supramarginal gyrus and adjoining part of angular gyrus, and posterior portion of first temporal gyrus
A: Severe anomic sensory aphasia, total alexia and agraphia; mixed the two languages in paraphasia, spoke mostly jargon C, and might answer questions spoken in either language in the other language.
AC:
C: +female −young +receptive +amnestic +discrepancy
   +Pitres −Ribot −switch +mixing

85
R: Pick, 1909 (Gloning & Gloning, 1965)
P/P: PJ, merchant
H:
MT: German
OL: Fluent Czech
N: Age 74, softening of angular and supramarginal gyri and second occipital gyrus and posterior half of second temporal gyrus on left side
A: Initially spoke only C with verbal paraphasias, then G returned, amnestic difficulties, literal and verbal paraphasias in both languages—answered questions in either language in the appropriate language, until deterioration in which C answered to G.
AC:
C: +amnestic +discrepancy +Pitres −Ribot ±switch

86
R: Pitres, 1895
P/P: 1
H:
MT: Patois until age 12
OL: French age 12, through work, residence, army, mainly used thereafter
N: Age 48, CVA, right hemiplegia; evaluated 3 years later
A: Expressive; dysarthria, agrammatism, word-finding difficulties in F; in P no speech; understanding fine in both.
AC:
C: +coordinate +expressive +amnestic +discrepancy +Pitres
   −Ribot +writing

87
R: Pitres, 1895
P/P: 2, baker
H:
MT: Patois and French
OL:
N: 1. Age 59, CVA, right hemiplegia;
   2. Age 62, hemiplegia lessened.
A: 1. Expressive (no spontaneous speech) and conduction in F;
   2. In F expressive (severe anomia), but word repetition possible; in P comprehension also good, but no production possible.

AC:
C: −young   +compound   +expressive   +conduction   +discrepancy
       −Ribot   +writing

88
R: Pitres, 1895
P/P: 3, woman
H:
MT: Basque
OL: Patois, French
N: Age 47, CVA. right hemiplegia; evaluated age 50.
A: Understood all three, spoke B with facility, less so F, not at all P; could read B and
       F, but not P.
AC:
C: +female   +compound   +expressive   +receptive   +discrepancy
       +Ribot   +writing

89
R: Pitres, 1895.
P/P: 4, traveling businessman
H:
MT: French
OL: Italian and Spanish, age 25, more used in business
N: Age 53, right hemiplegia
A: Severe dysarthria, some anomia in F and S; I entirely lost, both comprehension and
       production.
AC:
C: +polyglot   +compound   +expressive   +receptive   +amnestic
       +discrepancy   +Ribot

90
R: Pitres, 1895
P/P: 5, administrator
H:
MT: French, German
OL: Studied Greek and Latin, married a Basque and learned the language well, age 22,
       later learned for pleasure English, Spanish, Italian.
N: Age 56, CVA, right hemiplegia
A: From the start understood only F; after a year, began to produce French; could then
       express self, read and write in F.
AC:
C: +educated   +polyglot   +compound   +coordinate   +expressive
       +receptive   +discrepancy   +Pitres   +Ribot   +writing

91
R: Pitres, 1895
P/P: 6, officer
H:
MT: French
OL: English and German, reasonably well
N: Craniocerebral injury, age 36; then apoplectic attack, right hemiplegia

A: Agrammatism, trouble with reading comprehension, spontaneous writing; could tell if E or G was being spoken, but could not understand, translate, nor speak.

AC:

C: +young   +polyglot   +compound   +trauma   +expressive +receptive   +discrepancy   −switch

92

R: Poetzl, 1925 (Leischner, 1948; Minkowski, 1963; Gloning & Gloning, 1965)

P/P: Educated German teacher

H:

MT: German

OL: Czech, especially recently

N: Age 52, severe cranial trauma, paraplegia, then quadriplegia, coma, and death; left inferior parietal lesion.

A: Good understanding, mixed C nouns in speech, then apologized; next day amnestic.

AC: Recent intensive study of C

C: +educated   +amnestic   +discrepancy   +Pitres   −Ribot   +mixing

93

R: Poetzl, 1925 (Leischner, 1948).

P/P: Scholar

H:

MT: German

OL: French, Italian, English, Latin, Greek.

N:

A: All modern languages forgotten; L and Gr were best; however, they were agraphic and alexic (according to Herschmann).

AC:

C: +educated   +polyglot   +compound   +expressive   +receptive +discrepancy   −Ribot   +writing

94

R: Proust, 1872 (Pitres, 1895)

P/P: Woman

H:

MT: Italian

OL: Long French residence

N:

A: Slow recovery of usage of F, and of comprehension of I, but never expression of I

AC:

C: +female   +coordinate   +expressive   +receptive   +discrepancy +Pitres   −Ribot   +environment

95

R: Reichmann & Reichau, 1919 (Leischner, 1948)

P/P:

H:

MT: East Prussian, Low German

OL:

N: Age 21, gunshot wound

A: Expressive in LG, learned literary German (a new dialect) with therapy, much later LG returned, never with true consonants
AC:
C: +young +polyglot +trauma +expressive +?writing

96
R: Rinckenbach, 1866 (Pitres, 1895)
P/P:
H:
MT: German (Alsace)
OL: Fluent French, 25 years in army
N: Apoplectic ictus
A: G recovered first, both comprehension and speech; then comprehended F, but answered in G; F expression remained difficult.
AC:
C: +coordinate +expressive +receptive +discrepancy +Pitres +Ribot

97
R: Schwalbe, 1920 (Leischner, 1948)
P/P:
H:
MT: (German?)
OL: Hebrew in childhood, always used for prayers
N: Age 80
A: At first incoherent H words, then G gradually recovered
AC: (cf. French nun in Pitres)
C: −young +coordinate +expressive +discrepancy −Pitres −Ribot +automatic +writing

98
R: Simonyi, 1951 (Gloning & Gloning, 1965)
P/P:
H:
MT: German
OL: Hungarian predominantly, recently
N: Age 58, Pick's atrophy, diffuse damage
A: Only H spontaneous speech
AC:
C: +discrepancy −Pitres +Ribot

99
R: Shubert, 1940 (Chlenov, 1948; Minkowski, 1963)
P/P:
H:
MT: ?
OL: Georgian, Russian
N:
A: Wrote beginning of word in G, ended in R; as R writing and reading returned, G lost altogether.
AC:
C: +discrepancy +mixing +regression +writing

100
R: Smirnov & Faktorowicz, 1949 (Minkowski, 1963)
P/P:
H:
MT: Turkmenian
OL: Spoken Russian in army
N:
A: R returned before T.
AC: Minkowski: adaptation to Russian hospital.
C: +?coordinate +trauma +discrepancy +Pitres −Ribot
−writing +environment

101
R: Smirnov & Faktorowicz, 1949 (Minkowski, 1963)
P/P:
H:
MT: Kazakh
OL: Spoken Russian in army
N:
A: R returned before K.
AC: Minkowski: adaptation to Russian hospital
C: +?coordinate +trauma +discrepancy +Pitres −Ribot
−writing +environment

102
R: Smirnov & Faktorowicz, 1949 (Minkowski, 1963)
P/P:
H:
MT: Turkmenian
OL: Kazakh, Russian in army, both learned aurally
N:
A: Return in order: R, K, T.
AC: Minkowski: environment, adaptation to Russian hospital.
C: +?coordinate +trauma +discrepancy +Pitres −Ribot
+writing +environment

103
R: Stengel & Zelmanowicz, 1933 (Leischner, 1948; Goldstein, 1948)
P/P: Cook (woman)
H:
MT: Czech
OL: German, age 22, immigration, used C only rarely, then age 51 period of 4 years
returned to only C, then at 55 to G.
N: Age 57, cranial trauma, right Babinski
A: Motor, equal in both languages; mixing of words in spontaneous speech; repetition
worse in C; G words for daily life topics, C for more remote items and body parts.
AC:
C: +female −young +coordinate +trauma +expressive
+repetition ±discrepancy +mixing

104
R: Trousseau (Pitres, 1895)
P/P:
H:
MT: Russian
OL: French, quite well
N: Hemiplegia
A: Expressive—total in F, severe in R
AC:
C: +expressive   +discrepancy   +Ribot

105
R: Wald, 1958 (Minkowski, 1963)
P/P: "Lady"
H:
MT: Russian
OL: Fluent English, fairly good spoken French
N: Age 48, CVA
A: Initially spoke only E, even to answer R questions; then R recovered, E became
        difficult to express, though translation E to R was facile
AC:
C: +female   +discrepancy   −Pitres   −Ribot   ±switch   +regression
        ±environment   +writing

106
R: Weisenburg & McBride, 1935 (Goldstein, 1948)
P/P: Male, professor of Romance languages
H: Right for unimanual activities, left for bimanual
MT: English
OL: Spanish, French, Italian, German, Latin, Arabic
N: Age 49, lesion, probably subcortical, from thrombosis of left middle cerebral artery
A: Predominantly expressive Broca's and agraphia; disturbed in all languages, to
        degree he knew the language; repetition fairly good; improved in parallel;
        difficulty in translation from E to others, less vice versa; loss of accent in F and S
        but this returned gradually with general improvement.
AC:
C: +left   +educated   +expressive   ±discrepancy   +Ribot   +parallel
        +writing

107
R: Winslow, 1868 (Pitres, 1895)
P/P: "Lady"
H:
MT: English?
OL: French
N: Age 48, uterine hemorrhage, sick several months
A: E untouched, F global
AC:
C: +female   +discrepancy

108
R: Winterstein & Meier, 1939 (Minkowski, 1963)
P/P: "Lady"
H:
MT: Swiss German
OL: Italian residence, and friend, French; in school, literary German.
N: Age 35, craniocerebral accident, contrecoup fissure, lesion around Broca's area
A: I speech recovered first, then F with regression of I, then SG; answered G questions
        in F; however, mode of recovery same in all languages: dysarthria and paraphasias,
        perseverations, word-finding difficulties.
AC: Minkowski: affective factor of friends' recent visit.
C: +female   +young   +coordinate   +compound   +trauma
        +expressive   +amnestic   +discrepancy   −switch   +parallel
        +regression   +writing   −Ribot

STATISTICAL ANALYSES OF POLYGLOT APHASICS

INTRODUCTION

Since even the most careful review of cases (Paradis, 1977) admits that no single rule, or factor, can yet explain recovery patterns in polyglot aphasia, we determined to collect 100-odd cases of polyglot aphasia, and see if correlations could be found between personal factors (e.g., age and handedness), language history factors (e.g., age of learning L_2), neurological factors (e.g., hemisphere of lesion, lesion type), aphasic disturbances peculiar to polyglot aphasia (e.g., mixing languages in production), and recovery patterns.

The methodology was as follows: We abstracted information from the first 105 cases from the literature available to us. To these cases, 3 of our own were added. Each subject was coded for each of the 29 variables listed in the key to symbols (p. 110), and then the languages he or she knew were recorded, with the mother tongue labeled as such when that information was known.

A note of caution is in order with respect to interpretation of the results. Full details were not available in many cases, so some variables do not in fact tap all 108 patients. In correlating variables, only those subjects for whom we had data on each variable could be included, of course, so conclusions must sometimes be drawn on as few as 20 subjects. Needless to say, further systematic study may produce contradictory evidence. We have chosen to publish the data we have, in hopes of stimulating thought about the parameters involved in bilingualism.

In this section we first describe the subject population in terms of the various parameters we annotated when possible. Then we discuss correlations of the variables in terms of how they speak to various issues. Among the personal history issues are aging, age of L_2 acquisition, coordinate bilingualism versus compound bilingualism, and polyglotism versus monolingualism—and versus bilingualism in aphasics. Then follow the neurological issues: lesion site and type, aphasia types, and aphasic impairments peculiar to polyglot aphasia. Finally, recovery patterns are discussed.

GROUP DATA ON SUBJECTS

Of the 108 cases under study, 84 were men and 22 were women. In 2 cases the sex of the patient was not reported. It is important to note that complete details for each case were rarely available, so the totals on any given variable may not total 108. The patients' age at the time of the interview ranged from 15 to 94, with the median age being 51. Subjects' handedness was rarely explicitly mentioned; 7 of the patients were left-handers, 2 were ambidextrous, and 13 were noted to be right-handers. (We might assume, however, that the vast majority of the 86 remaining cases were right-handers.) The number of polyglots and bilinguals in our sample was similar: 50 polyglots and 48 bilinguals. Of the total, 51 had coordinate language histories; they had learned two languages in two different situations. Thirty-seven subjects had compound bilingual histories; they had learned two languages within the context of one situation. Fourteen subjects were labeled both compound and coordinate, because in their learning of multiple languages, some had been learned in compound fashion, whereas others had been learned coordinately. The precise age of second language learning was rarely recorded, so subjects were categorized as to whether they learned their second language in the preschool period, during school, or as adults. Nineteen subjects had learned their second language during early childhood, 32 had learned it in school, and 19 had learned a second language as adults. Table 5 gives a summary of personal data for all 108 cases.

Of cases in which the site of lesion was mentioned, or could be inferred from hemiparesis, 53 cases of left hemispheric lesion were reported, 7 of right hemispheric lesion, and 10 of bilateral lesions. The type of lesion was most frequently CVA and trauma. Table 6 summarizes lesion information.

As to the aphasic impairments evidenced, 64 patients had some sort of expressive, or production, difficulties; 45 had receptive, or comprehension, disturbance. Thirty-four patients showed amnestic or anomic symptoms, 10 were noted to have difficulty repeating speech

Table 5

Summary of Personal History Data

Sex:	84 male, 22 female
Age:	Range 15–94, median 51
Handedness (when noted):	7 left, 2 ambidextrous, 13 right
Polyglotism:	50 polyglots, 48 bilinguals
L_2 learning manner:	51 coordinate, 37 compound
L_2 learning age:	19 childhood, 32 school, 19 adults
Education:	40 well educated, 8 uneducated

Table 6

Summary of Lesion Information

Lesion side:	Left: 53		Right: 7		Bilateral: 10
Lesion type:	CVA:	26 cases 24%			
	Trauma:	23 cases 21%			
	Tumor:	13 cases 12%			
	Atrophy:	7 cases 6%			
	Infection:	3 cases 3%			
	Miscellaneous:	8 cases 7%			
	Unmentioned:	28 cases 26%			

upon command, and 8 were globally impaired to the point of being reduced to automatic speech. Agraphia was reported in 33 cases, and alexia in 29. Unfortunately, aphasic problems related specifically to polyglotism were tested only sporadically, so the percentage of cases reporting such problems cannot be taken to represent that which would be seen in a systematically tested population of polyglot aphasics. For example, only 5 case studies mentioned that the patient had translation problems; and regression of skills in a first-returning language upon increase of skills in a second language was cited in only 6 cases. Switching problems were reported in 29 cases. (In most of these cases the patient could not switch, but in some, the switching was sociolinguistically inappropriate.) Sixteen patients would mix elements of both languages as aphasics, whereas premorbidly they had not. The one polyglot variable that was mentioned in a large number of cases was the existence of a discrepancy between the aphasic state in the two languages. Discrepancy was reported for 79 cases, and reported explicitly **not** to obtain in only 20 cases. Of course these data, too, are not representative of an unselected polyglot aphasic population, because cases presenting discrepancy are the more interesting to report. Table 7 summarizes impairment data.

Table 7
Summary of Polyglot Aphasic Impairments

Impairments possible in monolinguals		Impairments specific to polyglots	
Expressive:	64	Translation:	5
Receptive:	45	Regression:	6
Anomic:	34	Switching:	29
Repetition:	10	Mixing:	16
Global:	8	Discrepancy:	79
Agraphia:	33		
Alexia:	29		

Recovery patterns could be abstracted for 47 patients, with respect to whether or not the recovery was parallel. For 20 patients, restitution followed parallel patterns in both or all languages; for 23 it clearly did not. As to the rules of Pitres and Ribot, 25 people followed the rule of Pitres, which states that the most recently used language returns first, while 13 people clearly contradicted this rule. Ribot's rule, that the earliest learned language returns first, was followed by 26 patients, and contradicted by 30 patients.

The set of languages spoken by the patients reflect the languages spoken by the authors who reported the case studies we compiled. We present the data, nevertheless, since they may be used to distinguish patterns in our population sample from patterns in other populations. Eighteen languages were represented as mother tongues of our subjects. Of these the most common were French (24 cases), German (22 cases), and English (17 cases). The next most frequent language was Russian, which was the mother tongue in 6 cases. In all, 43 languages were known to our particular subjects, when the second, third, fourth and so on, languages are taken into account. These languages were preponderantly Indo-European (93 cases). Slavic languages were known in 12 instances, Turkic in 6; mixed languages like Yiddish or Ladino were known in 4 cases. Sinitic and Semitic languages were each represented in two instances, and Basque and sign language each once.

CORRELATION OF VARIABLES

AGE   Among the personal data variables, sex provided no significant correlations, but age did. Two facts emerged that may be related. The elderly group evidenced no exclusively right-sided lesions, and they also were significantly more likely ($p = .02$) to contradict the rule of Pitres than were younger subjects. For the purposes of these calculations, subjects were divided into three groups: young (up to age 30), middle-aged (from 30 to 59), and elderly (from age 60). Table 8 suggests

Table 8
Rule of Pitres × Age (N = 41)

	Age		
	Under 30	30–59	Over 59
Recent L first (N = 28)	7 = 78%	15 = 68%	6 = 60%
Recent L not first (N = 13)	2 = 22%	7 = 32%	4 = 40%

that the percentage of people contradicting Pitres's rule increased with increasing age (see Obler & Albert, 1977). This may possibly be related, we have speculated, to the impairment in short-term memory that has been associated with aging. As to the side of lesion, the two older groups had a greater percentage of left lesions than did the younger group. Furthermore, the oldest group had no exclusively right-sided lesions (see Table 9).

We might conclude that younger polyglots are more likely to have aphasia from right hemispheric lesions than are younger monolinguals (cf. Boller, 1973; Brown & Wilson, 1973). This would imply that a greater percentage of polyglots than monolinguals have some right hemispheric representation of language. This statement is particularly true for younger polyglots; in the elderly, language may tend to be lateralized more in the left hemisphere.

AGE OF SECOND LANGUAGE ACQUISITION   We hypothesized that patients who had learned their second language early in life would be less likely to show a discrepant aphasic impairment between the two languages, since they were more probably compound bilinguals. This hypothesis was refuted; about 20% of the patients in each of the three groups of learning showed no discrepancy, whereas 80% showed some discrepancy (see Table 10).

Table 9
Age × Lesion Site

	Age		
	Under 30	30–59	Over 59
Left lesion	7 = 54%	31 = 80%	11 = 79%
Right lesion	3 = 23%	4 = 10%	0
Bilateral lesion	3 = 23%	4 = 10%	3 = 21%

Table 10

Discrepancy × *Age of L_2 Learning*

	Learned L_2 in childhood	School	Adult
Evidenced discrepancy	15	27	14
Evidenced no discrepancy	4	11	5

There was, however, a trend toward more parallel recovery related to the younger learning of L_2 ($p = 1.8$) (see Table 11).

There was no correlation between the type of aphasic disorders and the age of learning the second language (see Table 12). Thus, the age of learning the second language did not correlate with the type of aphasia, nor with the existence or nonexistence of discrepant aphasic impairment between the two languages. We may say that people who learned both their languages in childhood tended to show parallel recovery, whereas people who learned a second language in school or as adults tended to show nonparallel recovery.

POLYGLOTISM VERSUS MONOLINGUALISM   Only a few points can be made, in contrasting our polyglot aphasic population to an equivalent monolingual population. The reason for this difficulty in contrasting monolinguals and polyglots is that it is difficult to define what a group "equivalent" to our group would be.

Table 11

Parallel Recovery × *Age of L_2 Acquisition*

	Childhood	School	Adult
Parallel recovery	6	10	4
Nonparallel recovery	3	17	7

Table 12

Aphasic Problems × *Age of L_2 Acquisition*

	Childhood	School	Adult
Expressive problems ($N = 65$)	13	42	10
Receptive problems ($N = 45$)	8	31	6
Amnestic ($N = 34$)	5	23	6

An example of the problem arises when we search for an appropriate group to compare to ours with respect to sex distribution. Twenty-two percent of our population was female. Although many sociological factors may have entered into the underrepresentation of females in this or any aphasic group, we must consider the possibility that sex and bilingualism interact in brain organization for language. In a recent study of aphasic patients at the Institute of Physical Medicine and Rehabilitation, M. Sarno (personal communication, 1977) found 75 males and 59 females. This high percentage of females (44%) may be because her patients, unlike ours, were all stroke victims. In a study of sex differences in an aphasic population, McGlone (1976) included vascular and neoplastic etiologies but restricted her population to right-handers with unilateral lesions. No right-sided lesions resulted in aphasia, but 14 of the 29 left-lesioned males had aphasia, whereas only 2 of the 16 females did. Thus, McGlone's data showed an even smaller ratio of female aphasics (2:16= 12%) than did our population.

As to handedness, our population falls into the normal range for nonaphasics. If we assume that patients for whom no handedness was reported were right-handers, then 92% of the population was right-handed. Hécaen and Ajuriaguerra (1963) reviewed a number of handedness studies of healthy populations and found that they ranged from 5 to 30% non-right-handers. An unpublished study of ours restricted to aphasic patients seen at the Boston Veterans Administration Hospital, however, found 26 out of 354 patients, or 7% of aphasic male monolinguals to be left-handed or ambidextrous. The percentage of polyglot non-right-handers was strikingly similar to the percentage for monolinguals. Additionally, there was a high correlation (p=.08) between handedness and hemisphere of lesion in our small polyglot sample where data were available for both these variables (see Table 13). The distribution was much as one would find in a monolingual population (Hécaen & Albert, 1978).

Certain types of lesions led to certain types of aphasic disorder in

Table 13
Lesion Side × Handedness

	Left lesion	Right lesion	Bilateral lesion
Left-handed	2	3	1
Right-handed	11	1	0
Ambidextrous	2	0	0
Total	15	4	1

our population. Atrophy, for example, did not result in expressive aphasia for our population, whereas trauma, CVA, and, to a lesser extent, tumor did result in expressive impairments ($p = .0001$) (see Table 14).

To the best of our knowledge, the correlation between aphasia type and etiology has not been extensively studied in monolinguals. In fact, these data on expressive aphasia may relate to another parallel between a monolingual population and the polyglot aphasics. In the sample of monolingual veterans mentioned previously, we found that the exclusively Broca's aphasics were significantly younger than the exclusively Wernicke's aphasics (52 years and 63 years, respectively). In our polyglot sample, the 28 patients who were reported to have expressive impairment but not receptive impairment averaged 48 years old, whereas the 6 patients reported to have receptive impairment but not expressive impairment averaged 55 years old.

No definitive statements can be made regarding population differences between polyglot aphasics and monolingual aphasics. The proportional representation of females in the sample may differ in the two groups, and this difference may be due to neuropsychological repercussions of bilingualism. Handedness and age representation in our polyglot aphasic population were similar to that in a monolingual male aphasic population we have studied.

POLYGLOTISM VERSUS BILINGUALISM

We asked whether knowing only two languages had different consequences from knowing more than two languages. No significant differences emerged, but several curious tendencies can be described.

There was a tendency for discrepancy in aphasia types to be reported slightly more frequently in polyglots than in bilinguals (see Table 15).

The division, however, between polyglots and bilinguals was not

Table 14
Lesion Type × Aphasic Impairment

	Expressive	Definitely not expressive
Trauma	17	1
CVA	17	0
Tumor	6	2
Atrophy	0	3
Infection	3	0

Table 15

Discrepancy × Bilingual or Polyglot

	Discrepancy	No discrepancy
Polyglots	40 = 82%	9 = 18%
Bilinguals	33 = 75%	11 = 25%

significant. Neither the specific problems of polyglot aphasia (e.g., switching languages and mixing languages) nor the problems for the traditional aphasic (e.g., expressive, receptive, and amnesic) could be related to knowing only two, or more than two, languages.

With recovery patterns, however, some differences between the two groups could be seen. Polyglots were more likely to follow Pitres's rule than were bilinguals, and were more likely to contradict Ribot's rule (see Table 16).

Moreover, those five patients in whom regression of the first returned language was reported, when a second one started to return, were all polyglots. Where explicit mention was made of nonparallel recovery, it obtained in 17 polyglots and 9 bilinguals. In those cases where the handedness of our subjects was known, more polyglots were right-handers, whereas bilinguals were left-handers (see Table 17).

It would be difficult to explain why polyglot right-handers should have tended to become aphasics, whereas in the bilingual group, it was the left-handers who tended to become aphasic. Certain recovery patterns

Table 16

Recovery Patterns

	Polyglots	Bilinguals
Pro Pitres	22	18
Contra Pitres	5	7
Pro Ribot	17	17
Contra Ribot	20	14

Table 17

Handedness and Polyglotism or Bilingualism

	Polyglot	Bilingual
Left-handed	1	6
Right-handed	9	4
Ambidextrous	1	1

(regression and nonparallel recovery) were also more likely to occur in polyglots than in bilinguals. The polyglots, like the younger as compared to older subjects, were more likely than bilinguals to follow Pitres's rule that the recent language returns first. The polyglots were not significantly younger than bilinguals, however; polyglots averaged 45 years old, while bilinguals averaged 47.

COORDINATE VERSUS COMPOUND BILINGUALISM   The division of patients into compound and coordinate bilinguals provided no significant correlations, but several tendencies emerged. One difference between the two groups was that the compounds were more likely to show a discrepant aphasic picture than were the coordinates. Of the compounds, 81% showed discrepancy, while 71% of the coordinates showed discrepancy (see Table 18). For the aphasic syndromes, equal percentages of compound and coordinate subjects had expressive impairment (58% and 62%, respectively), but compounds were slightly more likely to evidence receptive impairment (38% of coordinates had receptive difficulties; 46% of compounds did). As to specifically bilingual problems, the largest difference between the compounds and coordinates was for the switching problem. A larger percentage of the compounds (33%) than of the coordinates (22%) were reported to have a switching problem. It is of interest to note that the proportion of subjects evidencing problems of mixing the two languages was approximately the same in both groups. More coordinates (28%) than compounds (18%) showed parallel recovery from polyglot aphasia (see Tables 19 and 20).

The compound bilingual is presumed to have had a fairly unified system for his two languages, whereas the coordinate has two or more separate systems. This being the case, one would have predicted that compound bilinguals would be more likely than coordinates to have parallel recovery from aphasia, since the two languages should be so closely bound. Compound bilinguals should also have shown less discrepancy rather than more. Perhaps the key to these contradictions lies in the fact that compounds had more switching problems with aphasia; learning a language in a compound situation may necessitate

Table 18
Compound–Discrepant Aphasic Pattern

	Coordinate	Compound
Discrepancy	41 = 71%	33 = 80%
Nondiscrepancy	17 = 29%	8 = 19%

Table 19

Aphasic Impairment and Compound–Coordinate

	Coordinate	Compound
Expressive	37 = 62%	24 = 58%
Receptive	23 = 38%	20 = 46%
Amnestic	20 = 33%	15 = 35%
Conduction	6 = 10%	3 = 7%
Central	4 = 7%	1 = 2%
Agraphia	16 = 27%	11 = 26%
Alexia	14 = 24%	13 = 30%

Table 20

Bilingual Aphasia Problems and Compound–Coordinate

	Coordinate	Compound
Automatic	6 = 10%	2 = 5%
Translation	3 = 5%	1 = 2%
Switch	13 = 22%	4 = 9%
Regression	2 = 3%	4 = 9%
Parallel recovery	17 = 28%	8 = 18%
Nonparallel recovery	16 = 27%	9 = 21%

development of a special mechanism for switch control, which the coordinate learner has somehow naturally provided in the two separate learning contexts.

LESION INFORMATION   The lesion information we obtained (when possible, type and etiology of lesion) speaks to two issues: discrepant aphasia and patterns of recovery from aphasia. First, however, we must underscore the high percentage of exclusively right hemisphere lesions found in our population. Where lesion site was known, or possible to infer from a hemiplegia, 53 cases of left hemisphere lesion were found, 7 cases of right hemisphere lesion, and 10 of bilateral lesion. Thus 10% of the known lesions resulting in aphasia were right hemispheric lesions. Of these 7 cases of right lesions, 3 were left-handers, 3 were right-handers, and for 1 the premorbid handedness was unknown. Three right-handers with right-sided lesions resulting in aphasia is a high percentage of crossed aphasia in a sample the size of ours. It implies that our polyglot aphasics had more language representation in their right hemispheres than monolingual populations regularly do.

Lesion type had no significant correlation with the various aphasic problems, but it did correlate with the discrepancy variable and with recovery according to the rule of Pitres. Tumor and atrophy were less likely to show a discrepancy between aphasic syndrome in each language, than were trauma and CVA (see Table 21).

There was a strong but not significant interaction between lesion type and Pitres's rule ($p = .25$). Trauma cases were very likely to follow the rule of Pitres, while CVA cases were as likely to contradict as to follow that rule (see Table 22). This may be related to the fact that many of the trauma patients in this population were young war-injured aphasics, whereas the CVA patients were older. The side of lesion, however, had no interaction with recovery by Pitres's rule. Side of lesion did interact with parallel recovery. Exclusively right hemisphere lesions were more likely to show nonparallel recovery, whereas exclusively left-sided lesions were more likely to show parallel recovery (see Table 23).

Table 21
Lesion Type × Discrepant Aphasia

	Discrepancy	No discrepancy
Trauma	20	3
CVA	22	4
Tumor	7	6
Atrophy	4	3

Table 22
Lesion Type × Pitres's Rule

	Follows Pitres	Contra Pitres
Trauma	12	0
CVA	10	7
Tumor	1	2
Miscellaneous	1	1
Atrophy	2	1
Infection	1	0
Seizures	1	0

Table 23
Parallel Recovery × Lesion Side

Type of recovery	Left	Right	Bilateral
Parallel	15	1	1
Nonparallel	11	4	2

We recognize that the data here are based on a small number of subjects; nevertheless, we must point out that the pattern seen in the data (namely, that right-sided lesions are more likely than left-sided lesions to result in nonparallel recovery) is consistent with a hypothesis that the right hemisphere is organized for language in the bilingual differently from the way in which the left hemisphere is organized for language. The differential patterns we see between performances in the two languages in the bilingual may be accounted for by their different organization, or degree of organization, in the right hemisphere.

APHASIC SYNDROMES IN POLYGLOTISM As a group, our polyglot aphasics looked like a monolingual group we studied at the Boston Veterans Administration Hospital, with respect to general aphasic impairments. Patients with expressive impairment outnumbered patients with receptive impairment, who outnumbered anomic patients (Obler & Albert, 1977). (Among the polyglots were 65 with expressive difficulties, 45 with receptive difficulties, and 34 with anomic difficulties.) The polyglot aphasic group differed from the monolingual group in having fewer conduction and global aphasics. The dearth of conduction aphasics may be because repetition was not tested in many patients. The number of global aphasics, or patients reduced to automatic speech, was probably small because such cases were not of interest to report.

The set of specific aphasic problems relevant to bilingualism distributed equally among the three basic aphasic groups: expressive, receptive, and amnestic. The only outstanding figure was the number of amnestic patients who evidenced a mixing problem, combining elements of words or sentences from each language (see Table 24). A more detailed analysis would be necessary to see if these amnestics were in fact mixing phonemes or morphemes within words or whether

Table 24
Bilingual Aphasic Problems × Aphasic Syndrome

	Expressive (N = 65)	Receptive (N = 45)	Amnestic (N = 34)
Translation	2	1	1
Switch	19	15	9
Mixing	9	7	9
Regression	3	0	3
Parallel recovery	11	7	9
Nonparallel recovery	22	16	8

they were simply picking a word from a second language as a strategy for overcoming their anomic problems.

We have mentioned certain tendencies related to recovery in our polyglot aphasics. For example, polyglots evidenced regression, whereas bilinguals did not. Additionally, parallel recovery was more likely in patients who had learned their second language during childhood.

As to the existence of discrepant aphasic syndromes, we have noted that there was no correlation between discrepancy and the age at which the second language was learned. Compound polyglots had somewhat more discrepant polyglot asphasia than did coordinate polyglots (81% and 71%, respectively).

There was a nonsignificant difference relating handedness and the existence of discrepancy. Of the 21 subjects for whom handedness was mentioned, the right-handers tended to show no discrepancy, whereas the left-handers tended to show a discrepant polyglot aphasic syndrome (see Table 25).

Although based on a small sample, these data suggest that left-handed and ambidextrous bilinguals are more likely than right-handers to have each of their several languages organized differently (perhaps more diffusely) in their brains. The bilateralizing effect of bilingualism may compound the bilateralizing effect of left-handedness (Zurif & Bryden, 1969).

THE RULES OF RECOVERY

In a previous study based on these data (Obler & Albert, 1977) we observed that the rule of Ribot, which states that the first language returns first in polyglot aphasia, does not hold more often than chance would predict. The rule of Pitres, on the other hand, which states that the most recently used language returns first, predicts the data with more than chance frequency. The rule of Pitres holds particularly for the nonelderly subjects in our population (i.e., those under the age of 60). Several other observations remain to be made about the correla-

Table 25
Handedness × Discrepancy[a]

	Discrepancy	No discrepancy
Left	5 = 71%	2 = 20%
Right	4 = 33%	8 = 67%
Ambidextrous	2 = 100%	0

[a] $p = .13$.

tions between Pitres's rule and other variables tested. First of all, it must be noted that there was no correlation between Pitres's rule and sex of subjects, nor between the rule and whether or not the subjects were compound or coordinate bilinguals. The age of acquisition of the second language did not correlate with the rule of Pitres, nor did the type of aphasic syndrome. The type of lesion, however, did tend to correlate, albeit insignificantly, with the rule of Pitres; trauma cases were particularly likely to follow Pitres's rule and recover the most recently used language first, whereas CVA patients were particularly likely to contradict Pitres's rule and recover first some language other than the recently used one. We have noted that this split between trauma and CVA patients with respect to Pitres's rule is possibly explained by the fact that patients with trauma were young, while patients with CVA were older. We have seen previously that older patients were most likely to contradict Pitres's rule, whereas young patients were most likely to follow it.

Amount of education was another factor which influenced the following of Pitres's rule. There was a nonsignificant trend for educated subjects to follow Pitres's rule but this was not true for the rule of Ribot (see Table 26). Finally, we note that Pitres's rule was slightly more likely to be followed in polyglots than in bilinguals (see Table 27).

Table 26
Education × Recovery Rules

	Educated	Noneducated
Pro Pitres	18	4
Contra Pitres	3	2
Pro Ribot	16	5
Contra Ribot	12	1

Table 27
Number of Languages × Recovery Rules

	Polyglots	Bilinguals
Pro Pitres	22 = 81%	18 = 72%
Contra Pitres	5 = 19%	7 = 28%
Pro Ribot	17 = 46%	17 = 55%
Contra Ribot	20 = 54%	14 = 45%

NEUROLOGICAL STUDIES OF NONAPHASIC POLYGLOTS

A series of postmortem studies on polyglot brains suggests that the bilingual brain may have a distinctive pattern of cerebral organization to house the extra knowledge. Scoresby-Jackson (1867) is credited with this hypothesis. He reported a case of motor aphasia in a monolingual illiterate farm servant who suffered cerebral trauma. The patient produced only "no," "yes," "dear," and "sair" ('sore'). Since the postmortem examinations revealed damage not in the anterior portion of the third frontal convolution, but only in the posterior part, and since Broca had suggested that any lesion in this convolution would lead to motor aphasia, Scoresby-Jackson suggested the possibility

that the functional activity of this convolution [the third frontal], beginning at its posterior extremity, is increased, in proportion to the acquisition of language, by an extension of its power towards its anterior end, so that whilst in the case of an illiterate man only the posterior part of the convolution would be in a state of activity, in the case of a linguist the entire convolution would be employed. It may be that a man acquires the ordinary power of speaking and writing his own language by the aid of the posterior third of his left frontal convolution, that by exercise in the art of speaking and writing, more and more of the convolution is utilized, whereby he not only acquires commensurate ease and elegance in the use of that language, but, moreover, adds to it other languages, dead and living. This is at present, of course, mere speculation [pp. 704–705].

Let us present the other cases in tabular form:

R: Retzius (Leischner, 1948; Kleist, 1934)
P/P: Statesman
H:
MT: (German?)
OL: Special talent for classical and modern languages, nonmusical
N: Second left temporal convolution especially well developed and irregular (postmortem), with marked furrows, as in third right frontal gyrus

R: Retzius (Leischner, 1948; Kleist, 1934)
P/P: Mathematician
H:
MT: Russian
OL: German, French, Swedish for scholarly writing, lecturing in G and S
N: Strong development of foot of third left frontal convolution, overdevelopment of left parietal and occipital lobes

R: Auerbach (Kleist, 1934; Leischner, 1948)
P/P: Stockhausen, singer
H:
MT:

OL: Fairly good spoken German, French, English
N: Additional right convolution between the first and second

R: Stieda (Leischner, 1948; Kleist, 1934)
P/P: Language scholar
H:
MT: (German?)
OL: Controlled about 26 languages in speech and script
N: Temporal and third frontal convolutions were markedly furrowed and
     cross-furrowed bilaterally

These studies imply that knowledge of numerous languages develops the brain, whereas illiteracy keeps it underdeveloped. The last two cases suggest that the increased furrowing is not necessarily restricted to the left hemisphere, but may obtain in the right or bilaterally. (It would be unwise, we believe, to generalize from a handful of cases. Yet the hypothesis is not implausible that learning a second language may influence patterns of cerebral development.)

Two case studies suggest that written Hebrew is treated differently from other languages. Stevens (1957) reported a case of primary reading epilepsy that was much more easily triggered by Hebrew than by English: an Orthodox Jewish-American woman of 24 with a history of reading that led to jaw twitching and then to a major motor seizure. Reading unfamiliar music could also cause the jaw jerks. Electroencephalographic studies revealed no dysrhythmia when various types of English print were read but the reading of Hebrew precipitated the jaw jerks and a dazed state after 30 sec. Spikes were most striking in the anterior leads, bilaterally. The author suggested that the differential effect was due to the fact that Hebrew was less familiar than English (the patient could read Hebrew aloud with fluency, but could not comprehend what she was reading) and "unconventional" in its right-to-left scanning direction. Even when she was treated with hydantoin, she would get equally frequent, though less severe, attacks of jaw jerking when reading and sometimes "when she was trying to recollect and relate to someone a partially forgotten incident." It is not uncommon for Jews to be taught to read Hebrew aloud fluently for prayers but with no analytic comprehension and this fact may serve to remind us that reading aloud may be independent from other language skills.

Streifler and Hofman (1976) reported the case of a Polish-born woman, long in Israel, who, after a minor car accident, displayed signs of spatial disorientation in addition to mirror-writing and mirror-reading in Hebrew only; her Polish and German remained unaffected. It may be important to note that this woman showed some signs of left-handedness. In addition to explaining this case on the basis of a separate cerebral organization for Hebrew reading and writing, different from that for English reading and writing, we refer to the hypothesis of Albert (1975). He stated that the right–left scanning direction of Hebrew reading may bring about a different organization for spatial tasks in cultures that regularly employ it, as compared to that organization in those cultures that read from left to right.

Two articles report successful recovery, under hypnotic age regression, of an early language which was presumed by the student to have been forgotten. A psychiatrist named As reported (1963) the case of an 18-year-old college student who spoke Swedish in his home until immigration to the United States at age 5. With the mother's remarriage, English soon became the predominant language in the home, and after age 6, Finnish was the only L_2 in the house. The experimenter composed a list of 56 questions in Swedish that a 5-year-old might be expected to answer. He judged the student's responses on a 4-point scale as to whether they were (a) not understood at all, (b) understood only in part, (c) understood but not answered, or (d) correctly understood and answered. Before hypnosis only 5 questions were at the past level, whereas 44 were in the first case of "no understanding." After five sessions of training in hypnotic age regression, the student answered correctly 25 questions and had reduced his noncomprehension to 26 questions (see Table 28). The student was assumed not to have been interested in, nor to have had the time to, study the language in the interval between the prehypnosis test and the test under age regression.

The five questions he answered correctly on the prehypnotic test were all to be answered by words which are phonetically close in the two languages (e.g., *klokka–clock*). Also, under age regression he could recall only six of the automatic sequence of numbers from 1 to 10 (although prehypnotically, he could recall none). Lastly, not unlike some aphasics, he did mix the two languages somewhat, answering the previously uncomprehended question "Do you have any brother?" with "No, I have no brother," where the *no* before *brother* was in English. This might be considered surprising, given the highly coordinate nature of this student's language history.

Table 28
Levels of Comprehension

	Level 1	Level 2	Level 3	Level 4
Prehypnosis	44	16	7	5
Under hypnosis	26	9	14	25

Fromm (1970) reported her experience with the age regression of a third-generation Japanese American whose experience in a relocation camp during World War II occurred when he was 3 or 4 years old. Under hypnotic regression to these ages he could talk fluently and at great length in Japanese and, afterwards, could not completely understand tapes made of the talk. As he became more comfortable with this part of his personality, his total amnesia for the hypnotic state broke, and he recalled his lips having moved in "funny shapes," his muscles having taken over the production of some words that he did not recognize even as he spoke them.

Gerson and Schweitzer (1972) recorded their observations on linguistic regression in multilingual psychotics in California. They noted that even long-term residents of the United States, for whom English was a second language, conversed in their native language (if at all) during acute psychotic episodes. They explained this on the basis of a greater automaticity of the native language, which rendered emoting and thinking in the first language easier than in the second. A second potential explanation for why the patients used their native language during psychotic episodes was that the use was in itself a display of hostility to the second-language environment. Such a case in which language choice was made for purposes of aggression was reported of a woman who refused to speak her native English with the institutional staff. Only later was it revealed that she was willing to converse, and lucidly, in her poor German.

We have discussed many clinical cases, and many reviews of clinical cases. Let us list the data any neuropsychological theory of bilingualism must account for:

1. Apparent loss of one language and not another;
2. Parallel recovery in most cases but not in all;
3. Regression in the first recovered language concurrent with recovery of the second;
4. The neuropsychology of affective factors;
5. The neuropsychology of Pitres's familiarity effect;
6. The possible split between use of informal and formal speech registers;
7. Possible differences from chronic, as opposed to traumatic, lesions;
8. The possibility of right hemisphere initiative in recovery or relearning of functions;
9. Apparent loss of switching facility;
10. Apparent loss of ability to translate upon command;

11. The possibility of losing a childhood language, and of regaining it through hypnosis;
12. Possible anatomical repercussions of multilingualism.

Experimental Neuropsychology

REVIEW OF CURRENT RESEARCH

Experimental studies of neuropsychological correlates of bilingualism are scarce. In those studies that have been done, methods appropriate to testing healthy subjects have been employed. In this section we first review studies in which response time was a major parameter. We then turn to tachistoscopic studies, which may use reaction time or correctness of response as a measure of degree of brain lateralization for visually presented stimuli. The third subsection details results of dichotic studies, in which auditory stimuli are presented simultaneously to both ears. The final subsection includes studies in which electrical measures (electroencephalographic or average evoked potentials) have been employed to test language lateralization.

RESPONSE TIME TESTS

In this section, we discuss tests in which subjects were instructed to perform a task in one or the other language. The time subjects took to perform the task in one language was compared to the time they took to perform it in the other language. Some of these tests have already been discussed in greater detail in Chapters 2 and 3. Lambert (1955), for example, compared the number of associations his French–English subjects could make in a limited time. This measure correlated with his reaction time test of comprehension in which subjects pushed buttons in response to commands.

In his dissertation Gekoski (1968) reported the results of reaction time analysis on a series of association tests. Although he found no difference between compound and coordinate subjects, he found that his native English speakers responded faster than native Spanish speakers. He attributed this difference to cultural factors. He also found that all subjects responded fastest when both stimulus and response items were in their native language. When the stimulus was in the second language and the response in the native language, subjects responded more slowly; and when the stimulus was in the native language and the response in the second language, the response was even slower. The results would support the common observation that passive, or perceptual, knowledge of a second language is more advanced than active, or productive knowledge.

In the same series of experiments, speed of translation was measured and found to correlate neither with type of bilingualism (compound–coordinate) nor with proficiency in the language. Three conditions were employed to measure translation speed, one simple translation task, the others requiring more information processing. Since there was a high correlation between the tasks, but none with the bilingualism type nor proficiency level, Gekoski suggested that some general mental dexterity factor underlies translation speed, but that this factor does not correlate with second language proficiency per se. (An alternate interpretation would be that speed in a translation task depends on practice in translation.)

Dalrymple-Alford (1967) ran two word recognition experiments with Arabic–English bilinguals at the American University of Beirut. (No further subject specifications were given.) In the first experiment, 10 subjects were exposed to single high-frequency words in Arabic or English, presented randomly by means of a tachistoscope to one hemifield or the other. They were instructed to speak the word as soon as possible. Under the cued condition, the subjects were told in advance the language-of-stimulus. Each word was exposed twice, once cued as to language-of-stimulus and once uncued. Reaction time measures showed responses for Arabic to be faster than those for English. No significant differences were found between the cued and uncued conditions. For Arabic words, the cued condition, in which the subject expected Arabic stimuli, resulted in slightly faster response than did the uncued condition (506 msec ± 51 cued, 522 ± 56 uncued). In English this tendency did not occur; knowing that the word would be in English seemed to have resulted in a slight delay (535 ± 50 cued, 533 ± 49 uncued).

In the second experiment, 16 subjects read cards aloud before being presented with the stimulus. Each card contained four words, either unilingual (four words in one language) or bilingual (two words in English and two in Arabic). The stimulus was one of the four words. The unilingual cards were considered to be the cued condition; the mixed cards, the uncued condition. In this experiment response time was greater with the cued items than with the uncued items for both languages (Arabic cued 527 ± 61, uncued 521 ± 46, English cued 529 ± 46, uncued 522 ± 48).

Dalrymple-Alford concluded that his results were inconsistent with a model of bilingualism in which the languages of the bilingual exist as separate systems. He based this conclusion on the hypothesis that the input switch might be expected to be primed by cuing; the subject could switch to the appropriate language processor before the stimulus was presented. Since, however, there was no significant difference between the cued and uncued conditions in either experiment, he suggested that the appropriate model was one of a single system, with no necessity for switching. His argument loses some of its force if we recall the experiment of Kolers (1966) in which artificial cuing (by color) proved ineffective. Even the second experiment of Dalrymple-Alford, in which subjects read four words aloud before the stimuli were presented, could hardly be considered a "natural" situation for encouraging a certain language set. Of interest in his results is the fact that responses to English stimuli took somewhat longer than response to Arabic stimuli.

Several tests discussed in Chapter 2 measured RT in response to mixed-language stimuli. The studies of Macnamara *et al.* (1968) and Kolers (1966) calculated an average time for input and output switching. The study of Wakefield, Bradley, Yom, and Doughtie (1975) demonstrated that, for Korean–English and Spanish–English subjects, sentences in which the language switch occurred at a major linguistic boundary took less time to process than sentences in which languages were switched within major constituents. These studies suggest a discontinuity in the cerebral processing of the two languages of the bilingual which would substantiate the linguistic notion of constituent structure.

One other set of experiments where time may enter as a major parameter are classical conditioning experiments: Unless the subject responds or inhibits response within a certain time, she will experience a shock. Lambert (1969), for example, reported the results of a test administered by Olton and himself in which French–English compound and coordinate subjects were expected to learn which words of a mixed-language series would precede an electrical shock. The shock could be avoided if the subject pressed a button in time. Among the words presented were translations of the critical words. These also elicited a response. No differences were found between the compound and coordinate groups, although Lambert and Olton had expected compound subjects to respond faster than coordinates.

Schvartz (1954) conditioned bilingual subjects to respond to the meaning of a word, then noted that the conditioning held for synonyms to the word and translation equivalents. The subjects also generalized for words similar in sound, but this generalizing response was extinguished after five to seven presentations. He then administered 1 gm of the anesthetic chloral hydrate and found that the semantic generalization no longer obtained, although the phonetic one was preserved. This differential suppression by anesthetic is clear support for a neuroanatomic substratum for the linguistic division of levels. As to bilingualism, this study and that of Lambert and Olton reinforce the data from the Stroop tests, which indicate that processing of words in both languages is unavoidable, and that translation equivalents are closely "associated" in the brain.

We refer to these time studies here because they serve as a transition from the psychological studies of the previous chapter to the neurolinguistic material we will discuss below. The three types of timed tests underline for us the physiological "reality" of the bilingual processes we have been discussing. These processes occur in real time, and some processes take longer than others. Reading mixed-language text takes longer even than reading in a language in which one is not fluent. Association and translation tasks may require different amounts of time from one or the other language depending on how proficient the bilingual is in each language. Inhibiting certain "automatic" semantic processing also requires time (or anesthesia).

TACHISTOSCOPIC TESTS

Tests which employ a tachistoscope are regularly used to measure cerebral lateralization for visual stimuli. The stimuli may be verbal or nonverbal, and may be presented in one or the other visual field, or bilaterally. Words may be presented vertically, in order to avoid the effects of visual scan. Subjects are sometimes obliged to report a central figure (in which case the examiner assumes that the subject's attention is on the central point). One difficulty with this procedure, however, which may be compounded with bilingual stimuli, is that oral report of the central figure may interfere with the perception and response to the test stimuli themselves. This section reviews tachistoscopic studies other than our own, which will be presented in detail.

One of a series of experiments reported by Mishkin and Forgays (1952) presented English and Yiddish words to bilingual subjects by means of a tachistoscope. The 19 bilingual subjects were all native speakers of English who had learned to read some Yiddish. The words from both languages were randomly exposed to one or the other visual field, and subjects were instructed to read the words. A point was given for each word correctly recognized. The scores for English words showed significant right visual field effect ($p < .01$), whereas the scores for Yiddish words showed an insignificant left visual field superiority (see Table 29). These results tell us that Yiddish and English words were treated differently by the subjects, but it is unclear whether that difference was due to some language-specific effect or to a second-language effect. The authors suggested that word beginnings are more crucial for word perception; Yiddish words begin on the right, English words on the left. This would imply that features specific to the languages induced differential lateralization. The authors also pointed out that subjects had poorer reading facility in Yiddish than in English. If differential proficiency brought about the differential lateralization reported in this experiment, one would have support for a second-language effect. Second-language effect might mean that a language only becomes strongly lateralized to the left hemisphere when it is fluently known.

Orbach (1953) expanded the Mishkin and Forgays (1952) study to include two groups of Yiddish–English bilinguals. He randomly presented single eight-letter (and in the second session five-letter) Yiddish and English words, by means of a tachistoscope, to one or the other visual field. For the entire population (N = 32) differential results obtained for the two languages. English words were better recognized in the right visual field (15.53 words out of 24 as compared to 8.18 in the left field), whereas for the Yiddish words no difference was seen (right field 9.90, left field 9.54). When the population was divided into those who had learned to read English first (N = 20), as opposed to those who had learned either Yiddish before English (N = 4), or both languages simultaneously, results closer to those of Mishkin and Forgays were found. Those for whom English was the first language had similar scores for English and Yiddish words (10.32 words for the right field, 7.65 for the left). The subjects who had not learned English first had the reverse tendency, that is, a left field superiority for Yiddish words (right field, 9.20 words; left field, 12.70). We are unfortunately not told their English scores. Orbach interpreted his results in terms of differential hemiretinal perceptual organization resulting from early reading habits. We suggest another possible interpretation: that some-

Table 29
Correctly Recognized Words[a]

	English		Yiddish
Left field	Right field	Left field	Right field
4.13	5.76	3.58	2.87

[a] Abstracted from Mishkin and Forgays (1952).

thing about the Yiddish language induced right hemisphere language dominance for subjects who learned it as their native language. English, on the other hand, induced a left hemisphere superiority for language, which was then built on in learning the second language.

Barton, Goodglass, and Shai (1965) studied 20 right-handed Israeli-born males who were fluent in English and were studying in the United States. The stimuli were common three-letter words in either language, and their three-letter equivalents in the other language. Words were presented vertically. Subjects were asked to respond orally. Results were compared with those of monolingual English speakers, tested only with English words. The authors found that vertical presentation resulted in a superiority of the right visual field for both languages. They concluded that reading scan direction is not so important in this task as is the left hemisphere dominance for language (see Table 30). (It is possible that left hemisphere dominance for oral response may be overriding a right hemisphere perceptual dominance for Hebrew.)

Also, although Israelis performed better on Hebrew than on English, they were worse in either language than the monolingual English speakers. This could be an artifact of the difficulty in balancing words across the languages, or of the structures of the two languages (Hebrew words of three letters would often be disyllabic, for example, whereas English words would rarely be so), or of the orthographic systems (written words in Hebrew are more likely to consist entirely of consonants; English words must contain one vowel). (Or could it be that a bilingual cannot perform as effectively as the monolingual in either language?)

Orbach (1967) performed another tachistoscopic study, this time using horizontal presentation of Hebrew and English words. Subjects were Israeli students who were academically proficient in reading

Table 30
Words Correctly Recognized out of 14[a]

| | | Field | | Degree of RVF |
		Left	Right	dominance (%)
Bilingual				
Israelis ($N = 20$)	English stimuli	3.67	4.85	14
	Hebrew stimuli	4.07	5.65	16
Monolingual				
Americans ($N = 10$)	English stimuli	5.90	7.85	14

[a] Abstracted from Barton et al. (1965).

English; 25 were right-handed, and 21 strongly left-handed. Instructions were to report the words or letters recognized, as quickly as possible after the stimulus exposure. The relevant data were the mean differences between the number of words correctly identified in the right and left fields (a positive number signified a right field effect). Table 31 is abstracted from his data.

Orbach concluded that the direction of scanning a language is a factor in the cerebral lateralization evidenced by tachistoscopic testing. That is, the right-to-left scanning direction of Hebrew script induces a left visual field effect, which counteracts the left hemisphere effect for language and results in a weak right field effect for visual stimuli for right-handers, and even in a slight left-field effect for Hebrew for the left-handers. This scanning effect, Orbach noted, may be reinforced by structural differences in the graphemes; significant features are likely to occur at word beginnings. Furthermore, English letters, he claimed, are more visually distinctive than are Hebrew letters, and the lack of vowels in Hebrew may have some influence. One wonders why there was no analysis presented of the letters identified correctly, since subjects were instructed to report letters when they could not report full words; and what a comparison with monolinguals would have shown. We also note the much greater mean differences between fields in English than in Hebrew, which seem to contradict Orbach's previous findings. This study implies that English, the second language, shows more pronounced left hemisphere dominance than does Hebrew.

Kershner and Jeng (1972) tested 40 right-handed graduate students in the United States. They had all spent most of their childhood in Taiwan and were "somewhat familiar with both written and spoken English." Stimuli were four-letter English words (in normal horizontal arrangement), two-character Chinese words (in normal vertical arrangement), and overlapping geometrical forms. Subjects were asked to write or draw what they saw. The scores of words correctly recalled for simultaneous (both visual fields) and successive (single visual fields) presentation showed similar patterns (see Table 32). The authors pointed to the double effect of scanning direction and hemisphere dominance; that is, the Chinese subjects showed a right visual field

Table 31
Mean Differences—Correct Scores, Right Minus Left Fields

	Right-handers	Left-handers
Hebrew stimuli	1.90 + 3.46	−.69 + 3.43
English stimuli	4.43 + 2.68	2.88 + 3.97

Table 32
Correct Responses[a]

Language	Visual field	Simultaneous	Successive
Chinese words	Right	15.22	21.56
	Left	6.17	16.25
English words	Right	15.35	22.25
	Left	6.25	16.34

[a] Abstracted from Kershner and Jeng (1972).

effect for Chinese as well as for English words when stimuli were presented successively, thus supporting a theory of left cerebral dominance for verbal material. Under stimultaneous bilateral presentation, however, in which English monolinguals had previously shown a left visual field effect (Heron, 1957), their bilingual subjects showed a right field effect for both languages. One supposes that this might be a result of the subjects not having the strong habit of English left-to-right reading. Nevertheless, these results were striking in that the scores for Chinese and English were so similar. One might have expected greater tendency toward a left visual field effect for Chinese, given the pictorial nonphonetic character of the orthographic system. The Lyman *et al.* (1938) aphasic case reported previously does give added support to the likelihood of Chinese characters being processed in the left hemisphere, although perhaps by a mechanism differing from that used to process the relatively phonological script of English.

Hamers and Lambert (1977) measured RT to unilaterally presented French and English words. Subjects were 15 right-handed balanced bilinguals (balance was judged by color-naming reaction speed, listener judgment of native speaker proficiency, acquisition before age 10, and personal usage reports). Subjects were asked to judge whether a word was a French word or an English word, and to indicate their answer by pressing one or another button. Concrete high-imagery words and their translation equivalents of close-to-equal length were employed as stimuli.

For these subjects, there was no difference in the amount of time taken to identify correctly a stimulus as being French or English, but words presented to the right field were identified significantly faster than words presented to the left visual field. Three of the 15 subjects, however, displayed a left visual field effect for both languages, whereas two subjects showed asymmetrical dominance for the two languages—both showed right visual field effect in English, and a mild left visual field effect in French.

The tachistoscopic study of Walters and Zatorre (in press) suggested that both English and Spanish are processed predominantly in the left hemisphere, regardless of which language is learned first, or the degree of fluency of the second language. Twenty word pairs were bilaterally exposed to 23 right-handed college volunteers. The instructions and the first series of pairs were in the native language (English for 13 subjects, Spanish for 10 subjects). Subjects were instructed to report first the number in the center of the card, and then as many of the words as they recalled. The mean recognition scores for both groups combined were 7.7 words for the right visual field, and 5.4 words for the left visual field, a significant difference for the total group. Error analysis showed that more errors of commission occurred in the right visual field, and more errors of omission in the left visual field. The authors pointed out that the degree of left lateralization for the two languages was less than that evidenced for right-handers in monolingual studies. In fact if we consider the distribution of subjects showing a right visual field effect (RVFE), as opposed to a left visual field effect (LVFE), or no visual field effect (OVFE), we see a low percentage of subjects with RVFE. A monolingual group of 10 monolingual English-speaking controls made for striking contrast (see Table 33).

The tachistoscopic studies we have reviewed present several contradictions. In all studies but one (Kershner & Jeng, 1972) some difference in laterality was found for the two languages of the bilingual. It is difficult to explain why, with some language-specific effect, French, Hebrew, and Yiddish speakers who also speak English show hemispheric asymmetries, whereas Spanish–English, Chinese–English, and other Hebrew–English bilinguals (those of Barton et al., 1965) do not. What may be important here is the fact that these contradictions exist.

Table 33
Subjects with Visual Field Effects[a]

| | Stimulus | Visual field effect | | |
Subjects	language	Right	Left	None
Native Spanish	English	9	1	0
speakers	Spanish	6	3	1
Native English	English	7	4	2
speakers	Spanish	6	7	0
Monolingual	English	9	1	0
English speakers				

[a] From Walters and Zatorre (1978).

They may be the result of different dominance patterns for individual bilinguals (we shall discuss this point in more detail in the next chapter). On the other hand, there are some bilinguals with a number of different language backgrounds who show weaker right visual field dominance for one or both of their languages than monolinguals of the same languages would be expected to show. It seems, also, that a greater percentage of right-handed bilinguals actually evidence some degree of LVFE than the right-handed monolinguals generally do.

A TACHISTOSCOPIC STUDY OF
HEBREW–ENGLISH BILINGUALS

Tirca Gaziel, Loraine K. Obler, and Martin L. Albert

INTRODUCTION

This study tested cerebral lateralization of Hebrew–English bilinguals for visual stimuli. A number of variables were employed that were expected, on the basis of previous tachistoscopic studies in monolinguals, to produce different dominance effects. Since familial handedness has been shown to relate to degree of lateralization for certain linguistic tasks (Zurif & Bryden, 1969), three groups of subjects differing in handedness were involved: left-handers, right-handers with no familial left-handedness, and right-handers with familial left-handedness. Subjects were also grouped according to different histories of bilingualism, and different relative proficiencies between the two languages. In addition to variables in subject selection, we studied variables in stimuli. Verbal and nonverbal materials were tested separately. For the verbal material, words, digits, and letters were tested. The words were presented both horizontally and vertically in order to examine the relative effects of scanning direction and cerebral lateralization for language. The questions we tried to answer were, how our bilingual subjects differed from monolinguals reported previously, and how our different bilingual groups differed from each other.

SUBJECTS FOR THE EXPERIMENTS

Fifty-four subjects of both sexes (30 males and 24 females) took part in the experiment. Their ages ranged from 17 to 30. They were seniors in high school and students of the Hebrew University in Jerusalem. None had any severe uncorrected visual or hearing defect nor any history of brain damage. All were paid volunteers and experimentally naive. They were informed that the experiment would involve two separate testing sessions of approximately 2 hours each, separated by at least 1 day in time.

Subjects were divided into six groups according to:

1. Their knowledge of Hebrew and English (knowledge of any other language was negligible);
2. Their handedness (the Edinburgh Handedness Inventory Questionnaire [Oldfield, 1971] was given to all left-handed subjects). Self-report was accepted for right-handed subjects with respect to familial left-handedness. Subjects were deemed to have familial left-handedness if any parent or sibling was left-handed.

Knowledge of the two languages was ascertained by means of a self-assessment scale. The subjects were asked to rate themselves on a scale from 1 to 7 for each of four skills (speaking, understanding, reading, and writing) in each language. In addition, note was made of the ages at which the subject used each language. Subjects were accepted in three groups: Americans, Israelis, and balanced bilinguals. The balanced bilinguals had learned both languages before the age of 13, and judged themselves at 6 or 7 on the self-assessment scale for both reading and writing. The Americans rated themselves 3–4 in Hebrew reading and writing on this scale, but 6–7 in English. Most of them had studied Hebrew in religious school as children. The Israelis, conversely, rated themselves 3–4 in reading and writing of English, but 6–7 in Hebrew.

The number of subjects in each group is shown in Table 34, together with the abbreviations we will use for each group.

GENERAL METHODOLOGY

The tachistoscopic stimuli were presented by means of a three-channel tachistoscope (model GB, Scientific Prototype M. G. F. Corp.).

Table 34
Subject Population

		Right-handers	
	Left-handers	With familial left	Without familial left
Balanced bilinguals	—	—	RBB 10
Americans—English-dominant bilinguals	LAB 7	RAB(L) 10	RAB 10
Israelis—Hebrew-dominant bilinguals	LIB 7	—	RIB 10

The subject activated a switch with his thumb which started the following succession: blank field (exposure time = 100 msec), fixation point (white cross on black background which coincided with the center of exposure field; exposure time = 100 msec), and then the stimulus (exposure times for the stimuli are discussed in the following). All stimuli were changed manually by the experimenter. The subject's reaction time was recorded on a Massey-Dickinson Modular millisecond counter; appearance of the stimulus triggered the counter to start counting. The subject's response stopped the counter. If the stimulus was negative and the subject did not react, the experimenter stopped the counter, by means of a switch near the experimenter's hand. The subject held a board on his knees on which three press-button switches were mounted. The middle switch permitted him to trigger the tachistoscopic sequence (blank field, fixation point, stimulus). The other two were for his reaction—the left switch was used during the session when left-handed responses were required, the right switch for right-handed responses. In all the experiments binocular viewing was employed.

In this tachistoscope, the exposure field was 1 m from the subject's eyes. The position of the subject's head was held constant by means of a special hood through which the subject looked at the stimuli. The blank field, field of fixation point, and stimulus field were each illuminated by two fluorescent lamps, one from above and one from below.

Throughout all the following studies, the method of successive pseudorandom presentation to left or right fields was employed, that is, on any one trial, the stimuli appeared either to the right or to the left of the fixation point, the order of left–right occurrence being pseudorandom. From a pile of small pieces of paper on which stimuli and their side of exposure were noted, we chose piece after piece and arranged the stimuli and their side of presentation as written on the pieces of paper on the stimuli list. We imposed the constraint never to expose more than two stimuli of the same kind on the same side in succession. Letters, words, and digits were chosen in the same manner. In the first session, subjects responded with their dominant hand; in the second, they reacted with the opposite hand.

The kinds of stimuli presented in each experiment and details of visual angle, duration of exposure, and mode of response are given in the section describing the individual experiments.

The exposure duration for each experiment was determined on the basis of a pilot study testing five subjects, and was chosen so as to yield a medium level of difficulty (see the following). The subjects in our pilot study were five medical students—two women and three men, all right-handed. During the experiments we changed the exposure time so that the subject could recognize at least half of the stimuli which were exposed; for this purpose we followed Orbach's (1967) technique—each subject was examined twice, once to find the optimal exposure time and once to recheck our findings. The exposure time used in our experiment was the mean exposure time for all five subjects. Each subject was tested on all the tests employed in our study, and the different tests were found to require different exposure times, ranging from 100 to 150 msec.

The testing procedure was as follows: The experimenter explained to each subject the structure of the experiments and mode of reaction. Communication with American subjects was in English; with Israeli subjects, in Hebrew; with balanced subjects, in a mixed language comfortably used between fluent bilinguals. In all the experiments to be reported below, subjects were tested individually in a quiet, isolated examining room. Sixty stimulus items, twenty each of single-digit numbers, words, and three-digit numbers, were included. They were presented in 10 trials, with six stimuli in each trial. Half of the stimuli presented in every trial in each experiment were positive and half negative. Stimuli were considered positive if they appeared on the stimuli list given to the subject, and negative if they did not appear on it. Before each trial the subject took one card from a pile of cards (with positive stimuli listed on them) placed before the subject on top of the tachistoscope. Each card contained a list of two or three stimuli, depending on the experiment. Only the stimuli written on the card were positive; the other two or three stimuli that did not appear on the card, but that were included in the trial, were negative. The subject was asked to respond, by pressing a response switch, only to the positive stimuli. The positive stimuli in the first session became negative in the second and vice versa. The time gap between the first and the second session was at least 48 hours.

Each subject was instructed to fixate her gaze on the central fixation point and to react as quickly as possible, trying not to make any mistakes. We allowed the subjects to trigger the exposure, in order to ensure that they were focusing on the fixation point at the time of exposure. Before triggering the exposure, the subjects were asked to state that they were ready, and only then were they allowed to press the starting key.

During each experiment, the experimenter reminded the subject several times to keep fixating. The switch which started the succession of the blank field, fixation point, and stimulus activated a Massey-Dickinson millisecond counter at the moment of stimulus exposure (the beginning of a step). The timer was stopped when the subject pressed the reaction key (the end of a step). A new step began 2 sec after the end of the previous one, whether or not the subject emitted a response. If within this interval the reaction switch was not pressed, the step was ended by the experimenter and the absence of response noted. After the first two experiments in every session, the subject was given a break of approximately 5 min during which he was engaged in conversation.

The testing order of all three experiments was constant for all subjects: (a) lines test; (b) letters and single-digit number test; (c) words and three-digit numbers test. Before each experiment in each session the subjects had four or five practice trials. Specifics of each test will be discussed in the appropriate sections to follow. The language stimuli were exposed in a predetermined random order with respect to position and language (letters and words in English or Hebrew). In this way the subject could not know beforehand whether the next stimulus (letter or word) would be Hebrew or English, nor whether it would appear in the left or the right visual field.

CEREBRAL DOMINANCE FOR PERCEPTION OF NONVERBAL MATERIAL

BACKGROUND   Our focus in this series of experiments was to be on language lateralization in bilinguals. Language lateralization in monolinguals is regularly found to be to the left hemisphere. In order to balance our tests of typically left hemisphere-dominant skills, we chose a test of line orientation which was expected to differentiate right and left visual field effects.

Kimura's (1973) findings on a test of line perception showed left visual field effect for identification of line slant. Her findings are contradicted by those of White (1969) who had found a right field superiority for identification of the slope of a line. The contradiction was resolved by the study of Umilta, Rizzolatti, and Marzi (1974), who found that line orientation that can be easily labeled verbally shows an RVFE, whereas line orientation that is hard to verbalize shows an LVFE.

In our study we used the same line orientations used by Umilta et al. (1974). The distinction between line orientations that are easy to verbalize (i.e., horizontal, vertical and 45° diagonal) and line orientations that are hard to verbalize (e.g., 30°) was made on the basis of Umilta's study.

There is some evidence that field differences obtainable with the tachistoscopic method are influenced by prior perceptual tasks (Kimura, 1973). So, in order to avoid the influence of verbal practice on our lines test, we gave the line test as the first test to each subject.

We expected to see in this experiment, since it involved spatial tasks, left visual field dominance in all six groups of subjects for the lines which were especially hard to verbalize, those at 15, 30, and 60° to horizontal. With lines at 90°, which could easily be labeled vertical, or 180 and 45°, which could be labeled horizontal and diagonal, respectively, we expected a right visual field effect on the basis of monolingual results.

METHODOLOGY The stimuli used in this experiment were black solid rectangles—.5 cm wide × 3 cm high—drawn on white cards. The rectangles were exposed either to the left or to the right of fixation point, and on a level with it. The distance between the fixation point and the nearest point of the rectangle was 2°21′ of visual angle.

The experiment consisted of four trials. In each trial four rectangles oriented in four different directions were exposed. The subjects were asked to discriminate between the different orientations of the rectangle by pressing a response switch following the appearance of the rectangle on two orientations previously specified as positive, and by refraining from pressing the key following the appearance of the rectangle in the other two orientations. Pressing the reaction switch stopped a millisecond counter that was started at the beginning of the 100-msec exposure period, thus providing an RT measure to the nearest millisecond.

In Trial 1 the four possible orientations were vertical (V), horizontal (H), right oblique (RO), and left oblique (LO). The two latter orientations resulted from a 45° clockwise and counterclockwise rotation of the rectangle in the upright position. The positive stimuli were RO and H in the first session and LO and V in the second session for each subject.

In Trial 2, the four possible orientations were 30 and 45° from the vertical to the right (30°R and 45°R) and 30 and 45° from the vertical to the left (30°L and 45°L)—the positive stimuli being 30°R and 45°L in the first session and 30°L and 45°R in the second session for each subject.

In Trial 3, the four possible orientations were 15 and 45° from the vertical to the right (15°R and 45°R) and 15 and 45° from the vertical to the left (15°L and 45°L)—the positive stimuli being 15°R and 45°L in the first session and 15°L and 45°R in the second.

In Trial 4, the four possible orientations were 30 and 60° from the vertical to the right (30°R and 60°R) and 30 and 60° from the vertical to the left (30°L and 60°L)—the positive stimuli being 30°R and 60°L in the first session and 30°L and 60°R in the second.

For symmetry, the rotations were clockwise for stimuli presented to the left of fixation point and counterclockwise for stimuli presented to the right of fixation point.

Each subject was tested twice on this test. In one session, the subject responded with the right hand; in the other session, with the left hand.

RESULTS   Measure was made of RTs for each line orientation. Reaction times for stimuli presented to the right visual field were subtracted from RTs for stimuli presented to the left visual field. Results are shown in Table 35.

COMPARISON OF LINE ORIENTATIONS

1. *Left Oblique–Right Oblique (LO–RO)*. All the groups showed LVFE for the diagonal line except the balanced bilingual groups—they showed almost no difference between the two visual fields for this line orientation. The LVFE was significant for right-handed and left-handed Americans ($p = .05$) and almost significant for right-handed Israeli bilinguals ($p = .055$).

2. *Horizontal Left–Vertical Right (HL–VR)*. All groups except the American bilinguals with sinistral relatives showed faster response to the line presented in the right visual field. They showed no difference between the two visual fields. The only significant RVFE, however, was for left-handed American bilinguals ($p = .05$).

3. *45°L–45°R*. In the first presentation of these orientations of line we can see right visual field effect in all the groups except for the balanced group. They showed no difference between the two visual fields. In the second presentation, results were very similar for all groups except that in this case balanced bilinguals showed an insignificant RVFE. The difference in the preferred visual fields, between oblique lines and 45° lines, we can explain by the context (i.e., the relative degree of easiness of verbalizing the 45° line as compared to other lines on the learning card—see Testing Procedure). The oblique lines were presented with horizontal and vertical lines, which were more easily labeled with a word than the oblique lines. In two other presentations 45° lines were presented with 30° and 15° lines. Compared to these two last orientations, 45° lines were more easily labeled with a word.

4. *30°L–30°R*. This orientation of line was presented twice in each session. In the first presentation, right-handed Americans showed an insignificant RVFE, and left-handed Israelis and balanced bilinguals showed no difference between the two visual fields. The three other

Table 35
Mean Difference in RT (msec) between the Visual Fields for the Same Orientations of Lines

Stimuli group	LO–RO	HL–VR	45L–45R	30L–30R	15L–15R	45L–45R	60L–60R	30L–30R
RAB	*MD = −229.21 SD = 76.09 p = .015	MD = 83 SD = 130.5 p = .541	MD = 155.55 SD = 137.59 p = .341	MD = 157.43 SD = 214.85 p = .491	MD = −249.0 SD = 119.29 p = .07	MD = 124.25 SD = 105.44 p = .277	MD = −97.55 SD = 171.6 p = .585	MD = −75.78 SD = 204.25 p = .72
RAB(L)	MD = 230 SD = 131.36 p = .114	MD = −1.24 SD = 125.58 p = .992	MD = 144.12 SD = 164.66 p = .41	MD = −110.12 SD = 138.31 p = .482	MD = −72.3 SD = 54.49 p = .217	MD = 183.44 SD = 82.36 p = .057	*MD = −169.85 SD = 63.63 p = .028	MD = −32.0 SD = 73.47 p = .676
LAB	*MD = −505.71 SD = 116.92 p = .005	*MD = 367.7 SD = 102.98 p = .012	MD = 26.33 SD = 121.67 p = .849	MD = −53.2 SD = 93.82 p = .601	*MD = −572 SD = 118.6 p = .003	MD = 345.33 SD = 260.64 p = .243	MD = −35.6 SD = 228.22 p = .844	MD = −252.75 SD = 217.86 p = .33
RIB	MD = −234.33 SD = 104.31 p = .055	MD = 112 SD = 145.05 p = .462	MD = 244.44 SD = 138.75 p = .116	MD = −201.6 SD = 223.73 p = .419	MD = −197.2 SD = 113.84 p = .117	MD = 345.0 SD = 152.28 p = .064	*MD = 285.67 SD = 76.51 p = .006	MD = −129.43 SD = 152.4 p = .428
LIB	MD = −150 SD = 155.65 p = .372	MD = 303.14 SD = 164.8 p = .115	MD = 113.33 SD = 164.85 p = .522	MD = 64.71 SD = 314.61 p = .846	MD = −69.0 SD = 134.8 p = .627	MD = 325.5 SD = 170.82 p = .113	MD = 98.0 SD = 38.77 p = .069	MD = −248.4 SD = 234 p = .348
RBB	MD = 15.75 SD = 115.27 p = .895	MD = 229.9 SD = 160.65 p = .186	MD = −15.0 SD = 252.19 p = .995	MD = 17.28 SD = 161.14 p = .918	MD = −43 SD = 158.64 p = .795	MD = 80.12 SD = 65.35 p = .26	*MD = 296.67 SD = 82.34 p = .015	MD = −202 SD = 103.02 p = .086

*p < .05.

174

groups showed an insignificant LVFE. In the second presentation of the line, all six groups showed an insignificant LVFE.

5. *15°L–15°R*. All six groups of subjects showed LVFE for this orientation of the line. This effect was significant only for left-handed American bilinguals ($p < .01$).

6. *60°L–60°R*. All three American groups showed LVFE for this line orientation, whereas the two Israeli groups and the balanced group showed a RVFE. The LVFE was significant for right-handed Americans with sinistral close relatives ($p < .05$). The RVFE was significant for right-handed Israelis ($p < .01$) and balanced bilinguals ($p < .05$).

Performance Differences between the Bilingual Groups

1. In general we can say that all the groups performed in a similar way on the lines test. There was one line orientation, however,—60°— that distributed our subjects into two groups: American bilinguals (showing LVFE), and Israeli and balanced bilinguals (showing RVFE).

2. When we divided our subjects into balanced bilinguals and nonbalanced bilinguals, we could see that results of nonbalanced bilinguals were similar to each other and the results of balanced bilinguals were different in the same measure from the results of all nonbalanced bilinguals. The balanced bilinguals were much more likely to show no mean differences between the two visual fields.

Performance Differences between Right-Handed and Left-Handed Subjects   When we looked at the results of right-handed subjects only (RAB, RIB and RBB), we could see that all three groups showed preference for the line presented in the right visual field (see column 2 of Table 35). For the easy-to-label stimuli (presented in columns 1, 3, and 6), all three groups of subjects together showed an RVFE in six cases and an LVFE in three cases. For hard-to-label stimuli (presented in columns 4, 5, 7, and 8), right-handed subjects showed RVFE only four times, and an LVFE eight times.

When we looked at the results of left-handed subjects only (LAB and LIB) we could see that the two groups preferred the stimulus presented in the right visual field (see column 2). For the easy-to-label stimuli (presented in columns 1, 3, and 6), all left-handed subjects showed an RVFE in three cases, an LVFE in two cases, and no field effect in one case. For the hard-to-label stimuli presented in columns 4, 5, 7, and 8, left-handed subjects showed RVFE in only two cases and an LVFE in six cases.

DISCUSSION

Since our experiment was based on an experiment done by Umilta *et al.* (1974), we will compare our results to those obtained by him and his colleagues. In order to do so, we must consider only the results of right-handed subjects. The trend of our results was very similar to the trend of the results reported in Umilta *et al.*'s experiment. For the line orientations that were easily described by verbal label (horizontal and vertical orientations), all our subjects showed RVFE. This effect became less and less frequent as we looked at the results of the stimuli that were more difficult to verbalize. In this case, the LVFE became more and more frequent. For the oblique line orientation (oblique was presented three times in our experiment), three groups of right-handed subjects showed RVFE in six cases and LVFE in three cases. For the last four orientations (30, 15, 60, and 30°, respectively), our subjects showed an RVFE only four times and an LVFE eight times. We can see a shift from the RVFE to the LVFE according to the ease with which the subject could describe the stimulus with the help of a verbal label. Line orientations that were easy to verbalize showed an RVFE since the left hemisphere usually deals with verbal tasks. As the stimuli became more difficult to code by verbal label, we might say, the right hemisphere gradually took this task on itself until finally we had almost only LVFE. If we look at the results of left-handed subjects, we can see a similar, but not identical, trend. There was a slightly greater tendency to LVFE for hard-to-label stimuli.

It is of interest to note that right-handed American bilinguals with sinistral relatives did not perform exactly as did the right-handed Americans. We may even say that their performances resembled more closely those of the left-handed Americans than those of the right-handed ones. We can explain this by speculating that right-handed Americans with left-handed close relatives may be less strongly lateralized and may occupy an intermediate position between right-handed and left-handed Americans with respect to cerebral lateralization.

One outstanding feature of our results was that there were almost no significant differences observed, unlike in the study of Umilta *et al.* We believe that the absence of significant differences on these tests has relevance to the understanding of the neurological basis of bilingualism. In this context we must note that other studies dealing with bilingual subjects also obtained insignificant results (see, for example, Mishkin & Forgays, 1952; Orbach, 1967—studies both dealing in Yiddish/Hebrew–English bilinguals). The fact that our subjects were bilinguals may have influenced their lateralization for visual perception of nonverbal material. There are two more trends pointing to the fact that bilingualism (and perhaps even Hebrew–English as opposed to English–Hebrew bilingualism) may have influenced the results. The results of one of the lines—60°—distributed our subjects into two groups: English–Hebrew bilinguals and Hebrew–English bilinguals. The first group showed an LVFE and the second, RVFE. Here we permit ourselves the following speculation: The set of lines 60°L–60°R is clearly dealt with by the right hemisphere. Americans (RAB, RABL, LAB) have left hemispheric dominance for language. This leaves their right hemisphere relatively free to process lines. So with this group we get mainly an LVFE. If Hebrew is more bilaterally distributed than English when Hebrew is the first language (RHB, LHB) or when it is acquired early (RBB), then less of the right hemisphere might be available for perception of line orientation. When we add to this the possibility that second languages may be learned by the right hemisphere, we use even more of the right hemispheric activity available for language. This would cause the left hemisphere to be more involved in spatial perception. Consequently with this group (RHB, LHB, RBB) we would have even more of an RVFE.

The second trend was visible when we divided our subjects into balanced and nonbalanced bilinguals. The results of nonbalanced bilinguals, Americans and Israelis, were similar to each other but both these groups differed in the same measure from the balanced group. Here, we may speculate that not only the kind of bilingualism but also the age at which the bilingual person acquires the second language might influence perception of nonverbal material. Another characteristic of balanced bilinguals is that they showed, in four instances, little or no difference between the two visual fields. We may speculate that both hemispheres of the balanced bilingual take part in the acquisition of the two languages known to her. Since the right hemisphere is occupied more than usually (i.e., as in a monolingual) with verbal tasks, then, when presented with lines, both hemispheres deal with the stimuli. This explanation accounts also for the fact that balanced bilinguals made the most errors.

If our speculations are correct, then we may say that monolingual subjects (from Umilta et al.'s experiment) and bilingual subjects, and different kinds of bilinguals among themselves, have different relative dominance for perception of nonverbal material.

RELATIVE INFLUENCE OF SCANNING VERSUS CEREBRAL
DOMINANCE FOR VISUAL PERCEPTION OF WRITTEN MATERIAL

BACKGROUND   Two hypotheses have been proposed to account for visual field asymmetries in the recognition of verbal material. One attributes the difference in recognition accuracy or in RT between the right and left visual fields to the directional orientation of the stimuli and thus to scanning tendencies. The second hypothesis claims that visual field preference for verbal material is associated with cerebral dominance for language. According to this hypothesis, verbal material is perceived better in the right visual field, since this field projects into the language-dominant left hemisphere.

The first hypothesis originated from reports by Mishkin and Forgays (1952) that scripts with opposed lateral orientations (Hebrew and English) yielded opposing lateral preference, and this was corroborated by Heron's (1957) findings, that English script was perceived better in the right visual field during unilateral exposure and in the left visual field during simultaneous exposures to both fields. It was suggested, therefore, that the observed visual field preferences were due to directional postexposure scanning tendencies. Harcum (1966) showed, by further manipulation of the usual experimental paradigm presenting words horizontally, that mirror images of English words were recognized better in the field opposite the one in which normally oriented words were more accurately recognized. These last findings support the association of visual field preference with the lateral orientation of the verbal stimuli.

The proponents of the cerebral dominance hypothesis utilized different methods to overcome the directional scanning tendencies in order to support their position. For example, manipulation of scanning by exposing words arranged vertically (Bryden, 1965; Barton, Goodglass, & Shai, 1965) resulted in right visual field preferences for verbal stimuli.

From the studies just mentioned it seems that neither of the two hypotheses alone can account for the observed asymmetries in visual recognition of verbal material, and that under conventional techniques, both cerebral dominance and directional scanning must play a role. In this experiment we tried to clarify, once again, the relative influence of scanning as opposed to cerebral dominance for visual perception of written material in terms of RT. Previous investigators tested monolingual subjects or bilingual subjects. Our subjects were bilingual subjects. The difference between the previous experiments with bilinguals and ours is that we specified two different levels of fluency in two different second languages and kept this variable constant throughout the study. We hypothesized that different levels of knowledge in the second language might influence the visual field effects. In the languages we were testing, reading habits were in opposite directions: English from left to right and Hebrew from right to left. This put us in a good position to look from another point of view at different influences of reading habits versus cerebral dominance. If the laterality difference effect was due only to cerebral dominance, we would get the same or similar differences between right visual field in both languages. If laterality differences were due to reading habits, we would expect shorter RT for English in the right visual field and for Hebrew in the left visual field.

SUBJECTS   The three groups that took part in this experiment were right-handed English bilinguals, right-handed Hebrew bilinguals, and right-handed balanced bilinguals. We were also interested in testing whether different levels of knowledge in any one of the languages used could influence in some way the laterality effects, and if so, in what way.

METHODOLOGY   Stimuli employed in this experiment were three-letter words (nouns only) in Hebrew and English, and three-digit numbers. Sixty white cards were prepared, on which a single stimulus was printed in black ink using a Normograph #4 stencil. There were 20 three-letter high-frequency words in Hebrew, selected from Raphael Balgur's (1968) *The Basic Word List for Elementary Schools*; 20 three-letter high-frequency words in English, selected from the Thorndike and Lorge (1944) Frequency Counts Category A; and 20 three-digit numbers, chosen with the restriction that no digit occurred twice in any three-digit number.

Within each group of stimuli, half were printed vertically and half horizontally, their order of orientation being chosen randomly. Half appeared to the left and half to the right of the fixation point. Each stimulus was 21 mm long (if horizontal) or high (if vertical) and subtended a visual angle of 1°2'. The angular distance from the fixation point to the beginning of the stimulus, if printed vertically, was 2°21'. All horizontal stimuli were printed on a level with the fixation point.

The Hebrew words (unvoweled) were

kli, mayim, zman, 'ir, derech, shemesh, kol, pa'am, yom, sefer, adam, sus, tseva, kesef, davar, sof, melech, 'ayin, aval, shir. (These words translate, respectively, to: 'tool,' 'water,' 'time' (noncount), 'city,' 'road,' 'sun,' 'voice,' 'time' (count), 'day,' 'book,' 'man,' 'horse,' 'color,' 'money,' 'thing,' 'end,' 'king,' 'eye,' 'but,' 'song'.)

The English words were

ice, sky, car, tea, pen, hat, map, net, leg, cow, key, age, art, toy, dog, bed, man, cup, egg, boy.

The three-digit numbers were

264, 847, 738, 517, 647, 536, 671, 651, 945, 918, 245, 917, 235,
832, 958, 613, 815, 436, 267, 982.

A pilot study indicated that word—number recognition was made substantially more difficult by the shift from a horizontal to a vertical situation. Accordingly, exposure duration for all stimuli in this experiment was 150 msec—50 msec longer than exposure period of stimuli in the two other experiments.

Each session consisted of four or five practice trials and 60 regular steps, divided into 10 trials. In each trial six stimuli (two Hebrew words, two English words, two numbers) were exposed. Only three of them were positive.

RESULTS In this experiment we looked at the results of right-handed subjects only. Right-handed American bilinguals showed an insignificant tendency toward an LVFE for Hebrew horizontal words and a significant ($p < .05$) RVFE for Hebrew vertical words (see Table 36).

Right-handed Israeli bilinguals showed significant RVFE ($p < .05$) for Hebrew words presented horizontally and insignificant RVFE for Hebrew words presented vertically. Right-handed balanced bilinguals showed an insignificant RVFE for Hebrew words presented horizontally and no difference between the two visual fields for words presented vertically (see Table 37).

Right-handed American bilinguals showed an insignificant RVFE

Table 36
Mean Difference in RT (msec) between the Two Visual Fields for Hebrew Words

	Stimuli	
Groups	HWH	HWV
RAB	$MD = -116.88$	$*MD = 1253.42$
	$SD = 76.55$	$SD = 165.2$
	$p = .641$	$p = .040$
RIB	$*MD = 763.66$	$MD = 308.6$
	$SD = 84.75$	$SD = 171.3$
	$p = .043$	$p = .583$
RBB	$MD = 160.86$	$MD = 79.01$
	$SD = 86.17$	$SD = 232.18$
	$p = .569$	$p = .919$

*$*p < .05$.

Table 37
Mean Difference in RT (msec) between the Two Visual Fields for English Words

	Stimuli	
Groups	EWHD	EWVD
RAB	MD = 570.52	*MD = −753.14
	SD = 138.51	SD = 98.13
	p = .225	p = .038
RIB	MD = 6.32	MD = −128.02
	SD = 148.26	SD = 165.72
	p = .990	p = .803
RBB	MD = 458.84	MD = 34.64
	SD = 187.57	SD = 247.56
	p = .450	p = .966

*$p < .05$.

for English words presented horizontally and significant LVFE ($p < .05$) for English words presented vertically.

Right-handed Israeli bilinguals showed no difference between the two visual fields for English words presented horizontally, and almost no difference between the two visual fields (slight tendency to LVFE) for English words presented vertically.

Right-handed balanced bilinguals showed an insignificant RVFE for English words presented horizontally and almost no difference between the two visual fields for English words presented vertically.

Right-handed American bilinguals showed an insignificant RVFE for numbers presented horizontally and vertically (in vertical presentation this tendency is smaller than in horizontal presentation)—see Table 38.

Right-handed Israeli bilinguals showed an insignificant RVFE for numbers presented horizontally and no difference between the two visual fields for numbers presented vertically.

Right-handed balanced bilinguals showed an insignificant LVFE for both vertical and horizontal presentation of numbers.

SUMMARY OF RESULTS   The right-handed American bilinguals showed an insignificant LVFE for horizontal presentation and a significant RVFE for vertical presentation of Hebrew words. In English, the pattern of their result showed exactly the opposite tendency: insignificant RVFE for horizontal presentation and significant LVFE for vertical presentation of English words. For numbers they showed an insignificant RVFE for both directions of presentation.

Table 38
Mean Difference in RT (msec) between the Two Visual Fields for Three-Digit Numbers

	Stimuli	
Groups	NHD	NVD
RAB	MD = 982.62	MD = 504.54
	SD = 232.95	SD = 285.53
	p = .215	p = .590
RIB	MD = 361.26	MD = 21.64
	SD = 151.45	SD = 287.95
	p = .470	p = .990
RBB	MD = −426.58	MD = 759.17
	SD = 130.58	SD = 155.67
	p = .328	p = .157

The right-handed Israeli bilinguals, on the other hand, showed a significant RVFE for horizontal presentation and an insignificant RVFE for vertical presentation of Hebrew words. For English words they showed no difference between the two visual fields in horizontal presentation. For numbers they showed an insignificant RVFE for horizontal presentation and no difference between the two visual fields for vertical presentation.

The right-handed balanced bilinguals showed an insignificant RVFE for Hebrew words presented horizontally and no difference between the two visual fields for Hebrew words presented vertically. Exactly the same pattern was seen in their results for English words. For both kinds of presentation of numbers they showed an insignificant LVFE. Note also that the number of mistakes in each language was greater in vertical presentation of the stimuli than in horizontal presentation for all three groups in the two visual fields (see Table 39).

Table 39
Comparison among the Three Groups

	Stimuli					
Groups	HWHD	HWVD	EWHD	EWVD	NHD	NVD
RAB versus RIB	*p = .047	p = .225	p = .391	p = .336	p = .489	p = .711
RAB versus RBB	p = .456	p = .209	p = .880	p = .368	p = .112	p = .235
RIB versus RBB	p = .197	p = .804	p = .552	p = .859	p = .229	p = .460

*p < .05.

There was a significant (p < .05) difference between American and Israeli bilinguals for Hebrew words presented horizontally. All other differences between these two groups and other groups were insignificant, but from the general trends in results we can see

1. The greatest differences were between Israeli and American bilinguals.
2. Balanced bilinguals fell in between these two (see Table 40).

From the preceding results we can see greater differences between the two visual fields in horizontal presentation of all kinds of stimuli than in their vertical presentation. The only exception is for the group of RAB, who showed less difference between the two visual fields for horizontal presentation of Hebrew words than for vertical presentation. This exception approaches significance ($p = .082$). The only significant result is in the same group, for English words. The difference between the two visual fields in vertical presentation is significantly ($p < .05$) smaller than the difference between the two visual fields in horizontal presentation.

DISCUSSION In this experiment we tried to determine (a) if the RVFE that was seen in previous studies of tachistoscopic presentation of verbal material is caused by reading habits only, cerebral dominance only, or both factors operating together; (b) if different levels of proficiency in the two languages are influential in the problem of scanning versus cerebral dominance.

In answering the first question, if we consider only the scanning

Table 40
Mean Difference in RT (msec) between Vertical and Horizontal Presentation

	Stimuli		
Groups	GHD	GED	GND
RAB	$MD = 1370.3$	$*MD = 1323.66$	$MD = -478.08$
	$SD = 221.28$	$SD = 146.6$	$SD = 394.97$
	$p = .082$	$p = .019$	$p = .711$
RIB	$MD = -395.06$	$MD = -66.12$	$MD = -339.66$
	$SD = 147.26$	$SD = 144.23$	$SD = 293.67$
	$p = .418$	$p = .894$	$p = .723$
RBB	$MD = -81.87$	$MD = -424.2$	$MD = -332.52$
	$SD = 177.83$	$SD = 144.04$	$SD = 175.32$
	$p = .887$	$p = .376$	$p = .563$

$*p < .05.$

hypothesis, we would predict that presentation of English words would yield an RVFE, and presentation of Hebrew words would yield the opposite effect, an LVFE, in all three groups of subjects. Our results, however, showed an RVFE for words and numbers presented horizontally in all three groups of subjects, with two exceptions: American bilinguals showed a slight LVFE for Hebrew words presented horizontally, and Israeli bilinguals showed no difference between the two visual fields for English horizontal words.

Since we did not see a reverse pattern of field effect for Hebrew stimuli and for English stimuli, we can conclude that reading habits are not the sole factor responsible for RVFE and that there is some other factor that contributes to this effect.

In order to eliminate the influence of scanning direction, we employed vertically presented words and numbers. If cerebral dominance for language were responsible for the RVFE, we might expect to see an RVFE for all kinds of stimuli, under both conditions of presentation, in all three groups of subjects. We did get a significant RVFE ($p < .05$) for Hebrew vertical words in the American bilingual group. No other significant results, however, were obtained. Instead we saw an insignificant RVFE for the same stimuli in the Israeli bilingual group, and no difference between the two visual fields for the balanced bilingual group.

For English words presented vertically, we got a significant LVFE ($p < .05$) in the American bilingual group, almost no difference between the two visual fields in the Israeli bilingual group, and no difference between the two visual fields for the balanced group.

The numbers presented vertically yielded an insignificant RVFE in the American and balanced groups, and no difference between the two visual fields in Hebrew bilinguals. We cannot conclude, therefore, that a simple cerebral dominance for language is the sole determining factor of visual field differences.

In order to evaluate better the relative influence of reading habits versus cerebral dominance, we compared the difference between the two visual fields under both kinds of presentation—vertical and horizontal—for all kinds of stimuli. If the only factor responsible for the RVFE were cerebral dominance, we would expect no consistent differences between these two kinds of presentation. From our results we can see that greater differences between the two visual fields occurred for all kinds of stimuli with horizontal presentation as compared to vertical presentation. The one exception was for Hebrew words in

American bilinguals. In this instance, there was a greater difference between the two visual fields in vertical presentation.

We can conclude that in conditions of horizontal presentation, reading habits and cerebral dominance are operating together and so yield a greater difference between the two visual fields. This kind of facilitation exists also in vertical presentation but is much less outstanding than in the horizontal presentation; therefore the differences between the two visual fields are also less outstanding. The differences between horizontal and vertical presentation must result from a relative difference of influence of reading habits versus cerebral dominance in the two conditions. The standard deviations with all kinds of stimuli were smaller in horizontal presentation than in vertical presentation, which means that there was more variability among the individual results in vertical presentation. We can explain this by the fact that our subjects were trained for the horizontal scanning of normal reading and not for reading vertically presented verbal material; so perhaps they used different strategies with more or less efficiency in order to deal with the vertical presentation task, while in the horizontal presentation task they used one well-trained strategy only.

We may conclude, furthermore, that cooperation between cerebral dominance and reading habits may have a facilitating effect, and that the horizontal presentation task is easier than the vertical presentation task. This is supported by: (a) our pilot study, where we saw that vertically presented stimuli required longer exposure time than horizontally presented stimuli; and (b) the fact that RTs for vertically presented stimuli were always longer than RTs for horizontal stimuli.

In answer to the second question, we cannot conclusively determine on the basis of our results the influence of different levels of proficiency in the two languages on cerebral dominance or on scanning habits. We are, however, in the position to say that such influence exists and that it operated differently in two groups of American bilinguals and in the group of Israeli bilinguals. American bilinguals showed an LVFE (insignificant) for Hebrew words presented horizontally and an RVFE (insignificant) for English words presented horizontally. For Hebrew words presented vertically they showed a significant RVFE and for English words presented vertically they showed a significant LVFE.

Israeli bilinguals, on the other hand, showed significant RVFE for Hebrew words presented horizontally and no difference between the two visual fields for English words presented horizontally. They showed an insignificant RVFE for Hebrew words presented vertically and no difference between the two visual fields for English words presented vertically. Our hypothesis of differential effects depending on learning history is reinforced by:

1. The results of the balanced bilinguals—they showed no difference in the preferred visual field between Hebrew and English words. In the case of horizontal presentation of stimuli in both languages, they showed an insignificant right visual field effect and in case of vertical presentation of stimuli in both languages, they showed no difference between the two visual fields.
2. The results of the number stimuli—all three groups showed right visual field effect (insignificant) for numbers presented both horizontally and vertically.

HANDEDNESS AND CEREBRAL DOMINANCE

INTRODUCTION The correlation between right-handedness and left cerebral dominance for language has been known for over a century (e.g., Bouilloud, 1864). The majority of left-handers display lateralization patterns like those of right-handers, but some left-handers show a converse pattern (i.e., right hemispheric dominance for language) or no dominance at all (e.g., Zangwill, 1960; Hécaen & Sauguet, 1971). Furthermore, it would appear that differences within the group of left-handers are related to the extent of familial left-handedness; left-handers with a parent or sibling who is left-handed are more likely to be right hemisphere-dominant for language than are left-handers with no left-handed family members (Bryden, 1965; Zurif & Bryden, 1969). There has also been some suggestion that right-handers with familial left-handedness are less strongly left lateralized for language than are right-handers with no familial left-handedness (Hécaen & Saguet, 1971). All the studies referred to in the preceding dealt either with differential severity and rapidity of recovery in aphasic patients (e.g., Hécaen & Saguet, 1971) or with experimental studies on healthy monolingual subjects (e.g., Bryden, 1965). Our study examined the interaction of handedness and familial left-handedness with lateralization in bilingual subjects. The methodology employed in this experiment was the same as that described previously, but we will consider only the results for horizontally presented words.

RESULTS For the problem of subject handedness, let us first exclude from consideration the group of Americans with familial left-handedness, so as not to confuse the issues of subject and familial handedness.

Hebrew Words. Hebrew horizontally presented words were perceived in similar manner, an insignificant RVFE, in three groups of subjects: LAB, LIB and RBB. Right-handed American bilinguals showed a slight tendency toward LVFE and right-handed Israeli bilinguals showed a significant ($p < .05$) RVFE.

English Words. There was no difference between the two visual fields for English words presented horizontally in two groups: LAB and RIB (see Table 41). RAB and RBB showed an insignificant RVFE for these stimuli and LIB showed a significant ($p < .05$) RVFE.

There were no significant differences among the groups (see Table 42). There were, however, two general trends: (a) differences between RAB and LAB were larger than the differences among all the other groups; (b) the differences between the left-handed subjects and balanced bilinguals were smaller than the differences between all the other groups.

In order to answer the question of the influence of familial handedness on cerebral lateralization, we compared the results of the three American groups for horizontal and vertical presentation of words. One

Table 41

Mean Difference in RT (msec) between the Two Visual Fields for Horizontally Presented Words

	Stimuli	
Groups	Hebrew	English
RAB	$MD = -116.88$	$MD = 570.52$
	$SD = \quad 76.55$	$SD = 138.51$
	$p = \quad .641$	$p = \quad .225$
LAB	$MD = \quad 435.24$	$MD = \quad 32.14$
	$SD = \quad 205.37$	$SD = 178.14$
	$p = \quad .595$	$p = \quad .963$
RIB	$*MD = \quad 703.66$	$MD = \quad 6.32$
	$SD = \quad 94.76$	$SD = 148.26$
	$p = \quad .043$	$p = \quad .990$
LIB	$MD = \quad 429.9$	$*MD = 769.83$
	$SD = \quad 203.65$	$SD = \quad 69.54$
	$p = \quad .596$	$p = \quad .027$
RBB	$MD = \quad 160.88$	$MD = 458.84$
	$SD = \quad 86.17$	$SD = 183.57$
	$p = \quad .596$	$p = \quad .450$

$*p < .05.$

Table 42
Comparison among Groups

	Stimuli	
Groups	HWHD	EWHD
RAB versus LAB	$p = .519$	$p = .493$
LAB versus RBB	$p = .749$	$p = .640$
RIB versus LIB	$p = .648$	$p = .229$
LIB versus RBB	$p = .750$	$p = .639$

group was left-handed; of the two right-handed groups one had familial left-handedness, while the other had none.

Hebrew Words. The results for Hebrew words presented horizontally were all significant. RAB showed a slight LVFE, and RAB(L) and LIB, an insignificant RVFE. Hebrew words presented vertically showed a pattern similar to that of Hebrew letters. RAB showed significant RVFE ($p < .05$), RAB(L) showed insignificant RVFE, and LAB showed insignificant LVFE.

English Words. There was an insignificant RVFE in all three groups for English words presented horizontally. The results for English words presented vertically were: RAB, significant ($p < .05$) LVFE; RAB(L), an insignificant RVFE, and LAB, no difference between the two visual fields (see Table 43).

Table 43
Mean Difference in RT (msec) between the Two Visual Fields for Horizontally and Vertically Presented Words

	Stimuli			
Groups	HWHD	HWVD	EWHD	EWVD
RAB	$MD = -116.88$	$*MD = 1253.42$	$MD = 570.52$	$*MD = -753.31$
	$SD = 76.54$	$SD = 165.2$	$SD = 138.5$	$SD = 98.13$
	$p = .641$	$p = .04$	$p = .225$	$p = .038$
RAB(L)	$MD = 360.01$	$MD = 497.54$	$MD = 137.28$	$MD = 430.01$
	$SD = 163.73$	$SD = 203.17$	$SD = 97.82$	$SD = 124.1$
	$p = .504$	$p = .668$	$p = .302$	$p = .302$
LAB	$MD = 435.24$	$MD = -1649.97$	$MD = 32.14$	$MD = 23.46$
	$SD = 205.37$	$SD = 238.24$	$SD = 178.14$	$SD = 184.89$
	$p = .595$	$p = .117$	$p = .963$	$p = .963$

$*p < .05$.

Comparison among the Three Groups. Almost all the differences between the groups were insignificant. The only significant difference was between RAB and RAB(L) for English words presented vertically (see Table 44). The general trend that we could see from these results was toward greater similarity between RAB(L) and LAB than between RAB(L) and RAB.

DISCUSSION   The differences between groups on these tasks were, in general, statistically insignificant. Nevertheless, we can note that two groups performed intermediate to the two extreme groups of left-handed Americans (all of whom had familial left-handedness) and right-handed Americans (without familial left-handedness). The two intermediate groups were the balanced bilinguals and the right-handed Americans with familial left-handedness. These results suggest an interaction between bilingualism and handedness that is consistent with the model of Annett (1964); she discusses a "dextral shift" in handedness, related to factors inducing hemispheric lateralization for speech. She assumes that these factors must depend on genetic mechanisms, inheritable in either a discrete or a scalar fashion. We suggest that linguistic factors such as learning a specific language first, or being bilingual from a young age, may interact with inherited brain substrate tendencies related to handedness, to determine eventual lateralization for language(s) in adults.

CEREBRAL DOMINANCE FOR HEBREW AND ENGLISH

INTRODUCTION   Elsewhere in this monograph, we discussed three articles that presented conflicting reports on the relative degree of lateralization for the two languages, in bilinguals who learn English and a language written in Hebrew script. Orbach (1953) reported an LVFE for Yiddish words and an RVFE for English words. Orbach (1967) reported an RVFE for English words, but no difference between the

Table 44

Comparisons among the Three Groups

Groups	Stimuli			
	HWHD	HWVD	EWHD	EWVD
RAB versus RAB(L)	$p = .419$	$p = .373$	$p = .430$	$*p = .029$
RAB(L) versus LAB	$p = .934$	$p = .064$	$p = .877$	$p = .594$

$*p < .05$.

fields for Hebrew words. Barton et al. (1965) found RVFEs for both Hebrew and English words. We suggested that the differences in their results may have been due to different relative degrees of proficiency in both languages on the part of their subjects, and perhaps to differences in structure between the Hebrew and Yiddish languages. In order to clarify the issue, we have looked at the data for three of our right-handed groups, the balanced bilinguals, the Israelis, and the Americans.

RESULTS   The data discussed here are presented in Tables 36 and 37.

Hebrew Words. The right-handed American bilinguals, for whom Hebrew was the second language, showed significant RVFE ($p < .05$) for Hebrew words presented vertically and a slight LVFE for Hebrew horizontal words. The right-handed Israeli bilinguals, for whom Hebrew was the mother tongue, showed a significant ($p < .05$) RVFE for Hebrew horizontally presented words, and an insignificant RVFE for Hebrew vertical words. Right-handed balanced bilinguals, who knew both languages equally well, did not show any significant field effect, but for Hebrew words presented horizontally there was an insignificant RVFE, and for Hebrew vertical words there was no difference between the two visual fields.

English Words. The right-handed American bilinguals, for whom English was the mother tongue, showed a significant ($p < .05$) RVFE for English words presented vertically, and an insignificant RVFE for English words presented horizontally. The right-handed Israeli bilinguals, for whom English was the second language, did not show any field effect in either kind of presentation of English words. The balanced bilinguals showed exactly the same pattern of results as for Hebrew words.

Summary of Results. Right-handed American bilinguals showed the following pattern: significant LVFE for English words presented vertically, significant RVFE for Hebrew words presented vertically, slight LVFE for Hebrew words presented horizontally, and an insignificant RVFE for English words presented horizontally.

The right-handed balanced bilinguals showed the same pattern for both languages.

The right-handed Israeli bilinguals showed a different pattern for each language: Hebrew horizontal words yielded significant RVFE and Hebrew vertical words yielded insignificant RVFE. For English words presented vertically and horizontally there was no difference between the two visual fields.

Comparisons among the Three Groups. The difference between Israeli bilinguals and balanced bilinguals, and the difference between

American bilinguals and balanced bilinguals, were all insignificant. The greatest differences, and those closest to significance, were between the Israeli and American bilinguals (see Table 45).

DISCUSSION   We discuss these data in terms of two hypotheses. First, we propose a second language hypothesis. A second language effect would mean that, due to right hemisphere participation in L_2 learning, the second language is less markedly left lateralized for language than is the first language. Second, we propose a balanced bilingual hypothesis. In the balanced bilinguals we would expect to see no differences in lateralization of the two languages, since both were acquired in the same manner.

The results of the American bilinguals for stimuli in their mother tongue showed insignificant RVFE for English words presented horizontally and significant LVFE for English words presented vertically.

Results of the same group for stimuli in Hebrew showed insignificant LVFE for Hebrew words presented horizontally and significant RVFE for Hebrew words presented vertically.

The results of the Israeli bilinguals for stimuli in their mother tongue showed significant RVFE for Hebrew words presented horizontally and insignificant RVFE of Hebrew words presented vertically.

The results of the same group for stimuli in English showed no difference between the two visual fields in vertical and in horizontal presentation.

The results of balanced bilinguals for the two languages showed the same pattern: insignificant RVFE for words presented horizontally and no difference between the two visual fields for words presented vertically.

In general, these data do not support the first hypothesis that there is a second language effect. The American bilinguals did not show less lateralization for their second language, Hebrew. Their pattern of results was unpredictable. They showed significant visual field effect

Table 45

Comparisons among the Three Groups

Groups	EWVD	EWHD	HWVD	HWHD
		Stimuli		
RAB versus RIB	$p = .336$	$p = .391$	$p = .225$	$*p = .047$
RAB versus RBB	$p = .368$	$p = .880$	$p = .209$	$p = .456$
RIB versus RBB	$p = .859$	$p = .552$	$p = .804$	$p = .197$

$*p < .05.$

only in vertical presentation, but the direction of this effect was opposite for the two languages: significant LVFE for English and significant RVFE for Hebrew. Two questions concerning these results remain:

1. Why did English vertical words show LVFE and Hebrew vertical words RVFE? On the basis of the doctrine of cerebral dominance based on monolinguals we would expect RVFE in both languages.
2. Why did only vertical stimuli yield significant visual field effects?

The results of balanced bilinguals do support the second, balanced bilingual hypothesis. There was no difference in lateralization between the two languages known by them; neither language was significantly lateralized. It may actually be significant that for balanced bilinguals we cannot see any difference in lateralization of each language; learning two languages from a young age, we may speculate, might involve more bilateral participation than learning only one language.

The results of Israeli bilinguals showed less lateralization of their second language, so these data support the first hypothesis (their results showed the second language effect). But why did the American bilinguals not behave in the same way? We have no answer to this question but propose the following speculation: It may be that learning Hebrew as a first language sets up the brain differently from the way learning English as a mother tongue would. American bilinguals learned English first and then Hebrew; Israeli bilinguals learned Hebrew first and then English. Perhaps the language which is learned first has some specific influence on the acquisition of the second language; so English as a mother tongue may have a different influence on Hebrew than that of Hebrew as a mother tongue on English. It is possible that each unique coupling of languages in the brain of bilinguals creates different mutual relationships and these serve as the basis of differences that we find in lateralization of each language in the brains of American and Israeli bilinguals.

Finally, we can conclude that difference in the lateralization of each language can be seen only in the brain of nonbalanced bilinguals. The difference in the lateralization of each language in the brain of bilinguals seems to be dependent on two factors:

1. *Age of acquisition of each language*—If the two languages are acquired simultaneously in the stage of development of cerebral dominance, we will see no difference in lateralization between them; if one language is acquired in the early period of de-

velopment of cerebral dominance and the second after the end of this stage, we will see differences in lateralization of each language.
2. Each pair of languages creates specific mutual relationships in the brain of bilinguals.

CONCLUSION

The fact that our bilingual subjects (especially the balanced bilinguals) often displayed insignificant differences in field effect, for verbal and nonverbal materials, may well be significant. We have argued that reading habits (i.e., scan direction) and handedness factors will influence tachistoscopic measures of dominance in bilinguals as they will in monolinguals. Factors specific to bilingualism itself may also affect tachistoscopic data on lateralization. More specifically, learning Hebrew and English fluently from prepuberty seems to result in symmetrical representation of each of the languages even in right-handers. Learning either of the languages at a later age, so that only one of the languages is fluent, will result in a more complex pattern of language lateralization. Although neither language will actually show a significant right visual field effect, one or both languages may show insignificant tendencies to left lateralization. One conclusion could be that learning a second language at any age involves right hemispheric mechanisms that would not have been involved in learning only one language. Such right hemispheric involvement in language learning could perhaps explain why our bilingual subjects performed differently from monolingual groups on a test of line orientation.

DICHOTIC STUDIES

In dichotic tests, different auditory stimuli are presented simultaneously to each ear. Testing of monolingual subjects has shown that a group of right-handed subjects will correctly perceive more of the items which had been directed to the right ear than to the left (Kimura, 1961). Subjects may be instructed as to which ear to report first, or they may report in any order they like.

Starck, Genesee, Lambert, and Seitz (1977) evaluated hemispheric dominance for the mother tongue of monolingual and trilingual Canadian children from ages 6 to 8. The trilingual children came from monolingual English Jewish homes, and were attending a language immersion school in which they were taught only in French and in Hebrew. The monolingual children, matched for socioeconomic status and IQ, were also Jews, but they attended English schools. At each age, in each group, eight students were studied. Stimuli were dichotically presented, English monosyllabic numbers. There were five simple pairs, five double pairs, and five pair-triads. Two studies were carried out, 1 year apart, each with different subjects. Analysis was made of accuracy of report, and order of recall. Total accuracy increased with age, but the degree of right ear dominance decreased with age for both groups. The results were inconclusive. Only one of the two studies showed trilingual subjects to perform better than monolingual subjects, and only one showed the trilinguals to have a stronger right ear advantage than the monolinguals. Order-of-recall results showed that right ear stimuli were reported first more often than were left ear stimuli. This was particularly striking in the trilingual subjects in one of the two studies. The authors concluded that trilingual education helps establish more reliable ear asymmetry effects at a younger age.

If we combine the accuracy results of their two tests, we see that at the younger ages, the trilinguals showed advantage in accuracy of report in English over the monolinguals. Although the degree of right ear dominance for the trilinguals was striking in their second year of immersion, by the third year it was no greater than that of the monolinguals. The monolinguals were more right ear dominant than the trilinguals, to start out with. Follow-up tests showed that the monolingual second graders were slowly approximating the adult pattern of monolingual right ear effect, whereas the trilingual second graders would develop greater cerebral symmetry, even in their mother tongue (see Table 46).

In Israel we ran a set of dichotic tests on 72 adult Hebrew–English bilinguals at the Aranne Laboratory for Human Psychophysiology and Neuropsychology, of Hadassah Hospital in Jerusalem. In the first half of the test Hebrew words and numbers were presented dichotically, and English words and numbers were presented dichotically. In the second half of the test, subjects heard a triad of English words in one ear while they heard a triad of Hebrew words in the other ear. The word triads

Table 46
Correct Responses[a]

Group	Stimulus presentation	Grade K	Grade 1	Grade 2
Monolinguals	Left ear	16.82	20.12	24.81
	Right ear	19.81	20.75	26.56
Trilinguals	Left ear	19.50	21.44	24.81
	Right ear	21.25	25.31	26.75

[a] Data summarized from Starck et al. (1977).

were composed of pairs chosen for difficulty of discrimination. Monosyllabic words were selected from a range of word frequencies (in order to provide the desired phonological contrasts). No word was so obscure that a high school graduate in the language would not recognize it. One-third of the pairs were minimally contrasted with feature contrasts existing in only one of the two languages (e.g., *thin–tin*; there is no /θ/ in Hebrew). One-third of the stimuli were minimal pairs with contrasts occurring in both languages (e.g., *big–pig*), and one-third of the stimuli were pairs containing no contrastive segment (e.g., *bet–sun*).

Our group of subjects was composed of 24 balanced bilinguals (who had learned both languages well before age 12, used both presently, and judged themselves equally fluent in both), 24 Americans who had fair knowledge of Hebrew, and 24 Israelis who had fair knowledge of English. The subjects were instructed to write down all the words they heard, in any comfortable order. The score was the number of correct words out of 72. The results for the intralingual condition are shown in Table 47.

We note that the Americans' total Hebrew performance was much better than the Israelis' English performance. This result is probably due to the fact that Americans in Israel have great need for auditory skills in Hebrew, whereas the emphasis for Israelis is on reading. All groups displayed a right ear advantage. We see, however, a difference between the balanced group and the two dominant groups. For the balanced group, a greater degree of lateralization was displayed in Hebrew, whereas the English was almost ambilateral. For the American-dominant and Hebrew-dominant subjects, on the other hand, English resulted in a greater degree of left hemispheric lateralization. We note that for the balanced bilinguals, the left ear performed equivalently in both languages, but the right ear performed better in Hebrew

Table 47

Results for the Intralingual Condition

	Stimuli							
	Hebrew words				English words			
Subject	Left ear	Right ear	Total	Difference (%)	Left ear	Right ear	Total	Difference (%)
Balanced	32.1	39.5	71.6	10.3	31.6	34.0	65.6	3.6
Americans	28.7	32.8	61.5	6.7	27.6	35.0	62.6	11.8
Israelis	31.5	39.1	70.6	11.3	12.5	18.2	30.7	18.6

than in English. For the American-dominant group, also, the right ear performed better in English than in Hebrew. (Because the Israelis performed relatively poorly in English, we cannot make such a comparison for them.) On the basis of these data alone, we could not support either a hypothesis of second language effect or one of language-specific effect. That is to say, it is unclear whether something about the Hebrew language results in its being more bilaterally represented than English (the language-specific effect) or whether learning a language second results in its being differently lateralized than the first language (the second language effect). We also note that the total of the balanced subjects' scores in Hebrew were just slightly better than those of the Hebrew-dominant group in Hebrew and those of the American-dominant group in English. The ear effect distribution pattern, however, was different for the balanced bilinguals and the two other groups. Furthermore, for the American-dominant and the balanced groups, one language was decidedly more asymmetrically distributed than the other.

If we consider the results of the tests that sent competing language stimuli into the two ears, with the subjects knowing in which ear to expect which language, we see the results shown in Table 48 (these tests have not been run on Israeli subjects). Both sets of data in Table 48 are consistent with the notion that the Hebrew language is more bilaterally represented than English is for these subjects. Hebrew was better processed by the left ear of both groups than was English. The only exception to this statement was the performance of the Americans in

Table 48

Competing Language Dichotics

	Condition							
	Predictably ordered				Randomly ordered			
Subjects	Left English	Right Hebrew	Left Hebrew	Right English	Left English	Right Hebrew	Left Hebrew	Right English
Balanced (N = 24)	28.8	47.4	34.9	35.2	8.4	20.5	15.8	11.2
Americans (N = 24)	29.7	38.8	29.7	38.2	10.6	16.9	15.8	12.4

	Total		Predictably ordered	
	Left	Right	Left	Right
Balanced	24.2	31.7	31.8	41.3
Americans	16.4	29.3	29.7	38.6

the predictably ordered condition. We suggest that they performed as well in Hebrew when it was presented to the left ear, either because Hebrew was for them a second learned language, with a major right hemispheric component, or else because, knowing their Hebrew was poor, they particularly attended to it.

The data for the different-type word pairs were analyzed for the first 12 subjects from the American and balanced groups. In Table 49, pairs of words that differed by a contrast in both languages (e.g., pig–big, where p–b contrast exists in both languages) are labeled "Both." Pairs of words that differed by a contrast in only one language (e.g., thin–tin, where there is no /θ/ in Hebrew) are labeled "One." Pairs of words where there were no shared phonemes (e.g., cat–pen) are labeled "No contrast." The largest consistent left–right discrepancy for both groups was between words that were contrasted by sounds one of which occurred only in Hebrew. Discrimination of these sounds, it would appear, is best treated in the left hemisphere.

This study suggests that language-specific and second language effects may contribute to dominance patterns. In addition, it suggests that these differential dominance patterns will be most striking when words of one language are pitted against words of another language. Finally, the study suggests that, while parts of the two languages may be handled in the right hemisphere, discrimination of phonemes particular to one or the other language remains primarily a left hemisphere task.

In another study differing auditory stimuli were presented to both ears. Lawson (1967) asked untrained subjects, fluent in Dutch and English, for simultaneous translation of a passage directed to one ear, when a conflicting passage was directed simultaneously to the other

Table 49
Number of Correct Responses by Contrast Type

	Left ear			Right ear		
Subjects	Both	One	No contrast	Both	One	No contrast
			Hebrew			
Balanced	11.2	9.8	11.6	11.6	13.9	12.9
Americans	10.0	8.6	8.8	9.0	10.8	8.0
			English			
Balanced	7.2	10.1	9.8	10.9	12.1	12.4
Americans	8.7	10.9	8.3	9.3	12.4	9.1

ear. Unfortunately she only used six subjects, and their handedness was not mentioned. She judged performance by the number of points omitted from the translation. More errors were made when the message played to the second ear was in the same language as that of the ear to be translated from, than when a different language went to each ear. It is, of course, impossible to determine whether the greater interference in the same-language dichotic condition was due to interference because of the dichotic input, or if it was due to interference between the speaking and listening.

It is of interest to compare this study to the Stroop studies (discussed previously) and especially to that of Preston and Lambert (1967), since the study involved auditory stimuli. In both Lawson's study and the Stroop studies, there is interference on a language production task from stimuli either in that language, or in another language known to the subject. On the Stroop test, however, interference resulted when the language of production and the language of stimulus were the same. On Lawson's test, since translation was required, most interference resulted when the language of production and the interfering language of perception were different. One explanation may be that the tests required two different tasks: translation in Lawson's study, labeling in the Stroop tests. Another explanation could be that the syntactic element involved in the continuous discourse of the Lawson test facilitated switching off the interfering language material, whereas such switching was more difficult when a limited set of lexical items was involved, as in the Stroop tests.

The three dichotic tests reported here speak to different issues. Ours and that of Starck et al. suggest that different languages may be organized differently in the brain. Lawson's study suggests that dichotic presentation of the same language to both ears results in more interference (i.e., worse translation) than does presentation of different languages to both ears. Our dichotic data support this notion, since the total scores for both the balanced and the American groups were somewhat higher in the cross-language condition than in the condition in which same-language stimuli were presented to both ears.

ELECTRICAL MEASURE STUDIES

Only two such studies have come to our attention. One employed electroencephalographic (EEG) measures of hemispheric activity in response to bilingual verbal stimuli; the second measured average evoked response (AER) to bilingual verbal stimuli.

Genesee *et al.* (1978) measured evoked potentials in 18 strongly right-handed adult French–English bilinguals who were exposed to a taped list of words. Subjects were asked to press a button corresponding to whichever language the word was in. The RT was also measured. The subjects were all judged to be equally fluent in both languages by self- and judge evaluation, and by a test of speed of encoding (Segalowitz & Lambert, 1969). They were divided into three groups on the basis of when they learned the second language, as infants; in childhood (age 4–6); and in adolescence, after age 12.

If we combine the RT results for both orders of button press (English button on the right and French on the left, and the opposite) we obtain the data shown in Table 50. There were no significant ear-by-language or ear-by-group interactions. The most striking result was the within-group consistency in judging any stimulus as belonging to one or the other language. At this task the subjects who started bilingual experience in childhood were best, and those who started in adolescence had the most difficulty, with those who started from infancy falling in between. Before we extract the conclusion that age 4–6 is the best time to expose a child to a second language, we must bear in mind the small size of the sample tested here, and the perhaps unnatural nature of the task. It does seem fair to suppose that the task required here may not be one that calls exclusively on differential use of each language, but rather one that demands a common cognitive skill of labeling.

The average evoked responses gave similar results for both N_1 and P_2 latency measures. These appeared earlier in the left than in the right hemispheres for all groups averaged together, but the adolescent group in fact had earlier right hemisphere occurrence. This group also had the briefest latency to both N_1 and P_2, which is interesting in the light of their having the largest RT. Measure of $N_1 - P_2$ amplitudes showed a

Table 50
Reaction Time (msec)[a]

Age of learning	English		French	
	Left ear	Right ear	Left ear	Right ear
Infancy	778.8	767.6	748.6	794.2
Childhood	719.7	712.5	701.6	698.2
Adolescence	834.6	834.7	828.6	852.8

[a] Data abstracted from Genesee *et al.* (1978).

language-specific effect. In the left hemisphere, French words resulted in higher amplitude than did English words. In the right hemisphere, however, there was no difference. The authors admitted to having no explanation for this effect. They suggested that the adolescent learners, albeit totally balanced, may have been using a different strategy for the task at hand, a strategy which relied on right hemisphere skills. Whether or not this different choice of strategy is based on a different neural organization of the two languages in these subjects is unresolved.

After a retest (described in their 1977 version of the study), which counterbalanced the button positions, Genesee, Hamers, Lambert, Mononen, Seitz, and Starck revised their interpretation of the average evoked response data, suggesting that the differences between the groups were differences in strategies adopted for the categorization task. Thus those who had learned the second language in adolescence "used a more right hemisphere-based, possibly gestalt-like, holistic, or melodic strategy," whereas the two groups who had learned the second language at a younger age used "a left-hemisphere, possibly semantic strategy."

Rogers (1977) tested for language lateralization by means of an electroencephalographic study. The subjects were Hopi–English bilingual children, from Grades 4–6. For all children, Hopi was the native language, and English the school language. Of interest to us were the two conditions in which EEG responses were recorded while the children were listening to two taped fables; one in English and one in Hopi. Listening to both stories elicited greater left hemisphere than right hemisphere activity, but the difference between the two hemispheres was more striking for the English story than for the Hopi story. This suggests that Hopi, the first language of these children, was more bilaterally represented than was English. The authors speculated that some language-specific effect was responsible for the asymmetrical dominance they found; they suggested that something about parts of the Hopi structure makes it particularly appropriate for right hemisphere representation.

Conclusion

The experimental neuropsychological studies we have reviewed are not strictly comparable with each other, since some have focused on certain questions and controlled for certain variables, whereas others have focused on other questions and controlled for other variables.

Nevertheless, a few points can be abstracted. First, it would appear that even in fluent balanced bilinguals, neuropsychological or neurolinguistic performance may vary in the two languages. Evidence from reaction time, tachistoscopic, dichotic, and electroencephalographic studies supports this statement. Second, there is evidence that this different performance may be a reflection of different cerebral lateralization for the two languages of the bilingual. This different lateralization may be influenced by a number of factors. In this chapter we have evidence suggesting that age of learning the second language and language-specific factors may play a role. Language-specific effects may interact with the order of learning two languages, to bring about one or another pattern of cerebral lateralization.

5

Theoretical Considerations

Introduction

Up until this point, we have categorized studies according to the discipline within which they were conducted. In each of the several disciplines (linguistics, psychology, and neuropsychology) we have clustered those experiments which treated the same basic phenomena (e.g., interference) or those which employed a similar experimental paradigm (e.g., list learning). In this chapter we focus on some of the issues in bilingualism which were discussed in the first chapter. Studies from the three disciplines are pulled together in order for us to evaluate neurobehavioral issues, such as cerebral lateralization; psycholinguistic issues, such as the relation between perception and production of language; definitional issues, such as the compound–coordinate dichotomy; and neurolinguistic issues, such as the language-specific effects on cerebral organization.

Bilingualism versus Monolingualism

It might be theoretically possible that bilinguals differ in no way from monolinguals except in controlling a second language. Let us draw up a balance sheet for skills and behavior tested in both monolinguals and polyglots. This permits us to discuss tasks for which differences have been found, and compare such tasks with those for which no differences are to be seen.

Bilinguals have the advantage over monolinguals in several language-related skills. Lerea and Laporta (1971) reported that bilinguals learn words presented auditorily in fewer trials, and with less foreign accent than do monolinguals. (The monolinguals, however, learned the visually presented stimuli in fewer trials). These data should mean that bilinguals are particularly skilled in setting up auditory associations and in imitating sounds. Kinzel (1964), however, reported that his bilingual 7-year-old child did not seem to have any advantage over monolingual children in a class for starting to learn a third language. Slobin (1968), on the other hand, saw that bilinguals do better on his phonetic symbolism task, intuiting meaning out of unknown foreign words.

Bilinguals also evidenced less semantic satiation than did monolinguals after continuously repeating a word many times (Jakobovits & Lambert, 1961). This might be taken to mean that the sense of relativity, necessitated in the bilingual who has two signs for every referent, permits him to maintain more clearly the integrity of the association of the sign with its referent. This hypothesis is in accord with Ianco-Worrall's (1972) finding that bilingual South African children of ages 4–6 were much more likely to judge word similarity on the basis of semantic instead of phonetic criteria, whereas the vast majority of children from both the monolingual groups were still making judgments on a phonetic basis or randomly.

Palmer's Spanish–English bilinguals (1972) recalled words from auditorily presented 40-item word lists in all language lists (Spanish, English, and mixed), better than did the English monolinguals. We also see in the report by Lambert and Rawlings (1969) that compound bilinguals performed better than monolinguals on core-concept labeling when they had been given lists of associated words in either language as well as mixed lists. In the study by Barton et al. (1965), however, the American monolinguals correctly recognized more tachistoscopically presented stimuli in either field than did the Israeli subjects, no matter whether the stimuli were Hebrew or English.

On the basis of tests such as these, it would appear that bilinguals have better developed auditory language skills than monolinguals, but that they do not necessarily differ from monolinguals in written skills.

The suggestion that the perceptual capacity of the bilingual is different from that of the monolinguals who speak the respective languages, can be made from a series of studies (the Caramazza et al., 1973, study of French–English synthetic-stop categorization, our replication of it on Hebrew—English bilinguals [Obler et al., forthcoming], and the Garnes, 1977, study on Finnish–English bilinguals). Whereas subjects in these tests may speak both their languages without a discernible accent, their perceptual phonemic categorization in either language environment appears to use criteria intermediate to those of the monolinguals.

On the test of Forster and Clyne (1968), however, the balanced bilinguals were seen to perform like the respective monolingual groups on a test requiring sentence completion. The monolingual German group had shown little difference with respect to degree of difficulty, whether the beginnings or the ends of complex sentences had to be recovered. The monolingual English speakers, on the other hand, took much longer to complete sentence ends than sentence beginnings. On this task of processing and production, then, the bilinguals were seen to have mastery over the two different sets of skills or strategies that the monolingual groups must use.

One test we discovered in which monolinguals performed better than bilinguals was that of Stafford (1968). The test was supposedly one of nonverbal problem solving, and the monolingual children had already been seen to have a higher nonverbal IQ than the bilingual children. Nevertheless, the monolinguals performed better than only one group of bilinguals, the compound bilinguals. Monolinguals took no fewer trials than did the coordinate bilinguals to solve the problems.

In summary, then, the evidence is strong that bilinguals function differently from monolinguals on a variety of cognitive tasks. Although it might appear that bilinguals have better performance scores than monolinguals on a greater number of the tests we have reviewed here, it would probably be incorrect to speak of a cognitive advantage of bilinguals over monolinguals. Rather, it seems to us more appropriate to speak of differences in cognitive style between bilinguals and monolinguals.

It is not impossible that these differences in cognitive style are related to differences in brain organization for language. As we will discuss in fuller detail (on p. 283ff) there is evidence that language is less lateralized in bilingual adults than in monolingual adults. The evidence from polyglot aphasic studies supports this view, since our study (Chapter 4) and that of Gloning and Gloning (1965) found a high proportion of right-handed polyglots in whom right-sided lesions led to aphasia. Such crossed aphasia occurs in a monolingual population at the rate of 1–2 cases in 100. Our study found 10% instances of crossed aphasia. The one experimental study which deliberately contrasted monolinguals and bilinguals contradicted a hypothesis of different cerebral organization in polygots and monolinguals. Barton *et al.* (1965) found equal degrees of right visual field dominance in the Israeli bilinguals (15%) and in the American monolinguals (14%). Other experimental studies (our own among them, see Chapter 4), however, contrasted fluent bilinguals with second language learners and did see differences in degree of lateralization for the two languages between the fluent and nonfluent learners. By logical extension, and by comparing the results of these subjects to those regularly obtained in tachistoscopic and dichotic tests, we suggest that bilinguals and monolinguals may yet be shown to have different cerebral lateralization patterns for language. This may further be related to early developmental differences between the monolingual and polygots. Starck *et al.* (1977) concluded from their dichotic data that trilingual children develop a reliable right dominance earlier than do monolingual children. Several reports implied that bilinguals mature (linguistically and perhaps cognitively) earlier than their monolingual counterparts. Both the Ianco-Worrall (1972) and Bain (1976) studies showed earlier linguistic abstraction in their bilingual children subjects.

In conclusion, then, bilinguals may differ from monolinguals by maturing earlier (both in terms of cerebral lateralization, and in acquiring linguistic abstraction skills). In adulthood, bilinguals may continue to be more verbally skillful than monolinguals. The greater verbal skills seen in bilinguals may be attributed to their cerebral organization for language, which seems to be more bilateral than that of the monolingual.

Degrees of Bilingual Proficiency

It is possible to have a general notion of what is meant when one says that someone is "better" or "worse" in one language than in another. We may mean that she speaks one of the languages haltingly, or with an accent, or with nonnative errors of grammar. We may mean that her reading and writing skills are not equivalent to those of her peers in the second language culture. As a rule, then, if we describe someone as a nonbalanced, or dominant, bilingual, we mean that one language is handled with the competence of the native speaker, while the second is not. In the course of this book, we have considered numerous studies that compared the performance of the balanced bilingual with that of the dominant bilingual. Some of these studies suggest that the balanced bilingual simply has "more" of some skill that the dominant bilingual has yet to fully master. Other studies, however, suggest that the balanced bilingual has **different** processing strategies from those that the dominant bilingual has for the nonfluent language.

Several studies suggest that the nonfluent speaker of a language has control over fewer processing strategies than a truly proficient speaker has. One result of this lack of strategies is that verbal memory seems to be worse in the nondominant language. On list recall tests, Nott and Lambert (1968), Palmer (1972), and Champagnol (1973) showed that increasing bilingual experience increased the number of items recalled (even on monolingual lists).

Another type of evidence that processing strategies are imperfect in the nonfluent bilingual comes from Macnamara (1970). In English-dominant college students, he found that the time necessary to judge whether or not a word flashed simultaneously with a picture was the label for the picture was longer in French (the nondominant language) than it was in English. Macnamara (1970) provided evidence that the speed of reading aloud was slower, in the Irish–English children he tested, in their less fluent language than in their fluent language.

Two studies suggest that concomitant with the imperfect processing skills just discussed is the inability of the dominant bilingual to take advantage of the full range of natural redundancy in a language. Mackay (1970) reported that dominant bilinguals experienced relatively greater difficulties in processing distorted speech when that distorted speech was in their nonfluent language than when the same degree of distortion was applied to their fluent language. Even in the simple task of shadowing (Treisman, 1965) more errors were made in the nonfluent language.

At the syntactic and semantic levels, too, higher level processing results in greater efficiency. Macnamara (1970) reported that English-dominant bilingual French–English college students evidenced less difference on reading speed between scrambled and unscrambled French passages than between scrambled and unscrambled English passages. Thus it would appear that for English, knowledge of linear, syntactic probabilities facilitated rapid reading, whereas for French, reading went on word by word. The sentence completion study of Forster and Clyne (1968) showed that dominant English bilinguals had not mastered the sentence reconstruction strategies of monolingual German speakers, but the balanced bilinguals had. Champagnol (1973) further demonstrated that the tendency to cluster words by semantic categories in both languages increased with proficiency in the L_2.

We suggest that the fluent speaker controls a wider range of processing strategies in his dominant language, and that these strategies permit optimal appreciation of the redundancies of a language. Our dichotic study suggested that some processing strategies did not approximate those of the native speaker as proficiency increased. Lambert (1956b) found, however, that in an association task, although the number of word responses increased in the L_2 as one became more fluent in the language, the word-type of response did not change, nor did the degree of accent, nor the stereotype, nor type of response (i.e., definitional or emotional).

Riegel (1968) theorized that all bilinguals develop from a compound state to become coordinate when and if they are truly fluent in a language. The test of release from proactive interference, that of Goggin and Wickens (1971), showed that balanced Spanish–English bilinguals benefited more from a change of language than did the dominant group. This supports Riegel's hypothesis, suggesting that the balanced bilinguals had greater language independence than did the nonbalanced bilinguals. Ervin (1961b), however, indicated the opposite, that dominant bilinguals have less compounding between the two languages than do balanced bilinguals. Her dominant subjects recalled individual words best in the language in which they had best been able to label them. We can draw no conclusion about Riegel's compound-to-coordinate developmental hypothesis from this contradictory evidence.

As to cerebral organization of the languages, although L'Hermitte et al. (1966) and Charlton (1964) have collected cases in which it appeared that aphasia impairs all languages to the degree that they were known before the onset of the aphasia, our tachistoscopic and dichotic studies showed different dominance patterns for the two languages of Hebrew—English balanced, as opposed to dominant, bilinguals. This discrepancy may be due to the fact that we were testing perceptual tasks, whereas the vast majority of the polygot aphasic subjects with equal impairment in both languages had expressive aphasias with impaired production. Thus, authors of polyglot case studies were dealing with production skills, while our experiments tested perception skills. We will suggest (p. 238ff.) that increasing fluency in a language correlates with a shift from bilateral representation toward greater left hemispheric lateralization for that language.

We conclude that the balanced bilingual has control of the processing strategies that a monolingual has for the respective languages, and perhaps also of superordinate strategies. The nonfluent bilingual does not have control of all these strategies and, as a result, will perform with decreased efficiency on a number of tasks in the second language.

Interference and Transfer

Of the many forms that bilingual interference may take, the one termed **transfer** may logically precede the rest. When we speak of transfer during second language acquisition, we mean that the learner imposes on the new language, structures which she transfers from the previous language or languages. This basic acquisitional strategy may result in erroneous productions in the second language in those instances in which the rules or structures of the second language do not coincide with rules or structures of the first language. Hakuta (1974) gave examples of facilitation for a Japanese child learning certain structures in English—those structures that occurred in Japanese—and delayed learning by the child of certain English structures that have no parallels in Japanese. Perceptual systems may also suffer from transfer; Scholes (1968) graphically displayed his evidence that the phonemic perceptual matrix of one's native language might structure the categorical perception of English phonemes.

With greater exposure to the new language, the learner may modify the rules that he originally transferred from the first language. With luck, he will successfully eliminate inappropriately transferred items and successively approximate the new language. Selinker (1972a) called the resulting language an "interlanguage" to emphasize that it is systematic; in fact, where interference occurs, it will usually occur systematically.

It must be emphasized that not all language acquisition is explained by direct transfer of the structures of the prior language onto the second language. In a series of articles, Dulay and Burt (e.g., 1974a,b,c,) and Kessler (1972) demonstrated that certain processes (they dealt with morphological ones) in second language acquisition follow the sequence that a native speaker of a language employs—not the sequence that contrastive analysis of the structures of the two languages would predict. We might argue that these data only contradict the notion of transfer at one level; in fact, they indicate that the learner may transfer to the task of learning a new language certain basic tools for language learning or predictions of what any language must be like, which permit him to grasp parts of the new language with native-like strategies.

In the face of the evidence that some structures of a second language are acquired with native-like order, some people never speak the second language with the proficiency of native speakers. Their problem is termed one of interference: They may have an accent in their daily speech; they may pause in search for a word or insert a word from

another language; they may inappropriately translate a syntactic structure from their first language into their second language. These are the
productive types of interference, and a listener will often label the
speaker "foreign" on the basis of such interference. Harder to measure,
but theoretically conceivable, is interference in the perceptual system;
essentially, the nonnative speaker may use nonnative strategies in
processing speech. The speaker notices the interference only if these
nonnative strategies result in misunderstanding. Although much description has been available on interference in speech production, work
remains to be done in sorting out the processes of perceptual and
processing interference. Beyond personal intuition, the hints we have
that perceptual interference exists are few. One example is the report by
Lambert and Preston (1967) that two words that are structurally close in
two languages (blue and bleu) provided more perceptual interference
(i.e., resulted in more errors) on a Stroop test than did structurally
distant words (e.g., green, vert). Segalowitz (1976) suggested that more
interference will be evidenced in the production systems than in the
perceptual–processing ones since production systems of the languages
must be more critically separated than perception systems.

It is probably important to distinguish between "natural," unconscious interference in the speech of the bilingual and interference that
is experimentally induced. By definition, the balanced bilingual
should rarely experience the natural interference, since she is assumed
to speak both languages as a native does. Particularly in the series of list
recall experiments, interference was deliberately induced by manipulating the variable of including translation equivalents for items on
the lists. This type of "interference" actually facilitated the recall task;
presentation of translation equivalents facilitated recall for French–
English, Spanish–English, and German–English subjects (Lambert et
al., 1958; Lopez & Young, 1974; Evers, 1970). In a second set of tests
one language was pitted against a second language in the hope that the
resulting "interference" would prove interesting. The Stroop test, in
both its visual and auditory forms (e.g., Lambert & Preston, 1967;
Preston & Lambert, 1969, for the visual modality; Hamers & Lambert,
1972, for the auditory modality), evidenced cross-language semantic
interference, although this interference was not so strong as within-
language semantic interference. A parallel finding was reported by the
Lawson (1967) study, which required simultaneous translation from
one ear under conditions of the same or a different language being
played to the second ear. When the second ear heard a passage that was
in the same language as that presented to the ear to be reported, more
errors resulted. The task of simultaneous translation must be consid-

ered a case of interlanguage interference because difficulties are experienced in addition to those resulting from mere listening and speaking simultaneously. This is seen in the reports by Gerver (1974a) and
Barik (1974), who found that shadowing a text resulted in fewer errors
and better comprehension than did simultaneous translation. Simultaneous translation may be seen as an intermediate type of interference
between experimentally induced and natural interference.

Several points remain to be made about natural productive interference. It must be borne in mind that two different processes may both
result in what is called interference; one is essentially the borrowing of
constituent items, while the other is the imposition of higher-level
rules. Item interference is best exemplified by lexical borrowing but
may also be seen in the systematic borrowing of a phoneme or idiom
structure, perhaps in translation. An example of higher-level interference would be a case in which a rule of phonological reduction or
expansion or an intonation pattern is inappropriately imposed on a new
language. The borrowing type of interference may be seen to result
from a search for a certain item during the process of speech; if the
speaker finds he does not have the item available in the second language, he may "choose" to borrow it from the first language. The
second type of interference has actually incorporated a productive
mechanism as a permanent feature of the second language for the
speaker. When interference is cited as a symptom of polyglot aphasia, it
is usually the first type of interference—a linear mixing of elements
from each language. We have seen clinically two cases in which senile
dementia apparently induced such mixing in an elderly bilingual.

One may ask how interference operates in the child learning two
languages at once. Several studies report that the youngest child may
mix words from both languages initially (Kinzel, 1964; Burling, 1959;
Obler & Rosenbaum, unpublished paper). By around the age of 3,
however, the concept of dual linguistic systems will develop in the
child, and she will make few obvious lexical interference errors from
then on. It is difficult to predict on theoretical grounds whether a
compound or a coordinate learning condition should result in more
interference of two languages later on. We might argue that the coordinate bilingual has the two languages better separated and so is less
susceptible to interference. Or we might argue that the compound
bilingual was obliged to develop and exercise some mechanism for
keeping the two languages apart and so becomes less susceptible than
the coordinate bilingual to interference.

Interference, then, may obtain at all linguistic levels. It is more
manifest in speech production but may also occur in speech perception

and processing. Nonfluent speakers will always be suspect of experiencing interference; balanced bilinguals may not be exempt either, however. Finally, more research must be done on the ways in which the second language may interfere with the first. It is our observation that several years in a foreign country may result in nonnative production of the speaker's native language. This phenomenon, in which recent usage sets the structures that predominate over earlier ones, may be a weak extension of the reported instances in which a child who is immersed in a new language at age 5 or 6 may subsequently entirely forget his first language.

The Switch Mechanism

By the concept of switch, we generally understand a mechanism which turns some system on or off. In the case literature on the polyglot aphasic, certain authors were prompted to suggest that some anatomically localizable mechanism must be responsible for the bilingual's skill in speaking only one or the other language (e.g., Poetzl, 1930). They based their argument on the fact that in some aphasics this "mechanism" was impaired. The patient either mixed languages as she had not premorbidly, or else she spoke only one language and could not switch to the other language. The aphasiologists' notion of a bilingual switch led psychologists to try to measure the effects of the switch. Kolers (e.g., 1966) and Macnamara and Kushnir (1971) manipulated subjects to compare "natural" spontaneous language switching with experimentally constrained switching and were able to calculate specific times for the switch (probably around .3 sec). Macnamara noted that the switch thus measured was in fact only a measure of time for switching in output production; he went on to measure an input switch as well. This switch would somewhat "automatically" set the bilingual language system to process any incoming material, no matter what language it was in.

We observed (Obler & Albert, 1977) that the alleged input switch was not as efficient as it might have been. In conditions in which it would have been particularly useful for the input switch to turn one language system off, processing at semantic level (in the language not being used) was nevertheless taking place. The best example of this is the bilingual Stroop test (e.g., Preston & Lambert, 1969), in which the optimal strategy is to ignore the interfering items in a labeling task. When the interfering items were in a language different from that in which the labeling was to be done, the input switch should simply have turned off the language system not in use. Instead, subjects regularly produced errors that indicated they had perceived the interfering stimuli, processed them semantically, and had gone on to translate and pronounce the translation item.

In order to explain this inconsistency in the alleged switch, we argue that a continuously operating monitor system controls the processing of input in the bilingual much as in the monolingual. All incoming stimuli are processed at the phonetic level and assigned to potential phonemes, which are then assigned to potential words, which are then interpreted syntactically; and in the light of linguistic and extralinguistic context, decisions are made about the likely meaning of incoming speech. Such a monitor would work most efficiently by assigning priorities in its interpretation. We suggest, for example, that if one were in France, the tendency would be to interpret incoming data as if they were French. Nevertheless, should stimuli from another known language enter the ear, the monitor system would soon realize that its processing strategies were not optimal, and it would reassign priorities so that the stimuli would be checked against the other language systems. It is conceivable that such a system holds for constraining speech output to a single system but permits borrowing and language switch where appropriate.

Aphasiologists are of two schools about the bilingual switch. Localizationists like Poetzl (1930) and Leischner (1948) maintained that the switching mechanism can be localized. Paradis (1977) pointed out that there is serious debate within the localizationalist school as to whether the location of the switch is frontal or posterior. We note that this discrepancy may be resolved if we consider that two very different types of switch impairment are being described. Poetzl (1930) located the switch mechanism in the parietal lobe near and including the posterior section of the Sylvian fissure. Leischner (1948) suggested that the switch is in the supramarginal gyrus, or the posterior parts of the second and third temporal convolutions. Both authors described cases in which the switching problem was that which Paradis labeled selective recovery; only one language returned. The cases in which an anterior lesion resulted in switching impairment, like that of Stengel and Zelmanowicz (1933), involved a very different type of impairment: mixing. Frontal disinhibition may explain this lack of an effective bilingual switch.

The theory of a second school of aphasiologists is more consistent with our notion of a bilingual input monitor system. This theory derives from Lashley's (1923) antilocalizationist, mass effect hypothesis. By Lashley's model, a lesion anywhere in the brain results in general cognitive impairment. The larger the lesion, the greater the general impairment. Goldstein (1948) specifically denied the possibility of localizing a bilingual switching mechanism; he suggested that the ability to switch languages appropriately, which is lost in some polyglot aphasics, is part of a general set-switching ability. Paradis (1977) expressed the antilocalizationist position particularly succinctly:

> The decision to switch from one language to another, just like the decision to speak in a particular language in the first place, is more economically explained by the functioning of a general neural mechanism than by a special mechanism for that specific purpose alone. There is no need to postulate an anatomical localization or even a specific functional organization, other than that which every speaker already possesses and which allows him, among other things, to switch registers within the same language [p. 91].

We conclude that multiple processes are involved in the conscious or unconscious decision to switch from one language to another, either in processing incoming language or in producing language. Some of these processes may involve general cognitive mechanisms; other processes may develop that deal more specifically with problems peculiar to bilingualism. In either case, no conclusive statement can be made at present as to the precise location of the mechanisms involved.

Language Set

There is no clear definition of what is meant by language set in bilingualism. Intuitively, set should be what is operating when a bilingual returns to a culture he has left for a considerable time and finds hesitation in speaking a once familiar language (e.g., Kinzel's child, 1964), or when one apparently loses a childhood language altogether. On the perception end, set may be what leads to initial lack of comprehension when we "hear" someone (because of nonlinguistic cues) speaking one language, but the person turns out to be speaking another, even though this other language is known to us (see Taylor, 1976).

Experimentally, set would seem to be what is at work when, as in Lopez et al. (1974), more translation errors are found in auditory paired-associate learning when the language of the items on the second list is different from the language of the first list. Such apparent inertia in switching from one language to the other may be considered set fixation.

Other studies that dealt with set attempted to control it experimentally. Macnamara et al. (1968) demonstrated that the bilingual could prepare himself for a certain language, since predictable alternation of stimuli resulted in shorter switch times. Artificial cues to change set, however, such as color cueing (Macnamara, 1971) or telling a subject the language label (Dalrymple-Alford, 1967) seemed to have no influence. The greatest influence on set, it would seem, is more a cumulative effect than a question of immediate environment. Davis and Wertheimer (1967) found that the number of association items to a given visual stimulus in a certain language depended more on the language in which the instructions had been given than on the language of the two words immediately preceding the stimulus. Segalowitz and Lambert (1969) trained one group of subjects in French and another in English and found performance on a task requiring the exclusion of English synonyms from learned category lists to be easier for those trained in French. Dalrymple-Alford (1967) found that by having subjects read cards in one or the other language before viewing a verbal stimulus presented tachistoscopically for oral recognition, he could not produce a shift of set, that is, RT did not speed up. Our failure and that of Caramazza et al. (1973) to evince perception differences by testing balanced bilinguals in two sessions, one in each language environment (speech, test booklets, magazine), may speak to a compound processing system rather than to a failure to induce set experimentally.

The preceding studies assumed that the ability to achieve language set is a natural part of bilingualism. The study of Sodhi (1969) viewed set phenomena as part of a general cognitive process. He evaluated Uznadze's (1966) definitions of psychological set fixation and extinction and found that only the latter—the ability to extinguish a set—correlated with successful college language learning. In the preceding discussion on switching, we alluded to the possible interplay between general cognitive processes involved in switching and more specific switching processes which may have developed in response to learning or using a second language. This explanation may reasonably be extended to account for the notion of language set. Although language set cannot be altogether dissociated from the general notion of cognitive set, we must expect that the speaker will perceive environmental and linguistic cues which will aid her in planning the processing priorities of the bilingual monitor system. This priority setting, then, would be the definition of language set specific to bilingualism.

Language Tagging

We may ask how a bilingual "knows" that he is speaking one or another language. We assume that such knowledge is involved, unconsciously, in his ability to continue speaking in only one of his languages. Do the individual words or structures have some sort of tag?

A number of reports provide evidence for the validity of the bilingual's claim that often she can remember the content of a conversation with another bilingual, without being able to remember the language they were speaking. It appears that, whether or not subjects are instructed to remember the language in which an item is presented, they cannot do this without making errors. For example, Heras and Nelson (1972) found that children would forget the language label of the final sentence of a paragraph, especially when the intermediate questions involved a switch to the other language, despite the fact that they knew they would be asked to remember language tags. Doob's (1957) presentation of statements to bilingual high school students resulted in better memory for content than for language of presentation when the subjects did not know in advance that either would be required.

Champagnol (1973) suggested that the ability to tag by language increases with age, since his more advanced second language students made the lowest number of translation errors on a recall task. Kolers' (1965) results supported this idea. His adult bilinguals achieved equal scores on unilingual and mixed lists, even though the mixed lists might have been expected to induce translation errors and, therefore, lower scores. Lambert et al. (1968) also showed that mixed lists in themselves posed adults no problems, although when list mixing was compounded with the problem of semantic categorization (i.e., in discordant lists, where the language split did not coincide with the category split), transition errors (i.e., inattention to language tag) resulted. Of course, it is difficult to judge whether it is simply greater age which aids subjects in attending to and recalling language tags, or whether their greater degree of education and/or greater knowledge of the second language is involved in their greater ability to recall language tags.

No experimental manipulation of language-tag conditions has been employed with aphasic polyglots, insofar as we know. It may be that the ability to keep languages tagged is impaired in those polyglot aphasics who mix languages within sentences.

We have not been able to speak to the question implicitly posed in the introduction to this section: whether, if language tagging exists in some real sense, it is at the lexical level or at a higher level (or both). If we conceive of language tagging at the lexical level, we may picture it as another feature appended to the individual lexical item, that is, the "tag" in whatever listing procedure accounts for the syntactic and semantic features of a given word. One could argue that such nonlexical information as the peculiar facial and, especially, buccal configuration employed for speaking each language, or the intonation system, or language-specific syntactic operations, also enters into what functions as language tagging.

Translation

Translation is a skill—and certainly not a primary language skill, since monolinguals regularly get along perfectly well without it. Teaching a second language by a method which encourages translation is only one of the ways to teach a second language. People in language learning programs of the direct method (where associations between the second language and real world elements are drilled, as are relations within the second language, but where translation is discouraged) are not likely to be bilinguals skilled at the task of translation.

Further evidence that translation is a special language skill is found in the mere existence of institutions devoted exclusively to the training of simultaneous interpreters; the people who undergo such training are adding a new skill to the fairly fluent bilingualism which they must possess prior to the course in simultaneous translation.

Consider also that proficiency in translation can be unidirectional; it can be better when translating from a certain fluent language (say, Uzbek) to another fluent language (say, Swahili) than vice versa (translating from Swahili to Uzbek).

Gekoski's (1968) dissertation speaks directly to the point that translation is a special language skill. He found no correlations between translation speed and the type of bilingualism (compound or coordinate) or even degree of proficiency in the two languages. This means that one could not predict how efficiently a subject could translate on the basis of whether or not he had learned the two languages under conditions likely to keep the two languages separate in his brain (coordinate) or under conditions likely to induce a single unified language system for both languages (compound). We must conclude that translation skills are not directly related to the degree of psychological "closeness" or "mixing" of two languages of the bilingual.

Treisman's (1965) study of simultaneous translations showed that subjects, of whom half were dominant in each language, made fewer errors when translating from French to English than when translating in the reverse direction. Barik (1974) showed that nonprofessionals had more difficulty translating from their weak to their dominant language.

These data highlight the highly specific nature of the skill of translation and imply that training or practice in the translation task itself, in the desired direction, is necessary to gain proficiency.

Further evidence for the dissociation of the skill of translation from other language skills comes from cases of polyglot aphasia in which speaking both languages is possible but in which translation is no longer possible. The case Goldstein (1948, p. 128) reported is a good example; the patient would switch, albeit somewhat inappropriately, from discourse in one language to discourse in the other language, but she could not translate upon command as she had been able to do premorbidly.

We must not conclude that all kinds of translation are learned only when specifically taught. There is considerable evidence that spontaneous use of translation by bilingual subjects can be documented, especially at the lexical level. Thus Burling (1959) reported that his 3-year-old son was willing and able to translate English items whose pronunciation he had not mastered so that his father would understand. Jakobovits and Lambert (1961) showed that semantic satiation with word stimuli extended to the translation equivalents of the words. Segalowitz and Lambert (1969) found that translation equivalent words were quickly incorporated in a task measuring RT or judgment as to semantic categorization. Evers (1970) provided evidence that presentation of translation items facilitated list recall, and Lopez and Young (1974) showed that this facilitation might operate in an unbalanced direction. In their study, English subjects who were dominant Spanish–English speakers (by a usage criterion) were aided more when the list to be learned was in English and the intial list in Spanish than vice versa. Additionally, we have seen that recall tests can induce translation errors (Lambert et al., 1968; Champagnol, 1973) and that association tasks often induce translation equivalents (Reigel & Zivian, 1972; Rüke-Dravina, 1971), especially for compound bilinguals (Gekoski, 1970). The results of Kintsch (1970) demonstrated that subjects who were led to expect translation equivalents to appear in a series of words that were to be judged for previous exposure were able to identify the translated words faster than altogether new words. This advantage was seen only on the second reappearance of the translation equivalent items, however, so perhaps some time was necessary to judge that in fact a translation equivalent item had been presented and was now being seen for the second time. The one study that suggested that spontaneous translation occurred at a higher linguistic level than the lexical level was that of MacKay and Bowman (1969). They showed that translation equivalents of sentences functioned like the sentences themselves in a sentence repetition task. They found that the translated sentences could be read aloud with speed equal to that of the sentences the subjects were translating after numerous repetitions in a task in which rapid reading was required. It was not exclusively the translation, however, of the primary, nontranslated sentences per se, which was acting in these cases, since, when the translated sentences did not share the same word order, the speed of reading after repetition was somewhat diminished.

One senses that the task of simultaneous translation must differ from a translation task in which the bilingual is free to work at her own pace. For example, in simultaneous translation there is advantage to be gained by translating each word as soon as possible after it has been uttered, so that a backlog of information to be translated will not accumulate. Nevertheless, Goldman-Eisler (1972) reported that simultaneous translators prefer to wait for constituent boundaries and translate larger-than-lexical units. Because of structural differences between languages, it is likely that simultaneous translators cannot take full advantage of the "natural" translation skills we have just discussed in preceding paragraphs. Gerver (1974a) has shown that shadowing speech was a less demanding task than simultaneously translating speech. The evidence was that more errors were made in translation than in shadowing. Moreover, we must note that the energy employed in spontaneous translation may actually conflict with the normal processing of speech for comprehension. Gerver reported that subjects were able to answer correctly more comprehension questions when they had been listening—or even shadowing—a passage than they could when they were simultaneously translating it.

Two contradictory ideas have been supported in our discussion of translation. We have argued that translation is an unnatural, educated skill and also that it can occur spontaneously, even in such experimental tasks in which translation causes undesirable confusion or errors. This contradiction may perhaps be resolved if we consider the monitor system described previously (p. 213). We argued there that the input system for processing will analyze incoming information in a number of ways, making hypotheses about what will follow, until it achieves a reasonable interpretation of any string of input. Association of a given word with its translation equivalent may be one of the spontaneous ways of processing that word. Thus the translation equivalent of a word (or even a sentence) might be available to the bilingual some time after he has heard or seen the language stimuli. Given that language tagging is an artificial task rarely called for in nonexperimental situations, the meaning underlying the pair of the word and its translation equivalent may be recorded in memory. In an experimental task, then, the translation equivalent may be mistakenly recalled. In a situation of simultaneous translation, on the other hand, the subject would have to inhibit production of translation equivalent items in order to be sure, on the basis of further linguistic context, that the appropriate equivalents have been selected.

Perception and Production

One fact that clinical neurology has contributed to theoretical linguistics is that the perceptual and productive language systems can be dissociated from each other to some extent. Systems for diagnosing monolingual aphasics divide patients into those who have more difficulty with language production (the expressive, or Broca's, aphasics), and those who have more difficulty with language comprehension (the receptive, or Wernicke's, aphasics). The linguist might well consider that different grammars may describe the two systems. It is conceivable that the production process-grammar and the perceptual process-grammar share only a deep semantic system and that the linguistic mechanisms involved in processing speech for comprehension differ in form and/or type from those involved in processing meaning for language performance.

Let us consider the bilingual evidence that production and perceptual processing systems exhibit independence of each other. We have reported (Albert & Obler, 1975) one particular aphasic case that is a striking example of the potential dissociation between production and perception; our patient evidenced primarily perceptual impairment (i.e., Wernicke's aphasia) in one of her premorbidly fluent languages and primarily production impairment (i.e., Broca's aphasia) in another fluent language. Two other cases are described in Chapter 4 (Silverberg & Gordon, forthcoming).

The perception–production dichotomy can also be observed in the logical progression of natural language acquisition: In the bilingual, as in the monolingual, comprehension skills regularly precede production skills. Tarone (1974b) explained the dissociation between production and perception skills in the second language learner by suggesting that different strategies are employed for the two procedures: Initially, perception of the second language (unlike production) relies on selective processing (i.e., of stressed words) and intelligent guessing of meanings. Studies of bilingual children also suggest that development of the perceptual and production systems may proceed differently. Both Leopold (1939–1949) and Kinzel (1964) reported that when their children returned from a trip to a country in which one language was used exclusively, the children could comprehend the language that they had not been using on the trip but were hesitant in producing the language. It would appear, then, that when one language was not practiced, production deteriorated in these children more than did perception.

These studies provide experimental evidence for the perception–production dissociation. Three studies which support this point followed a similar methodology, but dealt with different linguistic systems: Ervin (1961b) tested the distribution of lexical items, color words, whereas our study and that of Caramazza *et al.* (1973) tested a phonological variable, VOT of voiced–voiceless consonant pairs. In the perception task bilingual subjects and monolingual controls were asked to sort stimuli into categories. In all three tests the bilinguals were seen to have hazier boundaries between categories, and these categories were intermediate to those of the monolingual speakers of their respective languages. This implied that the bilinguals had a fairly unified perceptual system. In production in either language, on the other hand, the bilinguals performed more like the respective monolinguals. Thus their bilingual production system was dual, while their bilingual perception system was unified.

A third line of support for the perception–production split is Kolers' (1966) evidence from reading tasks. We assume that reading silently for comprehension is a perception task, whereas reading aloud can be purely a production task. Kolers timed silent and oral reading of sentences in either language and sentences in which words from two languages were mixed. In the silent reading condition, the nonfluent bilinguals took longer to read sentences in the nondominant language than they took to read the mixed sentences. In reading aloud, however, the converse was true: Reading mixed sentences took longer than reading sentences in the nondominant language. If we assume that the mixed sentences provided equal confusion in both conditions, then we can conclude that the skill of reading aloud may be mastered independently of the skill of reading for comprehension.

On the basis of the evidence accumulated from bilingual studies, we are convinced that perception and production systems are partially independent of each other. These studies would also suggest, however, that there is some interdependence between the two systems. Macnamara (1970) found that speed for reading aloud increased more in the slower second language with repetitions of the same sentence than it did in the first language. He suggested that the initial slowness in the second language resulted from a problem with input processing, which was then overcome with repetition of the sentences and permitted output processing to go on apace. We argue, however, that in repeating a sentence, reading was no longer the primary activity involved. Thus the children were simply gaining facility, perhaps from memory, in producing the necessary phonological sequence. In the various versions of the bilingual Stroop test, one might argue, subjects will often erroneously produce the translation equivalents of printed items. This seems to be a case of perceptive processing feeding uninhibited into the production system. Alternatively, however, this form of interference may be unnaturally induced because the subjects are instructed, essentially, to speak as fast as possible. Contact between the production and perceptive systems, we suggest, may obtain mainly at a deep semantic level.

Linguistic Levels and Categories

Structural linguists have envisioned the grammar of language as comprising a hierarchy of fairly distinct levels. The phonological level would contain a phonetic and a phonemic level. The morphological level, then, would incorporate elements of the phonological level. The next level would be syntax, operating on items produced at the morphological level. The lexicon might be an additional separate system, and semantics might be as well. Such a theoretical linguistic model of essentially separate levels and categories which may nevertheless interact is supported by evidence from a number of experimental and aphasiological studies of bilinguals.

The strongest evidence is for a dissociation between a phonological and a semantic level. In Schvartz's conditioning experiment (1954), phonetic association remained after semantic association, which was in fact the trained task, had been obliterated by administration of chlorohydrate. Ianco-Worrall (1972) found that bilingual children learned earlier than monolingual children to replace similarity judgments made on phonetic bases with those made on semantic bases. This lends support to the notion that phonetic processing is separate from, and developmentally earlier than, semantic processing. Riegel and Zivian (1972) saw that word association by similar initial letter was a more common strategy for languages in which the subject was not fluent, but that in languages in which she was fluent, semantic association took priority.

The aphasic case reported by Peuser and Leischner (1974) offers further proof of dissociation between linguistic levels. They described a linguist who was more severely agraphic in either of his two languages when writing to dictation in conventional orthography than he was when writing in phonetic transcription, a task that draws attention to the phonetic rather than the semantic features of language. The reading epilepsy case of Stevens (1957) can be interpreted similarly; severe attacks of epilepsy were brought on by reading Hebrew, a language that was apparently not processed semantically by the young woman. Reading in English, her native language and necessarily semantically processed, was much less likely to bring on an attack.

The lexicon has been assumed to be an independent system by many experimenters. Evidence for the validity of this position can be seen in Lambert's (1956a,b,c) studies in which he showed a change in paradigmatic behavior (the semantic type, and stereotypical nature, of association responses) as subjects advanced in knowledge of a second language. No changes in syntagmatic behavior (proportion of word categories) nor phonological behavior (accent) occurred, however.

The psychological reality of word class boundaries is justified in the light of Davis and Wertheimer's (1967) finding that paradigmatic association items (e.g., nouns with nouns, adjectives with adjectives) were more likely than syntagmatic ones, even across languages (i.e., when the stimuli were in one language and the response in another). Kolers (1963) provided support for a behavioral differentiation between concrete and abstract nouns, since the former were much more likely to result in translation equivalent responses than were the latter. This was true whether the subjects were speakers of Thai, Spanish, or German (in addition to English).

Thus there is neurolinguistic evidence that even within the lexicon, structures that have been posited to exist on theoretical grounds prove to have neuropsychological correlates. Phonetic mechanisms may be distinct from syntactic and semantic mechanisms. Lexical and syntactic processes may operate in different ways. Even such limited features as the one marking nouns as abstract or concrete must have neuroanatomical bases.

Linguistic levels, albeit autonomous, may be interlinked. Under certain experimental conditions, the interdependence of linguistic levels may be demonstrated. Evidence for the interrelationship of syntax and semantics is seen in Macnamara's (1970) study. He reported that complex syntactic structures in a nondominant language could result in mistaken comprehension, even when the individual lexical items and basic syntactic structures were known by the individuals. Indirect evidence for an interrelation between phonological production and syntax can be seen in Kolers' observation (1966) that under the unusual condition of reading aloud mixed-language syntax, his subjects read with a "new accent." This accent included phonological elements common to neither of the source languages. Further research may resolve the apparent contradiction and conclude that certain linguistic levels or entities are more interdependent, while others are more independent.

Language Modalities

We have seen that some dissociation between the perceptive language skills and the productive language skills is likely. Within both of these systems, different language modalities which focus on the different forms of language input or output can be sorted out. The English Language Institute of a large midwestern university, for example, recently converted its classes from a division along linguistic levels (vocabulary, syntax, pronunciation, etc.) to one along language modalities (reading, writing, speaking, and listening comprehension). Neurologists, too, expect cases of independent impairment in a single language modality. Even though linguists may consider writing skills to be secondary to speaking and aural comprehension, aphasiologists maintain that alexia and agraphia can occur, individually or together, with no impairment to the primary skills, and that expressive disorders for speaking (aphemia) can occur without agraphia, as can sensory aphasia for aural comprehension (word deafness) without agraphia (see, e.g., Hécaen & Albert, 1978, for review of this topic).

Among the bilingualism studies that reinforce the model of modality independence are those measuring switch time. Kolers (1966) found a large difference between the switch time necessary for reading mixed passages aloud and that necessary for creatively speaking them. Macnamara (1967b) showed that true–false judgments to mixed auditory sentences resulted in a slightly longer switch time than did judgment for visual stimuli. Terry and Cooper (1969) provided stronger evidence, for they found no correlation between reading skills and a capacity for perceptual differentiation in the second language.

Another piece of evidence that visual and auditory modalities may be processed differently comes from our experimental studies on Hebrew–English bilinguals. There was a discrepancy in the degree of cerebral dominance for Hebrew in our balanced bilinguals. For their tachistoscopic scores Hebrew was fairly ambilateral, whereas for their dichotic scores Hebrew was strongly right ear dominant.

Even within the written modalities, evidence that different neuroanatomical systems may underlie different orthographies comes from a number of aphasic cases. Lyman et al. (1938) described a patient who could deal much better with English orthography than with his native Chinese characters. The Englishman described by Hinshelwood (1902) evidenced Greek reading that was less impaired than reading of his languages that were written in Latin print.

We conclude that there is neurolinguistic support for the linguists' intuitive understanding that the visual and auditory modes of language are somewhat distinct.

Developmental Patterns of Bilingualism and Age of Acquisition

The individual nature of each reported case of bilingual aphasia, and the difficulty of delineating a simple set of rules to account for impairment or recovery patterns, lead one to suspect that bilingual language acquisition (as perhaps also monolingual language acquisition) differs from person to person. Nevertheless, certain patterns can be found in development toward balanced bilingualism.

One factor affecting acquisition patterns is age of acquisition. From the data of Genesee et al. (1978) we realize that even among preadolescents there are judgment reaction time differences between balanced subjects who learned their second language in infancy and those who learned theirs later, after age 6. From that study, too, we see that learning a language in adolescence can eventually result in balanced bilingualism, which contradicts Lenneberg's (1967) theory that puberty marks a crucial age after which learning a second language is unnatural and imperfect.

On the basis of the Leopold (1939–1949) and Kinzel (1964) studies (described in Chapter 2), we propose that children who learn both languages from infancy seem initially to assume they are learning a single system. This is evidenced in their mixed vocabulary, and occasional use of translation equivalents together (e.g., please bitte) in conjunction with absence of phonological interference, implying a single system containing all phonemes. Only at a later stage is there conscious realization that there are two language systems. This is evidenced especially by the fact that the children address different speakers differently. Unconscious differentiation between the two languages may take until around age 7 to work itself out entirely, for Kinzel found his daughter exhibiting interference until that time, even though she had been exposed only to monolinguals or nonmixing highly fluent bilinguals.

If, on the other hand, a child starts learning one language, and is then exposed to a second before the first has been completely learned, transfer errors can occur, as reported in Hakuta (1974) and Rosenbaum and Obler (unpublished paper, 1975). In such cases, the structures of the first language interfere for a time with those of the second language. At the same time, however, these children do not seem to need special lessons in order to acquire the second language. Given sufficient exposure to the second language, they will eventually become fluent speakers.

Children who are exposed to a second language at an early age do appear to develop precociously the capacity to deal with words semantically rather than phonetically (Ianco-Worrall, 1972). Furthermore, the developmental lateralization of language to the left hemisphere may occur earlier in bilingual children than in monolingual (Starck et al., 1977; Ben-Zeev, 1972).

In adults, interference at all linguistic levels can be documented when they learn a second language. Such interference is unlikely to disappear altogether, no matter how well they master the lexicon and syntax of a new language. Nevertheless, there is some evidence that language-specific features, such as a difficulty hierarchy of morphological items, may influence their acquisition patterns (Bailey et al., 1974). We infer that L_1 transfer need not altogether determine second language learning in adults, but that natural (inherent?) language-learning strategies from childhood also play some role in adult language learning. The pattern of learning in adults is seen to start with phonological associations and then to shift later to semantic associations (Riegel & Zivian, 1972).

Scovel (1969) reviewed the inadequacies of that literature which argues that the reason most adults cannot learn an L_2 without an accent, whereas children succeed in doing so, has to do with environment or "nurture." He pointed out that it cannot be merely the "unconsciousness" or unstructuredness of child learning, since even children learning in a school situation, and under some language-teaching method, will develop into fluent speakers. Nor is it a question of intelligence, since adults can master other parts of the grammar (syntax, style, etc.). Nor can it be merely a question of first versus all other language acquisition, since children may learn an L_2 years after L_1 but, after the initial period when phonological interference **does** manifest itself, will eventually achieve native-speaker fluency. Adults may have the ability to master the phonological patterns of another dialect of their language, but only children (and the rare adult) seem regularly to master those of an L_2. Scovel went on to review the basic principles of development of cerebral lateralization for language, and then to propose that it is no coincidence that puberty marks both the age after which foreign accent is likely to occur, and also the age after which the damaged brain may have lost some flexibility to reacquire language fluently. His hypothetical correlation remains to be proven, and it would seem that one place to start would be to examine the pattern of cerebral dominance in those adults who have managed to master an L_2 with little or no accent (e.g., the balanced bilinguals of Genessee et al., 1978, who had learned an L_2 in adolescence, perhaps had unusual brains to begin with).

Childhood bilingualism and adult bilingualism share some developmental features and differ in others. It may be that only in the child can a truly compound system develop, as the young child is exposed to two languages. Exposure to two languages, moreover, seems to make more demands on the bilingual child than on a monolingual child, and as a result the bilingual child will develop an abstract sense for language at a younger age and may start earlier to lateralize language to the left hemisphere.

The Compound–Coordinate "Dichotomy"

Today few would assert that individual bilinguals are **either** compounds or coordinates. To the original notion—that of a single language system comprising both languages in the compound bilingual **versus** dual noninterfering language systems, mediated only at the level of cognition, in the coordinate bilingual—have been added numerous modifications. These suggest that individuals lie along a continuum between the two poles, or that parts of systems are coordinate. The fact that many parameters have been proposed as having an influence on compound–coordinate status implies that the phenomenon may be a multidimensional continuum.

Diller (1974) was so distressed with the unclear definitions of the two groups, and with the inconclusive nature of the tests that correlate the dichotomy with language behavior, that he deemed the terms empty. Nevertheless, individual bilinguals do perform differently on many tests, and it would be unwise to discard the notions altogether when they may provide a reasonable, if partial, explanation for groupings of different performance patterns. Indeed, the careful experiment would run large numbers of bilinguals and then test for the significance of results under various subdivisions—by the different definitions—of the subjects.

Ervin and Osgood (1954a) first formalized the notion as one relating to the representational mediation processes or meanings synchronically operating upon input and output. They suggested that in the compound bilingual two sets of linguistic signs come to be associated with a single set of representational processes, meanings, or responses. In the coordinate, two separate meaning-level processors are maintained. Although this model limits itself to synchronic competence, it considers the two states to result from different language-learning situations.

Kolers (1968) suggested a water-tank metaphor to describe the two systems. In the compound bilingual different taps would release the same information but produce it through different rules (phonetic to syntactic). Coordinate bilinguals would possess two tanks, one each for receiving and dispensing information from each language. This metaphor makes clear the fact that it is largely lexicon which is considered when the compound or separate "language systems" are discussed, although Jakobowits (1968a) extended the model to include all realms (from phonological to attitudinal) of the bilinguals' language repertoire. Nevertheless, most of the work on these notions has dealt with the question of shared or separate lexicons.

Lambert (1969) summarized the development of his understanding of the compound–coordinate dichotomy. From the beginning, the problems of acquisitional context, acquisitional manner, and usage were all considered. In the extreme, the acquisitional context was thought to induce a different state depending on whether the subjects learned the two languages in the same or in different cultures. It could also be considered to apply when the subject spoke to one set of people in only one language and to another in only the other, or spoke one at home and one with peers. The manner of acquisition was also suspected to influence the bilingual's "state." A translation method, for example, could facilitate having each word or idiom filed near its translation equivalent in the other language. A language learned, even if in school, by an audiovisual method of direct learning (in which words were defined only in terms of objects or other words in the second language) would result in separated systems. The usage parameter suggested that rigid separation of usage environments (by culture or experience) should result in more separate systems (regardless of acquisition style), whereas daily mixing of the two languages (e.g., in a bilingual community, or as a professional translator) would result in a more compounded system.

Kirstein and de Vincenz (1974) considered the compound–coordinate dichotomy in the light of the generative–transformational hierarchy. They posited a model wherein the extreme coordinate bilingual controls two grammars which are unrelated except at the deepest levels of universal language processes and thought. For the compound bilingual, on the other hand, relations between the two languages obtain at all levels: both at the level of surface structure, and at the level of language-specific processes for the L_2. Therefore, deep encoding takes place in L_1 first, even if the language-specific rules in L_2 are the same as those of L_1. They presented this model graphically as follows.

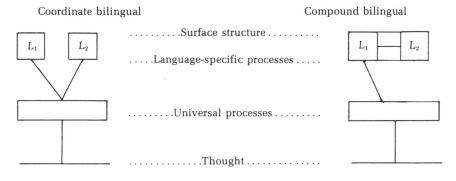

Kirstein and de Vincenz also suggested that spontaneous translation in the coordinate bilingual must go back through "**universal processes**" or "**thought**" (their emphasis), whereas spontaneous translation goes back only as far as the necessary L_1 level in the compound and proceeds to the corresponding L_2 level. It is unclear what is meant by "necessary" in this context.

While Diller (1974) would discard the compound–coordinate dichotomy altogether, others have suggested refining it by taking into account the multiple factors thought to be involved. Thus Genesee et al. (1978) defined their compound subjects as ones brought up in a thoroughly bilingual home from the earliest childhood, whereas the coordinates were those who learned one language after the other, usually after age 10 and also outside of the family. Beardsmore (1974) suggested that compounds might be considered those who **acquired** both languages "during the vital formative years," and coordinates those who **learned** their second language after this period.

Riegel (1968) proposed a developmental model for people who

learn one language before the other. In this model interrelationships develop between vocabulary items of L_1, and then, when a second language is introduced, a weak compounding interrelationship of translation equivalence may obtain. For the most part, however, L_2 develops internal relationships, so the bilingual achieving this stage of special language learning is essentially coordinate. Through appropriate usage conditions, a final compound stage may be reached where all items in the two languages are interrelated.

From a psycholinguistic point of view, the notion of partially compounded and partially coordinate systems is most attractive, since it provides for an efficient picture of what appears to go on in bilingual language processes. Diller (1974) attempted to convince the reader of the impossibility of a compound system accounting for anything but interference errors, by asserting that "no two languages are grammatically similar enough to be compoundable," and that "the same is true with regard to vocabulary." We propose that learning a language after the native one, **at whatever age**, cannot demand a repetition of all the same steps. In our argument, learning a language is like learning to ride a bicycle; once one has learned the basic principles of riding a bicycle (or of using language), one never again has to achieve certain elements of knowledge. At least to the extent that they are language systems, as differentiated from other cognitive systems, the two language systems of the bilingual can be considered to be compounded. Such possible universals of language process as the principle of transformation from underlying meaning to surface phonological realization need be grasped only once.

Furthermore, interference does obtain in bilinguals, even in fairly sophisticated bilinguals. At the more obvious levels (lexical, gross syntax, sometimes accent at the phonological level), the bilingual speaker may be sensitive enough to his own production errors to control them. In some instances, a compound system may be most efficient (e.g., the compounded phonemic processing systems reported by Caramazza et al., 1973). It may be in the interest of the bilingual individual to set up a single system and then generate rules to produce the L_2 on the basis of the single system. (When these rules are incorrectly abstracted, of course, interlanguage will result.) Thus, for example, it is unreasonable to suppose that entirely separate negation rules must be operating for the French and Spanish of bilingual speakers (since in both languages a negation item, ne and no, respectively, almost invariably precedes the verb), or that the Romance words like nation, liberty, and quality are originally learned as separate English and French items in English–French bilinguals, since their pronunciation does not differ enough to mask their similarity. To claim that such separation obtained would be like claiming that no English speaker recognizes the relation between *nation* and *nationality;* in fact such competence may reveal itself in the monolingual English speaker who can recognize Latinate words to which she has not been exposed previously and can generate derivational forms of them with no difficulty. We suspect that the ability to intuit correspondences between lexical items, and, moreover, between grammatical and phonological rules of the two languages, is part of the creative language acquisitional talent a human is born with.

With the foregoing as background, we shall now review the literature that pertains to differences seen between compound and coordinate subjects, as divided on the basis of one or more factors of their individual language histories (age of L_2 acquisition, change of culture, etc.).

Manner of acquisition, as Weinreich (1953) has suggested in his discussion of the bilingual individual, seems to influence later language skills, and is often tied to the compound or coordinate class fixation definitionally. In the study of Riegel *et al.* (1967), the native Spanish speakers who had been immersed in English were more proficient in L_2 in terms of vocabulary and oral fluency, than were the American subjects who had learned their second language in college. The native English speakers, however, seemed to have greater ability than the Latin Americans to identify conceptual structures. In the study by Lambert *et al.* (1968), Russian–English bilinguals who had learned their Russian predominantly for audiolingual fluency were seen to perform differently from French–English subjects, who were balanced in all modalities. Moreover, the audiolingual learners made many more translation errors.

The best evidence that age of acquisition influences later bilingual capabilities is in the study by Genesee *et al.* (1978). The authors found that in their subjects, who were all balanced bilinguals by performance measures and judgment, RT to a language-labeling task was different in the different groups. The differential reaction here implies that the groups employed different strategies. The average evoked responses, moreover, of the group who learned L_2 during adolescence, showed earlier right hemisphere participation in the task than did the evoked responses in two groups who learned L_2 before puberty.

We can see that differences exist between compound and coordinate subjects on a number of the psychological tests. Lambert *et al.* (1958) showed that bicultural coordinate bilinguals evidence greater semantic differential than either compounds or monocultural coordi-

nates. Jakobovits and Lambert (1961) saw that compound bilinguals manifested semantic satiation for words (and only slightly less for their translation equivalents), whereas coordinates evidenced less satiation
altogether. Instead of a significant decrease in meaning for the translation
equivalents of repeated words, the coordinate bilinguals showed an
increase. Lambert and Rawlings (1969) found compound bilinguals
(pre-age 6 learners) better able than coordinates to deal with the task of
abstracting core concepts, and in both conditions—from unilingual and
from mixed lists. Gekoski (1970) found compound subjects able to give
more translation equivalents than coordinates in a restricted association task. Stafford (1968) saw that his coordinate subjects performed
faster than compounds on an allegedly nonverbal problem-solving
task. In fact, he asked the subjects which language(s) they had used,
and found more than twice as many compounds as coordinates who
had used both languages.

Lambert and Fillenbaum (1959) pointed out that the majority of the
14 polyglot aphasic cases they studied could be accounted for by
Pitres's rule of recovery or Ribot's rule of recovery or both, whereas a
much lower percentage of the European cases could. They suggested
that this difference might be due to the fact that their Montreal cases
were likely to be compound bilinguals, whereas the Europeans were
likely to be coordinates. They argued that coordinates, being immigrants, might be more susceptible to affective factors than were the
compound North Americans.

In three studies no differences were seen between compound and
coordinate bilinguals despite the fact that the authors expected them.
Two of these (Gekoski,1968; Lambert & Olton, 1966; in Lambert, 1969)
involved translation, a task which we have argued is in no way
synonymous with, or naturally concomitant with, compound bilingualism. The third study is that of Segalowitz and Lambert (1969) in
which the task was to abstract and generalize core concepts from mixed
lists.

In the remainder of this section we shall weigh the evidence for a
compound system and that for coordinate systems. Here, these concepts are taken more to describe the synchronic "state" of the bilingual
mind than to relate to the history of learning the two languages.

The most compelling argument for coordinate systems is that of
the switch mechanisms, whose actions take a measurable amount of
time (e.g., Macnamara and Kushnir, 1971; Kolers, 1966), and which can
apparently be impaired in aphasia (e.g., Goldstein, 1948). It is difficult
to conceive of a switch without assuming that there are two separate
systems between which the switch operates. The language production

system, we have seen (e.g., bilingual Stroop testing [Preston & Lambert, 1969; Obler & Albert, 1977]), is a likely candidate for being a dual system.

The fact that translation is not necessarily an immediate response to a verbal stimulus also argues for some measure of separate systems at the level of lexical storage. Kintsch (1970) showed that even when subjects expected translation equivalents, they could not respond to them as quickly as they could to a repeated stimulus word. (In this task subjects were asked to judge whether or not a word had been exposed previously.) Barik (1974) discussed the particular difficulty caused in simultaneous translation by function words. This difficulty implies that there may be a syntactic component to language set; in fact, it would be an error to try to translate function words, because they are integrally tied to surface syntactic patterns.

Kolers (1963) demonstrated that in an interlingual association task, only one-third of the response items given by bilingual subjects were translation equivalents. (These cases of translation were usually for words referring to concrete objects.) This suggests that word association matrices may include items from both languages. In its extreme form, however, a compound model would predict that each word would be closely bound to its translation equivalent.

In the Tulving and Colotla (1970) study of free recall from monolingual, bilingual, and trilingual lists, subjects were found to be impaired in recall in inverse proportion to their facility in a language. The authors suggested that this came about not from difficulties in storing the items, but from differential accessibility, which in itself implies separate stores and/or separate rules for retrieval.

The study of Goggin and Wickens (1971) showed a parallel finding, when one paradigm was release from proactive interference in a mixed-list recall task. Changing the semantic category over four trials resulted, of course, in release, but so did changing only the language of presentation. Ervin (1961b) also showed a split between the recall of illustrated words. Those which were easiest to name in one language were easiest to recall in that language. Note that this was true for her dominant bilinguals, but not for the balanced bilinguals.

Kolers (1965) provided evidence that language tagging was more natural than color coding of words (although we have seen it to be less natural than semantic processing on p. 59). His subjects were more likely to recall the right word in the right language when it was in a mixed-language list than to recall it in the right colors when it was in a mixed-color list. This can be taken as additional, if weak, evidence of some degree of coordination or separation of the two language systems.

The bulk of the argument for compound systems comes from instances of interference and transfer. The documentation of lexical mixing and lexical and syntactic interference, in children exposed to two languages (Kinzel, 1964; Leopold, 1939–1949; Burling, 1959) in some aphasics (see Table 35, p. 109), and the hypnotic case of As (1963) implies an originally compounding system. That this interference may disappear after around age 6, tells us that some degree of coordination is later achieved.

The occurrence of translation errors on recall tasks (e.g., Champagnol, 1973; Tulving & Colotla, 1970) suggests the possibility of a compound storage system. Otherwise we must believe that translation errors indicate obligatory semantic processing to some cognitive level above and between two coordinate language systems. These two possibilities are sketched in the following diagram. Kolers' finding, that repetition of lexical items or their translation equivalents equally facilitated recall, likewise suggests a compound system at the lexical level.

A. Coordinate independence:

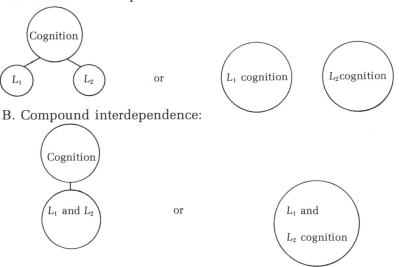

B. Compound interdependence:

The fact that translation equivalent associations are made in like fashion to associations from the same language (Schvartz, 1954; Davis & Wertheimer, 1967) is further evidence for a compound lexicon. The expanded evaluation judgments of correct phonological sequences, even in one's native language, are also evidence of a compounding of systems (Anisfeld et al., 1969).

Some studies start to give evidence for the more likely position that the two languages are compounded to some extent and coordinate to some extent. Nevertheless, the division for an individual or a group is fuzzy; it seems to cut across lines of modality, linguistic level, and word class or degree of abstraction to include elements of all of these. However, the correlation of compounding with perceptual systems and coordination with productive ones is evidenced.

The Caramazza et al. (1973) phonemic perception and production study gave ample evidence of compounding for input but coordination for output—since subjects spoke each language without an accent. The bilingual Stroop test (Preston & Lambert, 1969; Obler & Albert, 1977; Hamers & Lambert, 1972) reinforced this notion, since subjects consistently produced words in the assigned language, even if the wrong term was given due to semantic processing of the other language. Also, Slobin's (1968) finding, that bilinguals developed a "feel" for some universals of phonetic symbolism, supported the concept of a compounded phonological processor. His subjects had no knowledge at all of the third language from which the stimuli had been selected, so of course they had no productive system for that language.

We must conclude that notions of compound and coordinate bilingualism cannot be lumped together; some experiments have found significantly different psycholinguistic behavior in the two groups, and it is important to clarify why these differences obtained. It is not unreasonable to think that age of acquisition, manner of acquisition, and manner of practice of any skill should enter into the way that skill is represented neurologically.

Were we to speculate on the possible anatomical substrate permitting compound as opposed to coordinate language organization, we would consider the issue as it relates to cerebral dominance in bilinguals (see p. 238). If, with Fearey (1977), we consider two hypothetical cases, the argument can be made more clearly. Our compound bilingual would be the 5-year-old whose parents were both bilinguals who switched between the two languages. Moreover, the compound bilingual would live in a bilingual society with no politicolinguistic friction. Such a child would be equally fluent in both languages at all stages of her development. When her language started to become lateralized to the left hemisphere, it would be both her languages which were converging to some extent. In our hypothetical coordinate bilingual (an orphan who must start a new life with distant relatives in an alien country), left lateralization would occur at different times for each language. When he started to learn the second language, his right hemisphere would participate as it apparently does in language learning in any age. Eventually he could become fluent enough that the second language would start to lateralize toward the left. His brain, however, would have matured in the meantime, and the left lateralization of the second language would never permit such a degree of compounding as our ideal compound bilingual experienced.

Language-Specific Effects on Brain Organization

Whorf (1956) is credited with writing the strong form of the Whorf–Sapir hypothesis, which claims a correlation between the structures of a language and the patterns of cognition of its speakers. A bilingual should, by this theory, have command of two cognitive styles, which might account for a feeling on the part of the bilingual of changing set when changing languages. Vildomec (1963) refers us to Goldstein (1948) as one of the few neurologists who recognized that the intrinsic structure of a language may influence the form of the ensuing aphasia. Vildomec pointed out that one might expect different forms of agrammatism in an analytic language like English (in which function words mark syntax) than in a synthetic language like Turkish (in which the syntax is marked by affixation).

Acquisition studies also suggest that there are language-specific factors involved in bilingualism. The developmental studies of childhood bilinguals of Dulay and Burt (1974a,b,c) showed that acquisition of L_2 by the bilinguals paralleled monolingual acquisition of that language. Parallel acquisition was seen in Spanish and in Chinese children learning English. We might say that a difficulty hierarchy **within** English accounts for the order of acquisition of morphemes. Bailey et al. (1974) supported this theory with data from adults. Kessler (1972) also detailed discrepancies between Italian and English in bilingual children, which again showed that the intrinsic difficulties of the language in question determined the order of acquisition. Hakuta (1974) however, presented us with instances of transfer from Japanese that resulted in deviations from the English morphological hierarchy. It is likely, in fact, that language-specific effects interact with transfer effects in L_2 acquisition.

A number of the experimental studies reviewed in earlier chapters refer to behavioral differences resulting, or suspected to result, from differences between the two specific languages studied. We will discuss only those that provide strong evidence for language-specific effects.

Differential performance relating to word order differences between German and English were seen in two studies. Forster and Clyne (1968) demonstrated the relative difficulty subjects had in German as opposed to English in completing sentences when given the beginnings. Goldman-Eisler (1972) reported that the ear–voice span in simultaneously translating German was much longer than that in translating English, because the translator had to wait until a clause ended for predicate completion. Treisman (1965) reported similarly a greater ear–voice span for translation from English to French than vice versa in all her subjects, whether English-dominant or French-dominant.

Lambert (1956b) evinced more adjectival associations to French stimuli than to English in both native and nonnative groups; this finding may relate to structural differences between the two languages. It is not impossible that his finding of greater stereotypy to French stimuli may derive from structural differences as well. Different results were obtained by Lambert et al. (1968) for French–English and Russian–English subjects on a recall test. Genesee et al. (1978) found greater amplitude of average evoked response for their balanced English–French subjects when the word to be judged was French than when it was English. It is not impossible that a language-specific effect was responsible for these results.

Orbach's work with Yiddish (1953) clearly showed an asymmetrical dominance for Yiddish and English visual perception in his balanced subjects and in those who learned Yiddish first. Yiddish was more balanced between the hemispheres, whereas English showed the expected RVFE. The differential effects for Hebrew as opposed to the Latinate tongues are seen in Stevens's (1957) patient with the rare syndrome of reading epilepsy (her attacks were triggered more rapidly by Hebrew than English), and in Streifler and Hofman (1976) whose patient mirror-wrote in Hebrew but not in Polish or German. Orbach's (1967) measures of tachistoscopic dominance showed greater left hemisphere participation for visual Hebrew stimuli than for visual English stimuli in both left- and right-handers. Our tachistoscopic studies did likewise, and supported the belief that visual Hebrew is more equally lateralized than is English. The data of Barton et al. (1965) and Albert (1975) suggest that these cerebral differences in Hebrew speakers may be integrally tied to practice in reading scan direction.

Language-specific effects in the auditory domain were found for French versus English (Genesee, 1978), for Hopi versus English (Rogers, 1977), and for Hebrew versus English (in our own dichotic tests). In our experiments, for example, the balanced bilinguals evidenced stronger right ear effect in Hebrew than they did in English.

More work remains to be done to clarify what sorts of variables enter into what we call language-specific effects. On the one hand, we have evidence from contrastive linguistics that languages may share some structures and differ in other structures. What the anatomical correlates of such similarities or differences should be remains unclear. On the other hand, we have evidence that stimuli in one language may evince one lateralization pattern in bilingual speakers of that language, whether they are balanced or nonbalanced bilinguals, and a different lateralization pattern for another language in these same bilinguals. But it is hard to point to the precise structures in the languages that account for such asymmetrical lateralization. One approach for answering the dominance-asymmetry question may be to look for those tasks which the right hemisphere of monolinguals is supposed to deal with and see if the more symmetrically lateralized language contains a great number of such structures, or if such structures are crucial to processing the language. For example, Hebrew relies on internal vowel alternation for certain fairly common morphological derivations. Since vowels may be more bilaterally processed than consonants (Shankweiler & Studdert-Kennedy, 1967), such alternation may contribute to the more symmetrical lateralization of Hebrew, as compared to English. Rogers (1977) suggested that the greater spatial orientation of Hopi permitted the right hemisphere to take more of a role in language processing for the Hopi of her bilingual children, than for their English, which may be said to have a comparatively linear–temporal orientation. Such speculations must be tested in further research on language-specific effects.

Differential Cerebral Lateralization

Adult monolinguals who have had nonintensive introductions to foreign languages may assume that a foreign language is learned only with reference to the first language (i.e., by translation) and that therefore it would be absurd to expect that the second language could be in any anatomical way divorced from the organization of the first.

In the field of language teaching, however, it is understood that some students respond well to a method of teaching which relies on translation drill, whereas others become more fluent when the second language is taught in its own terms, with little or no reference to the first language. The fact that different students learn well under different methods implies that they are using different strategies—consciously or unconsciously—to acquire the new language. A simple example would contrast the student who learns a vocabulary item better when given visual reinforcement by writing down the word, with the student who learns it best by hearing and repeating it. It is legitimate to suppose that whatever these differing learning strategies may consist of, they may reflect some degree of differential involvement of brain organization.

Once we are willing to admit the possibility of individual variation in brain involvement for learning a second language, we may ask if different learning strategies eventually result in different neural representation of the language in question. To date, only the grossest measures have been made to test this possibility, namely, lateralization studies. Two basic points have emerged: first, that the language organization of the average bilingual may be more ambilateral than that of a monolingual; second, that the organizational systems of the two or more languages of the bilingual are not necessarily distributed equally with respect to cerebral language dominance. We raised a third point in attempting to account for these findings: Differential dominance patterns are not random; rather, they may be influenced by such acquisition parameters as age, manner, and modality of second language acquisition.

First, let us review the evidence which suggests that bilinguals are less strongly lateralized for language than are monolinguals. Two sorts of evidence, aphasiological and experimental, bolster this hypothesis. The aphasiological evidence derives from two studies, those of Gloning and Gloning (1965) and Nair and Virmani (1973). Gloning and Gloning reported that of the 4 left-handed subjects among the 11 polyglot aphasics whose cases they reviewed, 3 had exclusively right-sided lesions. As a rule, one might expect 60–70% of left-handers to have aphasia after a left-sided lesion; in the Glonings' admittedly small sample, only 25% of the left-handed subjects had left-sided lesions. This led the Glonings to postulate a high incidence of bilateral language representation at least in bilingual left-handers. Studying aspects of aphasia in unilateral hemiplegics of Indian nationality, Nair and Virmani found that 10 of the 12 right-handed left-hemiplegics evidenced aphasia. Since one would expect unilateral right-sided lesions to result in aphasic disorders in only .5–2% of monolingual right-handers, their finding of 83% in bilinguals is striking. Each of these studies argues in a different way that bilinguals are more likely than monolinguals to have their language less markedly left-dominant.

The experimental studies provide particularly strong support for the ambilaterality argument. Walters and Zatorre (1978) found that a full 54% of their native English-speaking Spanish bilinguals showed either an LVFE or no visual field effect on a tachistoscopic test of verbal material. With the same English stimuli only 10% of a group of monolingual controls failed to evidence a RVFE. The 1977 study of

Hamers and Lambert also reported a high percentage (33%) of French–English balanced bilingual subjects not evidencing the "predicted" RVFE in each language.

Aphasiological evidence can also be mustered to argue that at least some polyglots may have what we call asymmetrical lateralization, that is, a different lateralization pattern for each of their languages. Cases like those reported in Pitres (1895) in which one language recovers to some extent but the other does not may be explained in the following way: The recovering language was more bilaterally represented than the nonrecovering language and so was less severely impaired and recovered sooner. Cases like ours (Number 2, p. 111), in which a different aphasic syndrome was seen in each of several languages of one person, might also reflect asymmetrical lateralization for the language in question.

The experimental evidence for asymmetrical lateralization is even more compelling. A series of tachistoscopic and dichotic tests on bilinguals speaking languages from Hopi to Hebrew showed asymmetrical lateralization for different groups of subjects. Although "degree of lateralization" may be a suspicious concept if one wishes to label the individual subject, data from monolingual groups provide reliable test–retest lateralization percentages (Blumstein, Goodglass, & Tartter, 1975). More bilingual studies than test artifact can account for show significantly different lateralization percentages. Our own tachistoscopic study as well as those of Mishkin and Forgays (1952) and Orbach (1953, 1967) show a greater RVFE for tachistoscopically presented, horizontally displayed English words than for Yiddish or Hebrew words. One might counter that the results of Barton et al. (1965) and Kershner and Jeng (1972), who used vertical presentation and got no asymmetrical dominance, contradict our claim. We have argued elsewhere (Albert, 1975) that practice in reading-scan direction may influence cerebral organization for language. Rogers et al. (1977) provide evidence that Hopi is more bilaterally represented than English in native Hopi-speaking bilinguals.

Once we suspect that different languages may have different anatomical representation, we may begin to ask what factors are involved in determining that representation. Among the factors proposed to date are those of age of L_2 acquisition, manner of L_2 acquisition, usage patterns, language-specific factors, and order of language learning. Let us review studies pertaining to each of these factors.

Scovel (1969) suggested that it is not a coincidence that puberty marks the age after which L_2 learning becomes difficult. Rather, he argued, difficulty in L_2 learning must be related to the fixing of hemispheric lateralization believed by some (e.g., Lenneberg, 1967) to occur at around that age. Genesee *et al.* (1978) tested this hypothesis by means of an averaged evoked potential measure. They found that balanced bilingual adults who had learned their second language during adolescence showed an N_1 latency earlier in the right hemisphere than in the left hemisphere, unlike the bilinguals who had learned their second language before adolescence.

Hartnett's (1974) study of the interaction between manner of second language learning and cerebral dominance was reported by Krashen (1975) and Diller (1975). Students who were successful in a teaching program relying on "deductive" methods were likely to show eye movement to the right when mentally solving verbal problems. Students who were successful in a class conducted by an "inductive" method showed less consistent results.

The study of polyglot aphasics by Lambert and Fillenbaum (1959) suggested that language learning and usage circumstances may influence patterns of recovery from aphasia in polyglots. They supposed that their subjects in Montreal were for the most part compound bilinguals and differed from the European population represented in Leischner (1948), who were mostly coordinate bilinguals. The authors suggested that the differing language histories may have been responsible for the fact that a high percentage of their 14 subjects followed both the rules of Pitres and Ribot, whereas a high percentage of Leischner's cases contradicted these rules. Lebrun (1971) also reviewed a number of cases of polyglot aphasia and concluded that differently acquired languages may be "subserved by different cerebral circuits."

The effect of the order in which two languages are learned is seen in Orbach's (1953) study. He divided his subjects into two groups, those who had learned English first and those who had not. The latter group had learned Yiddish either before English or at the same time. He showed that the English-first group exhibited RVFE in both languages, whereas the other group displayed RVFE in English, but were balanced in Yiddish. Gaziel (1977) proposed that differences in the order of acquiring Hebrew and English interact with language-specific effects to produce the different dominance patterns she found in her several Hebrew–English bilingual populations.

Taken as a group, the studies discussed in this section argue forcefully in favor of the notions of cerebral ambilaterality of language representation in bilinguals, asymmetrical dominance for each language, and influence of language acquisition circumstances on dominance. In concluding, we must point out that two characteristics— bilingual cerebral ambilaterality and asymmetry of dominance for the languages of the individual—are not mutually exclusive. Use of the term ambilaterality of cerebral organization for language may be an exaggeration; in fact, the phenomenon we are describing may better be termed weak left lateralization, or greater right hemisphere participation. Whichever characterization may turn out to be more appropriate, ambilateralization may be seen as the result of that accident of language history which makes some people bilinguals while others remain monolinguals. Thus the learning of a second language can alter the "standard" lateralization pattern which we have come to expect in right-handed monolingual adults. Moreover, we have seen that the circumstances of the language learning may affect the eventual neural organization of that language. Since it is unlikely that one individual will learn all of her languages at precisely the same age, in precisely the same manner, with precisely the same affective considerations, it then seems likely that certain bilinguals have asymmetrical or different dominance patterns for their several languages.

6

Summary and Conclusions

Introduction

The main conclusion we have drawn from the evidence presented in this book is the following: Language is organized in the brain of a bilingual in a manner different from that which might have been predicted by studies of cerebral organization for language in monolinguals. Studies of monolinguals have indicated that the left hemisphere is dominant for language in most individuals. Studies of bilinguals demonstrate not only the left hemispheric role in language but also a major right hemispheric contribution.

The evidence suggests a need for revision of the traditional concept of cerebral dominance for language. The facts of bilingualism indicate that the right hemisphere plays a major role in the learning of a second language, even in adulthood. Further, the brain is seen to be a plastic, dynamically changing organ which may be modified by processes of learning. The brain does not have a rigid, predetermined neuropsychological destiny. The learning of a second language may alter patterns of cerebral organization even for the first-learned language. (For example, in certain individuals, cerebral dominance for the

first-learned language may shift from left to right hemisphere as the
second language is learned.) The pattern of cerebral dominance for a
given bilingual depends on a number of different factors, including age
of acquisition of L_2, manner of learning L_2, usage patterns, affective
relationship to both languages, order of language learning (i.e., the
final dominance pattern may vary depending on which language was
learned first), and language-specific factors (e.g., the different structural characteristics of Hebrew, Hopi, English, and French may have
qualitatively different impacts on the brain).

By way of speculation we propose the following schema for the
relationship of cerebral hemispheric activities to language in the bilingual. When someone who already knows a first language begins to
learn a second language, the right hemisphere plays the major role
initially, although the left hemisphere is also involved. As facility with
the second language increases, the left hemisphere begins to play a
more active role, although the right hemisphere continues to contribute. The fact of left hemispheric involvement in second language learning results in a modification of the functional organization of the first
language. The final pattern of cerebral dominance for either language is
not yet predictable but depends at least on the general factors enumer-
ated in the preceding paragraph.

We have found the study of bilingualism to be a useful tool for the
understanding of certain aspects of language and its neurological basis.
In the remainder of this chapter we shall summarize key points gleaned
from our analysis of bilingualism. First, we shall review each major
element of our (arbitrary) division, that is, linguistic, psychological,
and neuropsychological studies of bilingualism. Next, we shall list the
main conclusions of our theoretical discussions. Finally, we shall
speculate on possible implications of our observations.

Linguistic Aspects of Bilingualism

In the chapter on linguistic aspects of bilingualism we considered
studies relating to language patterns in bilinguals and second language
learners. With respect to acquisition of the second language it appears
that language-specific structures influence the learning of L_2 regardless
of the level and type of prior linguistic knowledge of the learner.

Children learning two languages from early childhood initially
develop a unified language system. The sorting out of two separate
languages starts at about age 3. Clear separation of two languages
may occur around age 7. From this age the language skill of the

child for the two languages and the stability of separation can be maintained.

It seems that separate productive phonological and morphological systems are mastered first, and somewhat later lexical and syntactic patterns are sorted out. We have seen evidence to support the theory that systems for language production and language perception are to some degree independent, although the picture of independence is far from complete. There is also a strong possibility that the bilingual builds a unitary system for perception and maintains two separate output systems.

Of interest to educators and to parents of bilingual children is the evidence that children learning two languages from infancy are not impaired cognitively or academically. It may even be possible to conclude that bilinguals have superior language skills to those of monolinguals.

Interference occurs differently at different linguistic levels and may even affect different word classes differently. Interference may be unidirectional between two languages or it may be asymmetrical, influencing one language in one way and the other in different ways.

The linguistic notion that a single competence may underlie the variable performance of a speaker must somehow be expanded to account for the bilingual. Models of bilingualism must take into account language-inherent structures, age of L_2 acquisition, and individual learning strategies.

Psychological Aspects of Bilingualism

In the chapter on psychological aspects of bilingualism we considered those studies relating to the area of overlap between language and cognition. In any analysis it must be kept in mind that bilingual capacity may be manifested differently on various tests depending on task requirements.

Mastery of a second language affects perceptual strategies and capacities. In the bilingual there is a loosening of perceptual constraints, a new openness and flexibility. Consistent with findings in the section on linguistic studies, we found strong evidence to suggest that bilinguals are better able than monolinguals to deal with abstract aspects of language, that there is greater cognitive flexibility on the part of bilinguals. Nonverbal skills are not impaired in young bilinguals, while verbal skills mature earlier. Bilinguals have greater linguistic sensitivity than monolinguals: Experience in study of a foreign language expands the individual's sensitivity to universals of phonetic symbolism.

Although the lexicons of the two languages of a bilingual seem to be more or less compounded, it appears that compound bilinguals and coordinate bilinguals may process words differently. On association tasks, for example, coordinates rely more on meaning, compounds, more on nonmeaning parameters such as language label or physical features. In list-learning tasks, coordinate bilinguals may learn more quickly via the visual modality, while compounds learn auditorily presented material better. Nonbalanced bilinguals are more likely to use different association strategies (phonetic or graphic elements in the stimulus item, translation) from those of balanced bilinguals (semantic strategies).

Linguistic input is processed for meaning in each language, regardless of the language of input, that is, semantic encoding is part of the usual procedure for processing language input, whereas language tagging is not. It is clear that words in one language, and their translation equivalents in the other (when such exist), are related in the brain in a nonrandom way, much as a word and its synonym in the same language may be connected in an associational network. This connection may be at a deep semantic level. At the same time, some independence of the two languages does occur, even in balanced bilinguals. In the lexical system, there is some independence for items that do not have precise translation equivalents. Different syntactic patterns serving the same function must also be stored somewhat independently for purposes of production. Likewise, we have seen, the productive phonological systems have a measure of dual (i.e., independent) organization.

Neuropsychological Aspects of Bilingualism

In the chapter on neuropsychological studies of bilingualism we considered those works relating to neuroanatomical and neurophysiological aspects of bilingualism. With respect to aphasia in polyglots, it would seem that the majority of bilingual aphasics lose and recover their separate languages in direct proportion to premorbid skill in each language. Many aphasics, however, have patterns of recovery which cannot be explained simply on the basis of extent of prior knowledge of the language. Alternative explanations are needed for this group.

The majority of single case studies of recovery from aphasia in polyglots show a diversity of recovery patterns. Most probably, this is due to the fact that the published cases were reported because they were unusual. Several explanations have been proposed to account for differential recovery patterns. We have discussed these in detail in Chapter 4. The explanations relate to which language was learned first, which language was used most recently, language of environment, affective factors, anatomical separation of languages, and degree of prior skill. No single rule can yet predict patterns of recovery in all the individual cases. This does not mean that patterns do not exist or that recovery patterns are totally random. Rather, there are many factors which contribute to the organization of the two languages in the brain of a bilingual, and it is as yet impossible to know or use these factors for prediction in a given case.

From our statistical analysis of clinical details of more than 100 polyglot aphasics (taken from our own observations and from cases reported in the literature), several points stand out. More aphasia was found following right hemispheric lesions in bilinguals (10%) than has been reported in monolinguals (1–2%). This argues for a greater right hemispheric contribution to language in bilinguals than in monolinguals. More aphasia was found in well-educated than in poorly educated bilinguals. (We wonder if there is a greater degree of left hemispheric lateralization for language in well-educated persons. If the poorly educated bilingual has greater cerebral ambilaterality for language than the well-educated bilingual, this fact may protect the poorly educated bilingual from aphasia.) Older (i.e., over age 60) bilingual aphasics were significantly less likely to follow the rule of Pitres, that the language used most recently returns first, than were younger bilinguals. (In this regard there is probably an interaction of declining memory in the aging person with patterns of recovery from aphasia.) Right-sided lesions were more likely than left-sided lesions to be associated with a differential recovery pattern.

In addition to the preceding studies of aphasics, we also found that brains of nonaphasic polyglots showed patterns of cerebral anatomy different from those of nonaphasic monolinguals; especially marked was a greater development of the third frontal gyrus and second temporal gyrus on the left, and the third frontal gyrus on the right. (We believe it would be reckless to generalize about anatomy from a handful of cases; however, the demonstrated anatomical differences are not without interest.)

Studies of experimental neuropsychology in bilingualism have used a variety of techniques. Evidence from reaction time tests, tachistoscopic and dichotic listening studies, and electroencephalographic studies have generally supported the following conclusions: The different languages may be organized differently in the brain of an individual bilingual. In particular, there may be differences in cerebral dominance that are not necessarily dependent on which language is learned first. Even in groups of fluent balanced bilinguals, performance on a variety of neuropsychological and neurolinguistic tests (e.g., tests of functional hemispheric asymmetry) may vary for each language.

In our own tachistoscopic study of Hebrew–English bilinguals conducted over a 2-year period (see pp. 167–193), we made a number of observations. Monolinguals and bilinguals and even different kinds of bilinguals have different relative degrees of cerebral dominance for perception of nonverbal material. In the bilingual the relative influence of cerebral dominance and reading habits (scanning patterns) on perception of written language varies with the language used and the degree of facility in that language. For Hebrew and English there is an asymmetrical pattern of cerebral dominance for language. It seems that the brain is "set up" differently for the learning of a second language, depending on which language is learned first. And, finally, again in this study, we saw that the learning of a second language at any age involves an active contribution of right hemispheric mechanisms.

Issues in the Field of Bilingualism

Chapter 5 was concerned with key issues in the field of bilingualism treated from a multidisciplinary point of view. In this summary we consider each issue as it appeared there.

BILINGUALISM VERSUS MONOLINGUALISM

Perceptual strategies of bilinguals differ from those of monolinguals. The bilingual seems to have mastery over the two different sets of skills or strategies which monolinguals use for each language. We do not mean, necessarily, to imply a perceptual advantage on the part of bilinguals. Rather, we would prefer to speak of differences in cognitive style. It is possible that the differences in perceptual strategy relate to differences in cerebral organization for language.

Bilinguals mature earlier than monolinguals both in terms of cerebral lateralization for language and in acquiring skills for linguistic abstraction. Bilinguals have better developed auditory language skills than monolinguals, but there is no clear evidence that they differ from monolinguals in written skills.

Even in adulthood bilinguals may continue to be more verbally skillful than monolinguals. The greater verbal skills may be attributed to many factors (e.g., greater practice effect on skills tested, perhaps). One of these factors may be that of cerebral organization for language, which seems to be more bilateral in the bilingual than in the monolingual.

DEGREES OF BILINGUAL PROFICIENCY

Evidence is presented to support the following conclusion: Not only does the fluent balanced bilingual have "more" of some skills that the unbalanced bilingual has yet to master, he has **different** processing strategies for the languages involved. We suggest, in addition, that the fluent bilingual speaker controls a wider range of processing strategies than does the nonfluent bilingual, and that these strategies permit optimal appreciation of the redundancies of a language.

Increasing fluency in a language seems to correlate with a shift from bilateral cerebral representation toward greater left hemispheric lateralization for that language.

INTERFERENCE AND TRANSFER

Not all language acquisition is explained by direct transfer of the structures of the prior language onto the second language. The learner may transfer to the task of learning a new language certain basic tools for language learning or predictions of what any language must be like, which permit her to grasp parts of the new language with native-like strategies.

Interference may obtain at all linguistic levels. Two different processes may both result in interference: a borrowing of constituent items, and the imposition of higher-level rules. Interference, for a given bilingual, may be different for each language, at various levels, and may obtain for perception as well as for production.

THE SWITCH MECHANISM

There is evidence to support the existence of an automatic input switch for perception and a semivoluntary output switch controlling production. Anatomical argument has been made that the switch may be located either in the area of the supramarginal or angular gyrus of the left hemisphere or in the dominant frontal lobe.

We do not accept this position. We would argue that a continuously operating monitor system, utilizing many parts of the brain, controls the processing of input in the bilingual much as in the monolingual. "Switching," then, is a constant activity in which choices of language, word, phrase, and so on, are continually being tested against their potential correctness. Such a monitor would work most efficiently by assigning priorities in interpretation and by being prepared to redirect decisions at any moment. Such a system could also constrain output to a single language while allowing borrowing of items and language switching where appropriate.

LANGUAGE SET

Language set cannot be altogether dissociated from the general notion of cognitive set. Nonetheless, a speaker perceives environmental and linguistic cues that aid his planning or ordering of priorities for the bilingual monitor system (see the preceding). This arrangement of priorities may be a definition of language set, specific to bilingualism.

LANGUAGE TAGS

The issue of language tagging is based on the question of how the fluent bilingual manages to speak only one language with only minimal mixing of another language. Secondarily, we may ask how the bilingual identifies incoming speech segments as belonging to one or the other of his languages, in order to process them according to the appropriate syntactic mechanisms. In each instance we must assume that there is some way of identifying language units as "belonging" to one or the other language. This identifying procedure, termed language tagging, is usually thought of as pertaining to the lexical system, but we have evidence that it may apply for distinctive phonemic and phonological units as well. In some sense those syntactic structures that occur in only one of the two languages must be "tagged" as pertaining to that language. At present we cannot determine whether this tagging involves a feature label associated with each individual item in question, whether it is achieved by contiguous anatomical storing of items within separate languages, or whether some other mechanism pertains.

TRANSLATION

The term **translation** can be used in two contexts. When we discuss the **skill of translation,** we emphasize that this is an "unnatural," trained or at least practiced, skill without which a fluent bilingual can get along. Good translation involves waiting to process phrase-length units. This may require inhibition of production of translation equivalents for specific lexical items. When we discuss translation equivalents, we must admit that the same lexical associative networks that a monolingual may demonstrate can be seen in the bilingual. For the bilingual, the network for a given item in one language may contain its translation equivalent (or near equivalent) in the other language, if such a term exists. As a result, on psycholinguistic tests of lexical skills such as association tests and list-learning tests, the translation equivalent of a word may be substituted for the word.

PERCEPTION AND PRODUCTION OF LANGUAGE

Although the perception and production systems must be connected to each other, there is evidence that they may function, at least in part, as two independent systems. This can be seen in three sorts of evidence. First, in language acquisition, some measure of comprehension must precede production. Second, in those situations in which a bilingual does not use a language for a period of time, the production system seems to suffer more than the perception or comprehension system. Third, we have demonstrated that, at least at the phonological level, the perceptual system of the bilingual is more unified, whereas the production system is more dual in nature.

LINGUISTIC LEVELS, CATEGORIES, AND MODALITIES

Several studies suggest that the phonological and semantic systems can be differentially affected or activated. For example, in Schvartz's (1954) classical conditioning paradigm, semantic associations were diminished when subjects were given chlorohydrate, whereas phonetic associations remained. On association tasks one can see different groups of bilinguals preferring different response strategies: Some (e.g., young children) will take advantage of phonological similarity while others (e.g., linguistically mature children) will rely on semantic similarities. Children will also make more syntagmatic associations, while adults and certain groups of bilinguals will make more paradigmatic ones. We may take these facts as evidence for "organizational" dissociation between different word categories in the bilinguistically mature individual.

The written modalities of language may be secondary to the auditory modalities, since one can be a fluent speaker of a language and yet be illiterate in it. Bilingual studies support this point, since auditory or visual systems may be selectively impaired in polyglot aphasia. Indeed, learning a second language through only its written system may facilitate return of that language in case of aphasia. In second language learners also, visual and auditory skills may progress with some degree of independence.

BILINGUAL LANGUAGE ACQUISITION

A young child who is exposed to more than one language is likely to develop an abstract attitude with respect to language at an earlier age than will a monolingual. This may correlate with earlier development of left lateralization for language in the bilingual child.

In the adult, second language acquisition will involve the right hemisphere as well as the left. Some linguistic strategies may be transferred from the earlier language, thus causing interference in the new language. Yet, in the adult as in the child, a certain sequence of mastering will transpire, based on structures inherent in the languages themselves.

COMPOUND AND COORDINATE BILINGUALISM

Although the notions of compound and coordinate may be difficult to define, they serve to remind us that acquisition parameters may influence the way in which a second language is organized in later life. Age of acquisition and manner of acquisition must be considered as factors influencing anatomical mechanisms for bilingualism. One must approach the issue of labeling an individual bilingual as compound or coordinate with caution, however. It is likely that certain systems (e.g., voice production, phonological perception, deep semantics) will be compound for all bilinguals, while other sytems (e.g., lexicon and syntax) will be coordinate to a greater or lesser extent.

LANGUAGE-SPECIFIC EFFECTS ON
CEREBRAL ORGANIZATION

Experimental studies and language acquisition studies suggest that language-specific structures may influence the eventual representation of a given language in the brain of the bilingual.

The acquisition studies document a "difficulty hierarchy" for acquiring specific structures in a given language. They note that this hierarchy is followed by native learners of that language and by second language learners, adult or child, regardless of what their first language is.

The experimental data in favor of language-specific effects include these findings:

1. Asymmetries in simultaneous translation, that is, translating from language A to B is different from translating from B to A;
2. The cerebral lateralization measures that suggest that asymmetrical hemispheric dominance may be brought about by language-specific factors. Particularly strong is the evidence that different orthographic systems (e.g., phonemic versus logographic, left-to-right versus right-to-left) may encourage different cerebral organization.

DIFFERENTIAL CEREBRAL LATERALIZATION

Four main points may be made:

1. Language organization in the brain of the average bilingual may be more bilateral than in that of a monolingual.
2. Patterns of cerebral dominance may be different for each language in the brain of a bilingual.
3. Differential cerebral lateralization for each language is not random but is influenced by many different factors, including age, manner, and modality of second language acquisition.
4. Cerebral dominance for language in the bilingual is not a rigid, predetermined, easily predicted phenomenon; it is, rather, a dynamic process, subject to variation throughout life and sensitive to environmental, especially educational, influences.

Speculative Suggestions

In summary, it would appear that learning a second language distinguishes the bilingual from the monolingual not only in language skills, but also in perceptual strategies and even in patterns of cerebral organization. If this is true, then certain consequences become apparent. We shall speak of three.

First, it would no longer be correct to accept the traditional dogma that the left hemisphere is necessarily dominant for language in right-handers. This doctrine was obtained from many years of study in monolinguals and it probably remains correct for most monolinguals.

Evidence from studies of bilingualism, however, suggests that the brain is a plastic, dynamic organ which continues to change throughout life as environmental (e.g., educational) stimuli impinge upon it. The right hemisphere may have as much capacity to acquire language in adulthood as it does in childhood. It may even be dominant for one of the languages of the bilingual. This may be related to the fact that the right hemisphere uses different strategies from those of the left for carrying out its linguistic functions. Even within the left hemisphere, as has been pointed out previously in studies of monolingual aphasics (Brown & Jaffe, 1975; Obler et al., 1978), patterns of cerebral organization for language may change throughout life.

Second, knowledge that cerebral organization for language differs for bilinguals and monolinguals may be useful therapeutically. It seems that the right hemisphere plays a major role in the learning of a second language. Perhaps a fruitful form of therapy for monolingual aphasics would be to teach them a second language (especially those aphasics who do not respond to traditional therapies in their usual language). We might predict, if this new approach to therapy were successful, either that the aphasic would learn the second language, or, alternatively, that the stimulation of the right hemisphere might serve as a "deblocking" technique to facilitate recovery of the patient's usual language.

Finally, the evidence presented in this book has implications for second language teaching. If it is true that the right hemisphere plays a major role in the acquisition of a second language, at any age, then it might be useful to develop a program of second language teaching that emphasizes so-called "right hemisphere strategies." For example, a second language might be more easily learned if it were taught through nursery rhymes, music, dance, or techniques emphasizing visuospatial skills.

Bibliography

Alajouanine, T., Pichot, P., & Durand, M. 1949. Dissociation des altérations phonétiques avec conservation relative de la langue la plus ancienne dans un cas d'anarthrie pure chez un sujet français bilingue. *L'Encephale, 38,* 245–265.

Alatis, J. (Ed.). 1970. *Bilingualism and language contact.* Washington, D.C.: Georgetown University Press.

Albert, M. 1975. Cerebral dominance and reading habits. *Nature, 256,* 403–404.

Albert, M., & Obler, L. 1975. Mixed polyglot aphasia. Paper presented at Academy of Aphasia, Victoria, B.C.

Anastasopoulos, G. 1959. Linkseitige Hemiplegie mit Alexie, Agraphie und Aphasie bei einem polyglotten Rechtshander. *Deutsche Zeitung fuer Nervenheilkunde, 179,* 120–144.

Anderson, N. (Ed.). 1968. *Studies in multilingualism.* Lyden: Brill.

Anisfeld, E. 1964. A comparison of the cognitive function of monolinguals and bilinguals. Unpublished doctoral dissertation, McGill University.

Anisfeld, M., Anisfeld, E., & Semogas, R. 1969. Cross-influence between the phonological system of Lithuanian–English bilinguals. *Journal of Verbal Learning and Verbal Behavior, 8,* 257–261.

Anisfeld, E., & Gordon, M. 1971. An effect of one German-language course on English. *Language and Speech, 14,* 289–292.

Anisfeld, E., & Lambert, W. 1964. Evaluational reactions of bilingual and monolingual children to spoken languages. *Journal of Abnormal and Social Psychology, 69,* 89–97.

255

Annett, M. 1964. A model of the inheritance of handedness and cerebral dominance. *Nature, 204,* 59–60.

Arkwright, T., & Vian, A. 1974. Les processus d'association chez les bilingues. *Working Papers in Bilingualism, 2,* 57–67.

Arsenian, S. 1937. Bilingualism and mental development. *Teachers College Contributions to Education No. 712.*

Arsenian, S. 1945. Bilingualism in the post-war world. *Psychological Bulletin, 42,* 65–86.

As, A. 1963. The recovery of forgotten language knowledge through hypnotic age regression: A case report. *American Journal of Clinical Hypnosis, 5,* 24–29.

Asayama, T. 1914. Ueber die Aphasie bei Japanern. *Deutsches Archiv fuer Klinische Medizin, 113,* 523.

Asher, J., & Garcia, L. 1969. The optimal age to learn a foreign language. *Modern Language Journal, 53,* 336–341.

Bailey, N., Madden, C., & Krashen, S. 1974. Is there a natural sequence in adult second language learning? *Language Learning, 24,* 235–243.

Bain, B. 1975a. Commentary: A Canadian education: Thoughts on bilingual education. *Journal of Canadian Studies, 10,* 57–62.

Bain, B. 1975b. Toward an integration of Piaget and Vygotsky: Bilingual considerations. *Linguistics: An International Review, 160,* 1–19.

Bain, B. 1976. Verbal regulation of cognitive processes: A replication of Luria's procedures with bilingual and unilingual infants. *Child Development,* Pp. 47, 543–546.

Balint, A. 1923. Bemerkungen zu einer Falle von polyglotter Aphasie. *Zeitschrift fuer die gesamte Neurologie und Psychiatrie, 83,* 277–283.

Barik, H. 1974. A look at simultaneous translation. *Working Papers in Bilingualism, 4,* 20–41.

Barton, M., Goodglass, H., & Shai, A. 1965. Differential recognition of tachistoscopically presented English and Hebrew words in right and left visual fields. *Perceptual and Motor Skills, 21,* 431–437.

Bastian, C. 1875. *On paralysis from brain disease in its common forms.* New York: Appleton.

Beardsmore, H. 1974. Development of the compound–coordinate distinction in bilingualism. *Lingua, 33,* 123–127.

Belgaev, B. 1964. *The psychology of teaching foreign languages.* New York: MacMillan.

Benton, A. 1969. Development of a multilingual aphasia battery: Progress and problems. *Journal of Neurological Science, 9,* 39–48.

Ben-Zeev, S. 1972. The influence of bilingualism on cognitive development and cognitive strategy. Unpublished doctoral dissertation, University of Chicago.

Berko, J. 1958. The child's learning of English morphology. *Word, 14,* 150–177.

Berlucchi, G., Heron, W., Hyman, R., Rizzolatti, G., & Umiltá, C. 1971. Simple RTs of ipsilateral and contralateral hand to lateralized visual stimuli. *Brain, 94,* 419–439.

Bernard, D. 1885. *De l'aphasie et de ses diverses formes.* Paris: Delahaye et Lecrosnier. P. 191.

Bertelson, P. 1972. Listening from left to right versus right to left. *Perception, 1,* 161–165.

Bianchi, L. 1886. Un caso di sordite verbale. *Rivista sperimentale di Freniatria, 12,* 57–71.

Bickerton, D. 1971. Cross-level interference: The influence of L_1 syllable structure on L_2 morphological errors. In G. Penen and J. Trin (Eds.), *Applications of linguistics.* Cambridge: Cambridge University Press.

Blumstein, S., Goodglass, H., & Tartter, V. 1975. The reliability of ear advantage in dichotic listening. *Brain and Language, 2,* 226–236.

Boller, F. 1973. Destruction of Wernicke's area without language disturbance. A fresh look at crossed aphasia. *Neuropsychologia, 11,* 243–246.

Bossard, J. 1945. The bilingual individual as a person. *American Sociological Review*, 10, 126–133.

Bourdin, C. 1877. Discussion sur l'aphasie. *Annales Médico-Psychologiques*, 17, 229–330.

Braine, L. 1968. Asymmetries of pattern perception observed in Israelis. *Neuropsychologia*, 6, 73–88.

Braun. 1937. Beobachtungen zur Frage der Mehrsprachigkeit. *Gottinische Gelehrte Unzeigen*, 119, 115–130.

Braun, L., & Klassen, B. 1973. A transfer material analysis of written syntactic structures of children representing varying ethno-linguistic communities. *Research in the Teaching of English*, 7, 312–323.

Broadbent, D. E. 1967. Notes on current knowledge concerning the psychology of learning modern languages. *Manpower and Applied Psychology*, 2, 148–157.

Brown, J., & Jaffe, J. 1975. Hypothesis on cerebral domance. *Neuropsychologia*, 13, 107–110.

Brown, J., & Wilson, R. 1973. Crossed aphasia in a dextral. A case report. *Neurology*, 23, 907–911.

Bryden, M. 1965. Tachistoscopic recognition, handedness, and cerebral dominance. *Neuropsychologia*, 3, 1–8.

Burling, R. 1959. Language development of a Garo and English speaking child. *Word*, 15, 45–68.

Buxbaum, E. 1949. The role of a second language in the formation of ego and superego. *International Journal of Psychiatry*, 18, 279–289.

Bychowski, Z. 1919. Ueber die Restitution der nach einem Schaedelschuss verlorgegungenen Sprachen bei einem Polyglotten. *Monatsschrift fuer Psychiatrie und Neurologie*, Bd. 45. Heft 4, 45, 183–201.

Cancino, H., Rosansky, E., & Schumann, J. 1974. Testing hypotheses about the nature of the second language learning process. *Working Papers on Bilingualism*, 3, 80–95.

Caramazza, A., Yeni-Komshian, G., Zurif, E., & Carbone, E. 1973. The acquisition of a new phonological contrast: The case of stop consonants in French–English bilinguals. *Journal of the Acoustical Society of America*, 54, 421–428.

Caramazza, A., Yeni-Komshian, G., & Zurif, E. 1974. Bilingual switching at the phonological level. *Canadian Journal of Psychology*, 28, 310–318.

Carmon, A., Nachshon, I., Isseroff, A., & Kleiner, M. 1972. Visual field differences in reaction times to Hebrew letters. *Psychonomic Science*, 28, 222–224.

Carmon, A., Nachshon, I., & Starinsky, R. 1976. Developmental aspects of visual hemifield differences in perception of verbal material. *Brain and Language*, 3, 463–469.

Carroll, J. 1961. Language acquisition, bilingualism, and language change. In S. Saporta, (Ed.), *Psycholinguistics: A book of readings*. New York: Holt, Rinehart, and Winston. Pp. 744–752.

Carrow, E. 1971. Comprehension of English and Spanish by preschool Mexican-American children. *Modern Language Journal*, 55, 299–306.

Carrow, M. 1957. Linguistic functioning of bilingual and unilingual children. *Journal of Speech and Hearing Disorders*, 2, 27–36.

Carrow, M. 1957. Linguistic functioning of bilingual and monolingual children. *Journal of Genetic Psychology*, 90, 143–150.

Champagnol, R. 1973. Organisation sémantique et linguistique dans le rappel libre bilingue. *Année Psychologique*, 73, 115–134.

Charcot, J. 1884. *Differente forme d'afasie*. Milan: Rummo (Ed.).

Charlton, M. 1964. Aphasia in bilingual and polyglot patients—a neurological and psychological study. *Journal of Speech and Hearing Disorders, 29*, 307–311.

Chlenov, L. 1948. Ob afazii u poliglotow. *Izvestiia Akademii Pedagogicheskikh Nauk RSFSR, 15*, 783–790.

Chomsky, C. 1969. *The acquisition of syntax in children from 5 to 10.* Cambridge, Mass.: MIT Press.

Clark, R. 1975. Adult theories, child strategies and their implications for the language teacher. In J. Allen & S. Corder (Eds.), *Papers in applied linguistics, Edinburgh course in applied linguistics*, Vol. 2. London: Oxford University Press. Pp. 291–347.

Clyne, M. 1968. Transference patterns among English and German bilinguals. *Review of the Institute of Applied Linguistics, Louvain, 2*, 5–18.

Clyne, M. 1969. Switching between language systems: *Actes du Xe Congrés International de Linguistes, 1*, 343–349.

Clyne, M. 1970a. Bilingual speech phenomena (with special reference to German–English bilinguals in Victoria). *Kivung, 3*, 99–111.

Clyne, M. 1970b. Some aspects of the bilingualism language maintenance of Australian-born children of German-speaking parents. *Review of the Institute of Applied Linguistics, Louvain, 9*, 35–47.

Cohen, S., Tucker, G., & Lambert, W. 1967. The comparative skills of monolinguals and bilinguals in perceiving phoneme sequences. *Language and Speech, 10*, 159–165.

Collins-Ahlgren, M. 1974. Teaching English as a second language to young deaf children: A case study. *Journal of Speech and Hearing Disorders, 39*, 486–499.

Cooper, R., & Greenfield, L. 1969. Word frequency estimation as a measure of degree of bilingualism. *Modern Language Journal, 53*, 163–166.

Coppola, A. 1928. L'afasia nei poliglotti e la simulazione nello 'Sconosciuto' di collegno. *Rivista di patologia nervosa e mentale, 33*, 359–393.

Critchley, M. 1974. Aphasia in polyglots and bilinguals. *Brain and Language, 1*, 15–27.

Cros, A. 1857. Recherches physiologiques sur la nature et la classification des facultés de l'intelligence et sur les fonctions spéciales des lobules antérieurs du cerveau. Unpublished doctoral dissertation, Paris 37.

Crothers, E., Suppes, P., & Weir, R. 1966. Latency phenomena in prolonged learning of visual representations of Russian sounds. *International Review of Applied Linguistics, 2*, 205–217.

Cummins, J. 1973. A theoretical perspective on the relationship between bilingualism and thought. *Working Papers in Bilingualism, 1*, 1–9.

Curtiss, S. 1977. *A psycholinguistic study of a modern day "wild child" Genie*: New York: Academic Press.

Czuchralski, J. 1971. Zur Sprachlichen Interferenz. *Linguistics, 67*, 5–15.

Dalrymple-Alford, E. 1967. Prestimulus language cuing and speed of identifying Arabic and English words. *Psychological Reports, 21*, 27–28.

Dalrymple-Alford, E., & Aamiry, A. 1969. Language and category clustering in bilingual free recall. *Journal of Verbal Learning and Verbal Behavior, 8, 6*, 762–768.

Dalrymple-Alford, E., & Aamiry, A. 1970. Word associations of bilinguals. *Psychonomic Science, 21*, 319–320.

Dalton, S. 1973. Language dominance and bilingual recall. *Journal of Psychology, 84*, 257–265.

D'Anglejan, A., & Tucker, G. 1973. Communicating across cultures: An empirical investigation. *Journal of Cross-Cultural Psychology, 4*, 122–130.

Darcy, N. 1953. A review of the literature on the effects of bilingualism upon the measurement of intelligence. *Journal of Genetic Psychology, 82*, 21–57.

Davine, M., Tucker, G., & Lambert, W. 1971. The perception of phoneme sequences by monolingual and bilingual elementary school children. *Canadian Journal of Behavioral Science, 3*, 72–76.

Davis, B., & Wertheimer, M. 1967. Some determinants of associations to French and English words. *Journal of Verbal Learning and Verbal Behavior, 6*, 574–581.

Dedić, S. 1926. Zur Aphasiefrage. *Zeitschrift fuer die gesamte Neurologie und Psychiatrie, 106*, 208–213.

DeGreve, M., & Van Passel, F. Quelques considérations sur le bilinguisme précoce. *Revue de l'Institut de Sociologie, Bruxelles, 10*, 125–136.

DeReuck, A., & O'Connor, M. (Eds.). 1964. *Disorders of language.* Boston: Little, Brown, and Co. Pp. 116–121, 248–250.

Diebold, A. 1961. Incipient bilingualism. *Language, 37*, 97–112.

Diebold, A. 1963. Code-switching in Greek–English bilingual speech. *Georgetown University Monograph Series of Language and Linguistics, 15*, 53–62.

Diebold, A. 1968. The consequences of early bilingualism in cognitive development and personality formation. In E. Norbeck, D. Price-Williams, & W. A. McCord (Eds.), *The study of personality: An interdisciplinary appraisal.* New York: Holt, Rinehart and Winston. Pp. 218–245.

Diller, K. 1970. "Compound" and "coordinate" bilingualism: A conceptual artifact. *Word, 26*, 254–261.

Diller, K. 1975. Criteria for adapting language teaching methods to the learning styles and abilities of students. Paper presented to the Fourth International Congress of Applied Linguistics, Stuttgart.

Dillon, R., McCormack, P., Petrusic, P., Cook, M., & Lafleur, L. 1973. Release from proactive interference in compound and coordinate bilinguals. *Bulletin of the Psychonomic Society, 2*, 293–294.

Dimitrijevic, D. 1940, Zur Frage der Sprachrestitution bei der Aphasie der Polyglotten. *Zeitschift fuer die gesamte Neurologie und Psychiatrie, 168*, 277–281.

Doob, L. 1957. The effect of language on verbal expression and recall. *American Anthropology, 59*, 88–100.

Dornic, S., Deneberg, G., & Hugglund, M. 1973. Visual search in dominant and nondominant languages. *Reports from the Institute of Applied Psychology, University of Stockholm, 37*, 10.

Dreifuss, F. 1961. Observations on aphasia in a polyglot poet. *Acta Psychiatrica Scandinavia, 36*, 91–97.

Dulay, H., & Burt, M. 1974a. Errors and strategies in child second language acquisition. *TESOL Quarterly, 8*, 129–136.

Dulay, H., & Burt, M. 1974b. Natural sequences in child second language acquisition. *Language Learning, 24*, 37–53.

Dulay, H., & Burt M. 1974c. A new perspective on the creative construction process in child second language acquisition. *Language Learning, 24*, 253–278.

Dyer, F. N. 1971. Color naming interference in monolinguals and bilinguals with matching and nonmatching interfering and naming languages. *Journal of Verbal Learning and Verbal Behavior, 10*, 297–302.

Emeneau, M. 1962. Bilingualism and structural borrowing. *Proceedings of the American Society, 106*, 430–442.

Entwisle, D., Forsyth, D., & Muus, R. 1964. The syntactic–paradigmatic shift in children's word associations. *Journal of Verbal Learning and Verbal Behavior, 3*, 19–29.

Epstein, I. 1916. *La pensée et la polyglossie; essai psychologique et didactique.* Lausanne: Payot.

Ervin, S. 1961a. Learning and recall in bilinguals. *American Journal of Psychology, 74,* 446–451.

Ervin, S. 1961b. Semantic shift in bilingualism. *American Journal of Psychology, 74,* 233–241.

Ervin, S. 1964. Language and TAT content in bilinguals. *Journal of Abnormal and Social Psychology, 68,* 500–507.

Ervin, S., & Landar, H. 1963. Navaho word associations. *American Journal of Psychology, 76,* 49–57.

Ervin, S., & Osgood, C. 1954a. Psycholinguistics: A survey of theory and research problems. In C. Osgood & T. Sebeok (Eds.), *Psycholinguistics.* Baltimore: Waverly Press.

Ervin, S., & Osgood, C. 1954b. Second language learning and bilingualism. *Journal of Abnormal and Social Psychology,* Supplement, 49, 139–146.

Ervin-Tripp, S. 1974. Is second language learning like the first? *TESOL Quarterly, 8,* 111–127.

Eskridge, J. 1896. Mind and word deafness after depressed fracture of the skull with subcortical hemorrhage-operation; complete recovery. *Medical News, 68,* 699–702.

Evers, K. 1970. The effects of bilingualism on the recall of words presented aurally. Dissertation, University of Minnesota. *Dissertation Abstracts,* 5197 A.

Fantini, A. 1977. *Language acquisition of a bilingual child: A sociolinguistic perspective (to age five).* Brattleboro, Vt.: Experiment Press.

Favez-Boutonier, J. 1967. Language. *Bulletin de Psychologie, 20,* 1378–1381.

Fearey, M. 1977. The formal evolution of the *tuyug* genre: Discourse structure in a bilingual poet. Paper presented at Harvard University.

Ferguson, C. 1959. Diglossia. *Word, 15,* 325–340.

Fishman, J. 1967. Bilingualism with and without diglossia; diglossia with and without bilingualism. *Journal of Social Issues, 23,* 29–68.

Fishman, J. 1969. Bilingualism in the barrio. *Modern Language Journal, 53,* 151–185.

Fishman, J., & Cooper, R. 1969. Alternative measures of bilingualism. *Journal of Verbal Learning and Verbal Behavior, 8,* 276–282.

Florenskaja, J. 1940. Sluczaj rasstorojstva rechi pri organicheskem zabolewanii s korsakovskim sindromen. *Trudy Tsentral 'nogo Instituta Psikhologii, 1,* 333–346.

Forster, K. 1970. Visual perception of rapidly presented word sequences of varying complexity. *Perception and Psychophysics, 8,* 215–221.

Forster, K. In press. Sentence completion in left- and right-branching languages. *Journal of Verbal Learning and Verbal Behavior.*

Forster, K., & Clyne, M. 1968. Sentence construction in German–English bilinguals. *Language and Speech, 11,* 113–119.

Forster, L. 1970. *The poet's tongues: Multilingualism in literature.* Cambridge-Otago: Cambridge University Press.

Fredman, M. 1975. The effect of therapy given in Hebrew on the home language of the bilingual or polyglot adult aphasic in Israel. *British Journal of Disorders of Communication, 10,* 61–69.

Freud, S. 1953. *On aphasia. A critical study* (E. Stengel, Ed. and trans.). New York: International University Press. (Originally published, 1891.) p. 60

Fromkin, V., Krashen, S., Curtiss, S., Rigler, D., & Rigler, M. 1974. The development of language in Genie: A case of language acquisition beyond the "critical period." *Brain and Language, 1,* 81–107.

Fromm, E. 1970. Age regression with unexpected reappearance of a repressed childhood language. *International Journal of Clinical and Experimental Hypnosis, 18,* 79–88.

Fudin, R. 1969. Critique of Heron's directional-reading conflict theory of scanning. *Perceptual and Motor Skills, 29,* 271–296.

Gali, A. 1928. Comment mésurer l'influence de bilinguisme. In *Le bilinguisme et l'éducation, travaux de la conférence internationale tenue à Luxembourg du 2 au 5 avril 1928.* Génève International d'Éducation. Luxembourg: Maison du Livre. Pp. 123–136.

Galstyan, Y. 1970. O uzaimootrushenii sistem rudnogo: Izuchaemugo yazykou pri duuyazychii [On interferences between the native and foreign language system in bilingualism], Russki Yazyk Acmyan. *Shkole, 14,* 28–38.

Gardner, R. & Lambert, W. 1959. Language aptitude, intelligence and second language acquisition. *Canadian Journal of Psychology, 13,* 266–272.

Gardner, R., & Lambert, W. 1965. Language aptitude, intelligence and second language achievement. *Journal of Educational Psychology, 56,* 191–199.

Garnes, S. 1977. Effects of bilingualism on perception. In O. Garnica (Ed.), *Papers on psycholinguistics and sociolinguistics.* Columbus, Ohio: Department of Linguistics. Ohio State University. Pp. 1–10.

Gekoski, W. 1969. Associative and translation habits of bilinguals as a function of language acquisition context. *Dissertation Abstracts,* University of Michigan, *30* (1-b), 404–405.

Gekoski, W. 1970. Effects of language acquisition contexts on semantic processing in bilinguals. *Proceedings of the Annual Convention of the American Psychological Association, 5,* 487–488.

Genesee, F., Hamers, J., Lambert, W., Mononen, L., Seitz, M., & Starck, R. 1978. Language processing in bilinguals. *Brain and Language, 5,* 1–12.

Gergely, J. 1970. Megfigyelesek a Franciaorszagban clo magyarok [Observations on the Hungarian spoken by Hungarians living in France]. *Magyar Nylev, 66,* 367–373.

Gerson, A., & Schweitzer, D. 1972. Linguistic regression in the multilingual psychotic. *Perspectives in Psychiatric Care, 10,* 236–237.

Gerstenbrand, F., & Stephan, H. 1956. Polyglotte Reaktion nach Hirnschedigung; ein kasnistischer Beitrag. *Wiener Zeitschrift fuer Nervenheilkunde, 13,* 167–172.

Gerver, D. 1974a. The effects of noise on the performance of simultaneous interpreters. *Acta Psychologica, 38,* 159–167.

Gerver, D. 1974b. Simultaneous listening and speaking and retention of prose. *Quarterly Journal of Experimental Psychology, 26,* 337–341.

Glanzer, M., & Duarte, A. 1971. Repetition between and within languages in free recall. *Journal of Verbal Learning and Verbal Behavior, 10,* 6, 625–630.

Gloning, I., & Gloning, K. 1965. Aphasien bei polyglotten. *Wiener Zeitschrift fuer Nervenheilkunde, 22,* 362–397.

Godkewitsch, M. 1972. The role of language habits in understanding letter sound sequences. *Journal of Experimental Psychology, 95,* 63–65.

Goggin, J., & Wickens, D. 1971. Proactive interference and language change in short-term memory. *Journal of Verbal Learning and Verbal Behavior, 10,* 453–458.

Goldblum, Z. 1928. Nach Treparation aufgetretene motor(ische) Aphasie (Hypolalie) mit Restitution bei progressive wachsenden Endotheliom im linken Zentrofrontallappen. *Schweizer Archiv fuer Neurologie und Psychiatrie, 22,* 227–268.

Goldman-Eisler, F. 1972. Segmentation of input in simultaneous translation. *Journal of Psycholinguistic Research, 1,* 127–139.

Goldman-Eisler, F., & Cohen, M. 1974. An experimental study of interference between receptive and productive processes relating to simultaneous translation. *Language and Speech, 17,* 1–10.

Goldstein, K. 1933. L'analyse de l'aphasie et l'étude de l'essence du langage. *Journal de Psychologie Normale et Pathologique, 30,* 430–496.

Goldstein, K. 1948. *Language and language disturbances.* New York: Grune and Stratton.

Goodglass, H., & Quadfasel, F. 1954. Language laterality in left-handed aphasics. *Brain, 77,* 521–548.

Gorlitzer, V. 1959. Ein 94 jahriger mit einem deutschen Sprachzentrum und mit wahrscheinlich slowenischen Sprachzentren. *Wiener Medizinische Wochenschrift, 109,* 358.

Graham, R. 1956. Widespread bilingualism and the creative writer. *Word, 12,* 369–381.

Grasset, J. 1884. Contribution clinique à l'étude des aphasies. *Montpellier Médical,* janvier. 33–34.

Greene, J., & Zirkel, P. 1974. The use of parallel testing of aural ability as an indication of bilingual dominance. *Psychology in the Schools, 11,* 51–55.

Greenson, R. 1950. The mother tongue and the mother. *International Journal of Psychiatry, 31,* 18–23.

Guiora, A., Brannon, R., & Dull, C. 1972. Empathy and second language learning. *Language and Learning, 22,* 111–130.

Gumperz, J. 1967. On the linguistic markers of bilingual communications. *Journal of Social Issues, 23,* 48–57.

Gumperz, J. 1973. The communicative competence of bilinguals: Some hypotheses and suggestions for research. *Language in Society, 2,* 143–154.

Hakuta, K. 1974. A preliminary report on the development of grammatical morphemes in a Japanese girl learning English as a second language. *Working Papers in Bilingualism, 3,* 18–38.

Hallowell, A. 1951. Cultural factors in the structuralization of perception. In J. Rohrer & M. Sherif (Eds.), *Social psychology at the crossroads.* New York: Harper & Row. Pp. 164–195.

Halpern, L. 1941. Beitrag zur Restitution der Aphasie bei Polyglotten im Hinblick auf das Hebraeische. *Schweizer Archiv fuer Neurologie und Psychiatrie, 47,* 150–154.

Halpern, L. 1949. La langue hébraïque dans la restitution de l'aphasie sensorielle chez les polyglottes. *Semaine des Hôpitaux de Paris, 58,* 2473–2476.

Halpern, L. 1950. Observations on sensory aphasia and its restitution in a Hebrew polyglot. *Monatschrift fuer Psychiatrie und Neurologie, 119,* 156–173.

Hamagan, E., Markmar, B., Pelletier, S., & Tucker, R. 1976. Differences in performance in elicited imitation between French monolingual and English-speaking bilingual children. *Working Papers on Bilingualism, 8,* 30–58.

Hamers, J. 1973. Interdependent and independent states of the bilingual's two languages. Unpublished doctoral dissertation, McGill University.

Hamers, J., & Lambert, E. 1974. Bilingual's reactions to cross-language semantic ambiguity. Unpublished research report, McGill University.

Hamers, J., & Lambert, W. 1972. Bilingual interdependencies in auditory perception. *Journal of Verbal Learning and Verbal Behavior, 11,* 303–310.

Hamers, J., & Lambert, W. 1977. Visual field and cerebral hemisphere preferences in bilinguals. In S. Segalowitz & F. Gruber (Eds.), *Language development and neurological theory.* New York: Academic Press.

Harcum, E. 1966. Visual hemifield differences as conflicts in direction of reading. *Journal of Experimental Psychology, 72,* 479–480.

Harcum, E., & Finkel, M. 1963. Explanation of Mishkin and Forgays result as a directional reading conflict. *Canadian Journal of Psychology, 17,* 224–234.

Harris, M., & Hassemer, W. 1972. Some factors affecting the complexity of children's sentences: The effects of modelling, age, sex, and bilingualism. *Journal of Experimental Child Psychology, 13,* 447–455.

Hartnett, D. 1974. The relation of cognitive style and hemispheric preference to deductive and inductive second language learning. Master's thesis, University of California, Los Angeles.

Hasselmo, N. 1969. How can one measure the effects which one language may have on the other in the speech of bilinguals? In M. Kelly (Ed.), *Description and measurement of bilingualism: An international seminar, University of Moncton, June 6–14, 1967.* Toronto: University of Toronto Press.

Haugen, E. 1950. The analysis of linguistic borrowing. *Language, 26,* 210–231.

Haugen, E. 1954. Some pleasures and problems of bilingual research. *International Journal of American Linguistics, 20,* 116–122.

Haugen, E. 1956. *Bilingualism in the Americas: A bibliography and research guide,* Publication No. 26 of the American Dialect Society. University, Alabama: University of Alabama Press.

Haugen, E. 1974. Bilingualism, language contact, and immigrant languages in the United States: A research report 1956–1970. *Current Trends in Linguistics, 10,* The Hague: Mouton.

Hécaen, H., & Ajuriaguerra, J. 1963. *Les gauchers.* Paris: Presses Universitaires de France.

Hécaen, H., & Albert, M. 1978. *Human neuropsychology.* New York: Wiley.

Hécaen, H., Mazars, G., Ramier, A., Goldblum, M., & Merienne, L. 1971. Aphasie croissée chez un sujet droitier bilingue (Vietnamien–français). *Revue Neurologique, 124,* 319–323.

Hécaen, H., & Saguet, J. 1971. Cerebral dominance in left-handed subjects. *Cortex, 7,* 19–48.

Hegler, C. 1931. Zur aphasie bei polyglotten. *Deutsche Zeitschrift fuer Nervenheilkunde, 117,* 236–239.

Heras, I., & Nelson, K. 1972. Retention of semantic, syntactic, and language information by young bilingual children. *Psychonomic Science, 29,* 391–392.

Heron, W. 1957. Perception as a function of retinal locus and attention. *American Journal of Psychology, 70,* 38–48.

Herschmann, H., & Poetzl, O. 1920. Bemerkungen ueber die Aphasie der polyglotten. *Neurologisches Zentralblatt, 39,* 114–120.

Hickey, T. 1972. Bilingualism and the measurement of intelligence and verbal learning ability. *Exceptional Children, 39,* 24–28.

Hill, J. 1970. Foreign accents, language acquisition and cerebral dominance revisited. *Language Learning, 20,* 237–248.

Hinshelwood, J. 1902. Four cases of word-blindness. *Lancet, 1,* 358–363.

Hoenigswald, H. 1962. Bilingualism, presumable bilingualism and diachrony. *Anthropological Linguistics, 4,* 1–5.

Hoff, H., & Poetzl, O. 1932. Ueber die Aphasie eines zweisprachigen Linkshaenders. *Wiener Medizinische Wochenschrift, 82,* 369–373.

Hoffman, N. 1934. The measurement of bilingual background. In *Contributions to education.* New York: Bureau of Publications, Teachers College, Columbia University, 623–675.

Hofman, S., Shapira, T., & Streifler, M. 1975. Sinistrad mirror writing and reading after brain concussion in a bi-systemic (oriento–occidental) polyglot. Mimeographed paper.

Hornby, P. (Ed.). 1977. *Bilingualism: Psychological, social, and educational implications.* New York: Academic Press.

Ianco-Worrall, A. 1972. Bilingualism and cognitive development. *Child Development*, *43*, 1390–1400.

Imedadze, N. 1967. On the psychological nature of child speech formation under condition of exposure to two languages. *International Journal of Psychology*, *2*, 129–132.

Impellizzeri, I. 1970. Use of the verbal summator technique with language and non-language majors in college. *Journal of General Psychology*, *83*, 143–149.

Ingram, E. 1975. Psychology and language learning. In J. Allen & S. Corder (Eds.), *Papers in applied linguistics, The Edinburgh Course in Applied Linguistics* (Vol. 2). London: Oxford University Press. Pp. 218–289.

Isserroff, A., Carmon, A., & Nachshon, I. 1974. Dissociation of hemifield reaction time differences from verbal stimulus directionality. *Journal of Experimental Psychology*, *103*, 145–149.

Jakobovits, L. 1968a. Dimensionality of compound–coordinate bilingualism. *Language Learning*, *3*, 29–56.

Jakobovits, L. 1968b. Implications of recent psycholinguistic developments for the teaching of a second language. *Language Learning*, *18*, 89–109.

Jakobovits, L. 1969. Second language learning and transfer theory: A theoretical assessment. *Language Learning*, *19*, 55–86.

Jakobovits, L. 1970. *Foreign language learning, a psycholinguistic analysis of the issues*. Rowley, Mass.: Newbury House.

Jakobovits, L., & Lambert, W. 1961. Semantic satiation among bilinguals. *Journal of Experimental Psychology*, *62*, 576–582.

Johnson, G. 1953. Bilingualism as measured by a reaction-time technique and the relationship between a language and a non-language intelligence quotient. *Journal of Genetic Psychology*, *82*, 3–9.

Johnson, N. 1974. Zombies and other problems: Theory and method in research on bilingualism. *Language Learning*, *24*, 105–133.

Jones, R. 1966. Situational vocabulary. *International Review of Applied Linguistics*, *4*, 165–173.

Jones, W. 1959. *Bilingualism and intelligence*. Cardiff: University of Wales Press.

Junge, B. 1972. The effects of bilingualism on selected verbal learning tasks. *Dissertation Abstracts International*, *33*, *(4-A)*, 1516.

Kainz, F. 1956. *Linguistisches und sprachpathologisches zur Problem der Sprachlichen Fehllenstrungen Sitzungsheriche der Oesterreichischen Akademie der Wissenschaften*. Philosophisch–historische 230, 1–134.

Kauders, O. 1929. Ueber polyglotte Reaktionen bei einer sensorischen Aphasie. *Zeitschrift fuer die gesamte Neurologie und Psychiatrie*, *122*, 651–666.

Kausler, D., & Kollasch, S. 1970. Bilingual verbal discrimination transfer: Implications for verbal discrimination theory. Paper presented at the Annual Meeting of Psychonomic Society, San Antonio.

Keets, D., & Keats, J. 1974. The effect of language on concept acquisition in bilingual children. *Journal of Cross-Cultural Psychology*, *5*, 80–99.

Keiting, G. 1973. A comparison of four methods of teaching word recognition to bicultural, bilingual adults. *Dissertation Abstracts International*, *33*, *(7-A)*, 3242.

Kellaghan, J., & Macnamara, J. 1967. Reading in a second language. In M. Jenkinson (Ed.), *Reading instruction: An international forum*. Newark, Delaware: International Reading Association. Pp. 231–240.

Kelly, L. (Ed.). 1969. *Description and measurement of bilingualism: An international seminar, University of Moncton, June 6–14, 1967*. Toronto: University of Toronto Press.

Kelly, M., Tenezakis, M., & Huntsman, R. 1973. Some unusual conservation behavior in children exposed to two cultures. *British Journal of Educational Psychology, 43,* 181–182.

Kenyeres, A. 1938. Comment une petite Hongroise de sept ans apprend le français. *Archives de Psychologie, 26,* 321–366.

Kershner, J., & Jeng, A. 1972. Dual functional hemispheric asymmetry in visual perception; effects of ocular dominance and post exposural processes. *Neuropsychologia, 10,* 437–445.

Kessler, C. 1971. *The acquisition of syntax in bilingual children.* Washington, D.C.: Georgetown University Press.

Kessler, C. 1972. Syntactic contrasts in child bilingualism. *Language Learning, 22,* 221–233.

Kimura, D. 1961. Cerebral dominance and the perception of verbal stimuli. *Canadian Journal of Psychology, 15,* 166–171.

Kimura, D. 1973. The asymmetry of the human brain. *Scientific American, 228,* 70–78.

Kinsbourne, M. 1974. Direction of gaze and distribution of cerebral thought processes. *Neuropsychologia, 12,* 279–281.

Kinsbourne, M., & Cohen, V. 1971. English and Hebrew consonant memory span related to the structure of the written language. *Acta Psychologica, 35,* 347–351.

Kintsch, W. 1970. Recognition memory in bilingual subjects. *Journal of Verbal Learning and Verbal Behavior, 9,* 405–409.

Kintsch, W., & Kintsch, E. 1969. Interlingual interference and memory processes. *Journal of Verbal Learning and Verbal Behavior, 8,* 16–19.

Kinzel, P. 1964. *Lexical and grammatical interference in the speech of a bilingual child.* Seattle: University of Washington Press.

Kirstein, B., & de Vincenz, A. 1974. A note on bilingualism and generative grammar. *International Review of Applied Linguistics, 12,* 159–161.

Kline, C., & Lee, N. 1972. A transcultural study of dyslexia: Analysis of language disabilities in 277 Chinese children simultaneously learning to read and write in English and in Chinese. *Journal of Special Education, 6,* 9–26.

Kolers, P. 1963. Interlingual word associations. *Journal of Verbal Learning and Verbal Behavior, 2,* 291–300.

Kolers, P. 1965. Bilingualism and bicodalism. *Language and Speech, 8,* 122–126.

Kolers, P. 1966. Reading and talking bilingually. *American Journal of Psychology, 79,* 357–376.

Kolers, P. 1968. Bilingualism and information processing. *Scientific American,* March, 78–86.

Kovac, D. 1967. Psychological aspects of multi-lingualism. *Pszichologiai Tamulmanyok, 10,* 51–58.

Kovac, D. 1969. Command of several languages as a psychological problem. *Studies of Psychological Problems, 11,* 249–258.

Krapf, E. 1957. A propos des aphasies chez les polyglottes. *Encéphale, 46,* 623–629.

Krashen, S. 1973. Lateralization, language learning, and the critical period: Some new evidence. *Language Learning, 23,* 63–74.

Krashen, S. 1975. Additional dimensions of the deductive/inductive controversy. *Modern Language Journal, 59,* 440–441.

Kuo, E. 1974. The family and bilingual socialization; a sociolinguistic study of a sample of Chinese children in the United States. *Journal of Social Psychology, 92,* 181–191.

Lambert, E. 1955. Measurement of linguistic dominance of bilinguals. *Journal of Abnormal and Social Psychology, 50,* 2, 197–200.

Lambert, W. 1956a. Developmental aspects of second-language acquisition. *Journal of Social Psychology, 43,* 83–89.

Lambert, W. 1956b. Developmental aspects of second-language acquisition: II. Associational stereotype, associational form, vocabulary commonness, and pronunciation. *Journal of Social Psychology, 43,* 91–98.

Lambert, W. 1956c. Developmental aspects of second-language acquisition: III. *Journal of Social Psychology, 43,* 99–104.

Lambert, W. 1969. Psychological studies of the interdependencies of the bilingual's two languages. In J. Puhvel (Ed.), *Substance and Structure of Language.* Berkeley: University of California Press. Pp. 99–125.

Lambert, W., & Fillenbaum, S. 1959. A pilot study of aphasia among bilinguals. *Canadian Journal of Psychology, 13,* 28–34.

Lambert, W., Gardner, R., Barik, H., & Tunstall, K. 1962. Attitudinal and cognitive aspects of intensive study of second language. *Journal of Abnormal and Social Psychology, 66,* 358–368.

Lambert, W., Havelka, J., & Crosby, D. 1958. The influence of language-acquisition contexts on bilingualism. *Journal of Abnormal and Social Psychology, 56,* 239–243.

Lambert, W., Havelka, J., & Gardner, R. 1959. Linguistic manifestations of bilingualism. *American Journal of Psychology, 72,* 77–82.

Lambert, W., Ignatow, M., & Krauthammer, M. 1968. Bilingual organization in free recall. *Journal of Verbal Learning and Verbal Behavior, 7,* 207–214.

Lambert, W., Just, M., & Segalowitz, N. 1970. Some cognitive consequences of following the curricula of the early school grades in a foreign language. In J. Alatis (Ed.), *Monograph series on languages and linguistics.* Washington D.C.: Georgetown University Press. Pp. 229–262.

Lambert, W., & Preston, M. 1967. The interdependencies of the bilingual's two languages. In K. Salzinger & S. Salzinger (Eds.), *Research on verbal behavior and some neurological implications.* New York: Academic Press. Pp. 115–120.

Lambert, W., & Rawlings, C. 1969. Bilingual processing of mixed-language associative networks. *Journal of Verbal Learning and Verbal Behavior, 8,* 604–609.

Lamonthe, P. C. 1974. Semantic generalizations in French and English bilinguals. *Canadian Journal of Behavioral Science, 6,* 414–419.

Lashley, K. 1923. *Brain Mechanisms and Intelligence,* Chicago: University of Chicago Press.

Lawson, E. 1967. Attention and simultaneous translation. *Language and Speech, 10,* 29–35.

Lebrun, Y. 1971. The neurology of bilingualism. *Word, 27,* 179–186.

Lebrun, Y. 1976. Recovery in polyglot aphasics. In Y. Lebrun and R. Hoops (Eds.), *Recovery in aphasics.* Amsterdam: Swets and Zeitlinger, B.V.

Lecours, A. R., & Lhermitte, F. 1976. The "pure form" of the phonetic disintegration syndrome ("pure anarthria"); anatomo-clinical report of a historical case. *Brain and Language, 3,* 88–113.

Lehiste, I. 1970. Grammatical variability and the differences between native and non-native speakers. *Working Papers in Linguistics, Ohio State University, 4,* 85–94.

Leischner, A. 1948. Ueber die Aphasie der Mehrsprachigen. *Archiv fuer Psychiatrie und Nervenkrankheiten, 180,* 118–180, 731–775.

Lenneberg, E. 1967. *Biological Foundations of Language.* New York: John Wiley.

Leopold, W. 1939–1949. *Speech Development of a Bilingual Child* (4 vols.). Evanston, Ill.: Northwestern Press.

Lerea, L., & LaPorta, R. 1971. Vocabulary and pronunciation acquisition among bilinguals and monolinguals. *Language and Speech, 14,* 293–300.

Levinson, B. 1960. Comparative study of verbal and performance ability of monolingual and bilingual native born Jewish children of traditional parentage. *Journal of Genetic Psychology, 97,* 93–112.

L'Hermitte, R., Hécaen, H., Dubois, J., Culioli, A., & Tabouret-Keller, A. 1966. Le probleme de l'aphasie des polyglottes: Remarques sur quelques observations. *Neuropsychologia, 4,* 315–329.

Liedtke, W., & Nelson, L. 1968. Concept formation and bilingualism. *Alberta Journal of Educational Research, 14,* 225–232.

Liepmann, D., & Saegert, J. 1974. Language tagging in bilingual free recall. *Journal of Experimental Psychology, 103,* 1137–1141.

Lisker, L., & Abramson, A. 1964. A cross-language study of voicing in initial stops: Acoustical measurements. *Word, 20,* 384–422.

Lopez, M., Hicks, R., & Young, R. 1974. Retroactive inhibition in a bilingual $A-B$, $A'-B'$ paradigm. *Journal of Experimental Psychology, 103,* 85–90.

Lopez, M., & Young, R. 1974. The linguistic interdependence of bilinguals. *Journal of Experimental Psychology, 102,* 981–983.

Luria, A. R. 1960. Differences between disturbance of speech and writing in Russian and French. *International Journal of Slavic Linguistics and Poetics, 3,* 13–22.

Lyman, R., Kwan, S., & Chao, W. 1938. Left occipito-parietal brain tumor. *The Chinese Medical Journal, 54,* 491–516.

MacKay, D. 1970. How does language familiarity influence stuttering under delayed auditory feedback? *Perceptual and Motor Skills, 30,* 655–669.

MacKay, D., & Bowman, R. 1969. On producing the meaning in sentences. *American Journal of Psychology, 82,* 23–39.

Mackey, W. 1953. Bilingualism and linguistic structure. *Culture, 14,* 143–149.

Mackey, W. 1962. The description of bilingualism. *Canadian Journal of Linguistics, 7,* 51–85.

Mackey, W. 1965. Bilingual interference; its analysis and measurement. *Journal of Communication, 15,* 239–249.

Mackey, W. 1966. The measurement of bilingual behavior. *Canadian Psychologist, 7,* 75–92.

Macnamara, J. 1967a. The bilingual's linguistic performance: A psychological overview. *Journal of Social Issues, 23,* 58–77.

Macnamara, J. 1967b. The linguistic independence of bilinguals. *Journal of Verbal Learning and Verbal Behavior, 6,* 729–736.

Macnamara, J. 1967c. Problems of bilingualism. *Journal of Social Issues, 23,* 58–77.

Macnamara, J. 1969. How can one measure the extent of a person's bilingual proficiency? In L. Kelly (Ed.), *Description and measurement of bilingualism: An international seminar, University of Moncton, June 6–14, 1967.* Toronto: University of Toronto Press. Pp. 80–97.

Macnamara, J. 1970. Comparative studies of reading and problem-solving in two languages. *TESOL Quarterly, 4,* 107–116.

Macnamara, J., Feltin, N., Hew, M., & Klein, M. 1968. An analytic comparison of reading in two languages. *Irish Journal of Education, 2,* 41–53.

Macnamara, J., Krauthammer, M., & Bolgar, M. 1968. Language switching in bilinguals as a function of stimulus and response uncertainty. *Journal of Experimental Psychology, 78,* 208–215.

Macnamara, J., & Kushnir, S. 1971. Linguistic independence of bilinguals: The input switch. *Journal of Verbal Learning and Verbal Behavior*, 10, 480–487.

Major, R. 1977. Phonological differentiation of a bilingual child, in O. Garnica (Ed.), *Papers in psycholinguistics and sociolinguistics*. Columbus, Ohio. Department of Linguistics, Ohio State University, Pp. 88–123.

Massad, C., Yamamoto, K., & Davis, O. 1970. Stimulus modes and language media: A study of bilinguals. *Psychology in the Schools*, 7, 38–42.

McGlone, J. 1976. Sex differences in functional brain asymmetry. *Research Bull.*, 378, Department of Psychiatry, University of Western Ontario.

Meillet, A. 1934. Le bilinguisme des hommes cultivés. *Conférences de l'Institut de Linguistique de l'Université de Paris*, 2, 5–8.

Middleman, F. 1969. Linguistic relativity in psychotherapy. *Comprehensive Psychiatry*, 10, 31–43.

Milner, E., Taylor, L., & Sperry, R. 1968. Lateralized suppression in presented digits after commissural section in man. *Science*, 161, 184–186.

Minkowski, M. 1926. Ueber den gegenwaertigen Stand der Aphasiefrage. *Schweizer Archiv fuer Neurologie und Psychiatrie*, 18, 328–342.

Minkowski, M. 1927. Klinischer beitrag zur Aphasie bei Polyglotten, speziel im Hinblick auf des Schweizerdeutsch. *Schweizer Archiv fuer Neurologie und Psychiatrie*, 21, 43–72.

Minkowski, M. 1928. Sur un cas d'aphasie chez un polyglotte. *Review of Neurology*, 35, 361–366.

Minkowski, M. 1933. Sur un trouble aphasique particulier chez un polyglotte. *Revue Neurologique*, 40, 1185–1189.

Minkowski, M. 1936. Sur des variétés particulières d'aphasie chez des polyglottes. *Schweizerische Medizinische Wochenshrift*, 2, 697–699.

Minkowski, M. 1949. Sur un cas particulier d'aphasie avec des réactions polyglottes de fabulation et d'autres troubles après un traumatisme cranio-cerebral. *Comptes rendus du Congrès des Méd. Alien. et Neurol. de France*, Clermont-Ferrand-Neiisles-Brains. Pp. 315–328.

Minkowski, M. 1963. On aphasia in polyglots. In L. Halpern (Ed.), *Problems of dynamic neurology*. Jerusalem: Hebrew University. Pp. 119–161.

Minkowski, M. 1964. Sur un nouveau cas d'aphasie avec des réactions polyglottes particulières. *Comptes rendus du Congrès de Psychiatrie et de Neurologie de Langue Française*, Marseilles. Pp. 1264–1274.

Minkowski, M. 1965. Considérations sur l'aphasie des polyglottes. *Revue Neurologique*, 112, 486–495.

Mishkin, M., & Forgays, D. 1952. Word recognition as a function of retinal locus. *Journal of Experimental Psychology*, 43, 43–48.

Monteverde-Ganoza, L. 1974. Aspectos sicolinguisticos en la afasia de los bilingues. *Languaje y Ciencias*, 14, 1–9.

Mossner, A., & Pilch, H. 1971. Phonematisch–syntaktisch Aphasie: Ein Sonderfall motorischer Aphasie bei einer Zweisprachigen Patientin. *Folia Linguistica*, 5, 394–409.

Moulten, W. 1962. What standard for diglossia? The case of German Switzerland. *Georgetown Monograph Series on Languages and Linguistics*, 15, 133–144.

Nair, K. R., & Virmani, V. 1973. Speech and language disturbances in hemiplegics. *Indian Journal of Medical Research*, 61, 1395–1403.

Neufeld, G. 1973. The bilingual's lexical store. *Working Papers on Bilingualism*, 1, 35–65.

Nielsen, J. 1962. *Agnosia, apraxia, aphasia.* New York: P. Hoeber.

Nielsen, J., & Raney, R. 1939. Recovery from aphasia, studies in cases of lobectomy. *Archives of Neurology, 42,* 189–200.

Nott, C., & Lambert, W. 1968. Free recall of bilinguals. *Journal of Verbal Learning and Verbal Behavior, 7,* 1065–1071.

Obler, L. 1977. *Polyglot aphasia.* Paper presented at the North East Conference on Language Acquisition. Boston.

Obler, L. Forthcoming. Right hemisphere participation in second language learning. In K. Diller (Ed.), *Individual differences and universals in language learning aptitude.* Rowley, Mass.: Newbury Press.

Obler, L., & Albert, M. 1977a. Influence of aging on recovery from aphasia in polyglots. *Brain and Language, 4,* 460–463.

Obler, L., & Albert, M. 1977b. Aphasia type and aging. Paper presented at Academy of Aphasia, Montreal.

Obler, L., & Albert, M. 1978. A monitor system for bilingual language processing. In M. Paradis (Ed.), *Aspects of bilingualism.* Columbia, S.C.: Hornbeam Press.

Obler, L., Albert, M., & Gordon, H. 1975. *Asymmetry of cerebral dominance in Hebrew– English bilinguals.* Paper presented at the thirteenth annual meeting of the Academy of Aphasia, Victoria, B.C.

Oldfield, R. 1971. The assessment and analysis of handedness. The Edinburgh inventory. *Neuropsychologia, 9,* 97–113.

Orbach, J. 1953. Retinal locus as a factor in the recognition of visually perceived words. *American Journal of Psychology, 65,* 555–562.

Orbach, J. 1967. Differential recognition of Hebrew and English words in right and left visual fields as a function of cerebral dominance and reading habits. *Neuropsychologia. 5,* 127–134.

Ore, P. 1878. Fracture du crane. *Bulletin de l'Academie de Médecine, 7,* 1131–1138.

Osgood, C., & Sebeok, T. 1954. *Psycholinguistics.* Baltimore: Waverly Press.

Ovcharova, P., Raichev, R., & Geleva, T. 1968. Afeziya u Poligloti (Bulg.). *Neurohirurgiia, 7,* 183–190.

Palmer, M. 1972. Effects of categorization, degree of bilingualism and language recall of select monolinguals and bilinguals. *Journal of Educational Psychology, 63,* 160–164.

Paradis, M. 1977. Bilingualism and aphasia. In H. Whitaker & H. Whitaker (Eds.), *Studies in neurolinguistics* (Vol. 3). N.Y.:Academic Press.

Partilov, V. 1970. Vzaimodesitvue yazykov pri ovuyazychii s tochki zreniya vzaim ootnosheniya yazyka i myshleniya [The interaction of languages in bilingualism relationship between language and thought]. *Izv. Akad. Nauk, Lit. Yazyka, 29,* 203–209.

Pavlovitch, M. 1920. *Le langage enfantin; acquisition du serbe et du français par un enfant serbe.* Paris: Champion.

Peal, E., & Lambert, W. 1962. The relation of bilingualism to intelligence. *Psychological Monographs, General and Applied, 76* (No. 546).

Penfield, W. 1953. A consideration of the neurophysiological mechanisms of speech and some educational considerations. *Proceedings of the American Academy of Arts and Sciences, 82,* 5, 201–214.

Penfield, W., & Roberts, L. 1959. *Speech and brain mechanisms.* Princeton, N.J.: Princeton University Press.

Peters, A. 1974. Research report: University of Hawaii study of the beginnings of speech. *University of Hawaii Working Papers on Linguistics, 6,* 93–99.

Peuser, G. 1974. Vergleichende Aphasieforschung und Aphasie bei Polyglotten. *Folia Phoniatrica, 26,* 167–168.

Peuser, G., & Leischner, A. 1974. Stoerungen der Phonetischen Schrift bei einem Aphasiker. *Neuropsychologia, 12,* 557–560.

Pick, A. 1903. Fortgesetzte Beitrage zur Pathologie der Sensorischen Aphasie. *Archiv fuer Psychiatrie und Nervenkrankheiten, 37,* 468–487.

Pick, A. 1909. Forgesetzte Beitrage zur Pathologie des Sensorischen Aphasie. *Archiv fuer Psychiatrie und Nervenkrankheiten, 37,* 216–241, 468–487.

Pick, A. 1921. Zur Erklarung gewisser Ausnahmen von der sogenannten Ribotschen Regel. Abhandlungen aus der Neurologie, Psychiatrie, Psychologie und ihren Grenzgebieter. *Monatsschrift fuer Psychiatrie und Neurologie, 13,* 151–167.

Pitres, A. 1895. Etude sur l'aphasie. *Revue de Médecine, 15,* 873–899.

Poetzl, O. 1925. Ueber die parietal bedingte Aphasic und ihren Einflug auf das Sprechen mehrerer Sprachen. *Zeitschrift fuer Neurologie, 96,* 100–124.

Poetzl, O. 1930. Aphasie und mehrsprachigkeit. *Zeitschrift fuer die gesamte Neurologie und Psychiatrie, 124,* 145–162.

Pohl, J. 1965. Bilinguismes. *Revue Roumaine de Linguistique, 10,* 343–349.

Politzer, R. 1965. Some reflections on transfer of training in foreign language learning. *International Review of Applied Linguistics, 8,* 333–340.

Postman, L. 1961. The present status of interference theory. In C. N. Cofer & B. Munsgrove (Eds.), *Verbal learning and verbal behavior.* New York:McGraw-Hill. Pp. 152–179.

Preston, M., & Lambert, W. 1969. Interlingual interference in a bilingual version of the Stroop Color-Word Task. *Journal of Verbal Learning and Verbal Behavior, 8,* 295–301.

Proust, A. 1872. De l'aphasie. *Archives Générales de Médecine, 19,* 303–318.

Rabbitt, P. 1968. Three kinds of error-signalling responses in a serial choice task. *Quarterly Journal of Experimental Psychology, 20,* 179–188.

Rao, T. 1964. Development and use of the directions test for measuring degree of bilingualism. *Journal of Psychological Research, 8,* 114–119.

Reichmann, R., & Reichau, E. 1919. Traubstummenlehrer: Zur Uebungsbehandlung der Aphasien. *Archiv fuer Psychiatrie, 60,* 8–42.

Reynolds, A. 1971. Information processing when translating or transforming sentences. *Dissertation Abstracts International, 32 (1-B),* 594.

Ribot, T. 1882. *Diseases of memory; An essay in the positive psychology.* London: Paul.

Riegel, K. 1968. Some theoretical considerations of bilingual duplication. *Psychological Bulletin, 70,* 647–670.

Riegel, K. 1971. Psychological studies in bilingual performances and cross-linguistic differences. *Studies in Language and Language Behavior, Phase VI,* 1–49.

Riegel, K., Ramsey, R., & Riegel, R. 1967. A comparison of the first and second languages of American and Spanish students. *Journal of Verbal Language and Verbal Behavior, 6,* 536–544.

Riegel, K., & Riegel, R. 1963. An investigation into denotative aspects of word meaning. *Learning and Speech, 6,* 5–21.

Riegel, K., & Zivian, W. 1972. A study of inter- and intralingual associations in English and German. *Language Learning, 22,* 51–63.

Riese, W. 1949. Type, evolution and localization of aphasia following neurosurgical relief in a 60 year old scientist, affected by paralysis agitans. *Confinia Neurologica, 9,* 216–225.

Rinckenbach, J. 1866. Observation d'aphasie. *Archives Générales de Médecine, 8,* 105–106.

Rogers, L. 1977. *EEG hemispheric asymmetries and bilingualism.* Paper presented to International Neurological Society, Santa Fe.

Ronjat, J. 1913. *Le développement du langage observé chez un enfant bilingue.* Paris: Champion.

Rose, R., & Caroll, J. 1974. Free recall of mixed language list. *Bulletin of the Psychonomic Society, 3,* 267–268.

Rüke-Dravina, V. 1960. Mehrsprachigkeit im Vorschulalter. *Travaux de l'Institut de Phonétique du Lund.*

Rüke-Dravina, V. 1971. Word associations in monolingual and multilingual individuals. *Linguistics, 74,* 66–84.

Russell, W., & Jenkins, J. 1954. *The complete Minnesota norms for responses to 100 words from the Kent-Rosanoff word association test. Studies in the role of language in behavior* (Tech. Rep. N. 11, N. 8, 66216). University of Minnesota.

Saegert, J., Kazarian, S., & Young, R. 1973. Part/whole transfer with bilinguals. *American Journal of Psychology, 86,* 537–546.

Saegert, J., Oberneger, J., & Kazarian, S. 1973. Organizational factors in free recall of bilingually mixed lists. *Journal of Experimental Psychology, 97,* 397–399.

Saer, H. 1923. The effect of bilingualism on intelligence. *British Journal of Psychology, 14,* 25–38.

Saer, H. 1931. An experimental inquiry into the education of bilingual peoples. In W. Rawson (Ed.), *Education in a changing commonwealth.* London: The New Education Fellowship. Pp. 116–121.

Salomon, E. 1914. Motorische Aphasie mit Agrammatismus und sensorische Storungen. *Monatsshrift fuer Psychiatrie, 35,* 181–208.

Salzinger, K. 1967. *Research in verbal behavior and some neurological implications.* New York: Academic Press.

Samargi, W. 1972. Variation and variables in religious glossolalia. *Language in Society, 1,* 121–130.

Sauvageot, A. 1934. Le bilinguisme des hommes cultivés. *Conférences de l'Institut de Linguistique de l'Université de Paris, 2,* 5–14.

Sauvageot, A. 1939. Problemes de la structure interne (innere Sprachform) et du bilinguisme. In *Ve Congrès International des Linguistes* (2e publication). Rapports: Bruges. Pp. 19–39.

Scherrer, G., & Wertheimer, M. 1964. *A psycholinguistic experiment in foreign-language teaching.* New York: McGraw-Hill.

Schneerson, F. 1939. Lapsikhulogie shel du-haleshoniut baaretz. *Hakhinukh, 12,* 1.

Scholes, R. 1967. Categorical responses to synthetic vocalic stimuli in speakers of various languages. *Language and Speech, 10,* 252–282.

Scholes, R. 1968. Phonemic interference as a perceptual phenomenon. *Language and Speech, 11,* 86–103.

Schuell, H., & Jenkins, J. 1961. Relationship between auditory comprehension and word frequency in aphasia. *Journal of Speech Hearing Research, 4,* 30–36.

Schulze, H. A. 1968. Unterschiedliche Ruckbildung einer sensorischen und einer ideokinetischen motorischen Aphasie bei einem Polyglotten. *Psychiatrie, Neurologie und Medizinische Psychologie, 12,* 441–445.

Schvartz, L. 1954. K voprosu o znachenii slowa kak uslownogo razdrazitela. *Bulletin of Experimental Biology and Medicine, 38,* 15.

Schwalbe, J. 1920. Ueber die Aphasie bei Polyglotten. *Neurologisches Zentralblatt, 39,* 265.

Scoresby-Jackson, R. 1867. Case of aphasia with right hemiplegia. *Edinburgh Medical Journal, 12,* 696–706.

Scott, S. 1973. *The relation of divergent thinking to bilingualism: Cause and effects.* Mimeographed paper, McGill University.

Scovel, T. 1969. Foreign accents, language acquisition, and cerebral dominance. *Language Learning, 19,* 245–253.

Segalowitz, N. 1977. Psychological perspectives on bilingual education. In B. Spolsky & R. Cooper (Eds.), *Frontiers in bilingual education.* Rowley, Mass.: Newbury Press.

Segalowitz, N., & Lambert, W. 1969. Semantic generalization in bilinguals. *Journal of Verbal Learning and Verbal Behavior, 8,* 559–566.

Selinker, L. 1972a. Interlanguage. *International Review of Applied Linguistics, 10,* 209–231.

Selinker, L. 1972b. Second-language learning experiments and mathematical learning theory. *Language Learning, 22,* 291–299.

Shai, A., Goodglass, H., & Barton, M. 1972. Recognition of tachistoscopically presented verbal and non-verbal material after unilateral cerebral damage. *Neuropsychologia, 10,* 185–191.

Shankweiler, D., & Studdert-Kennedy, M. 1967. Identification of consonants and vowels presented to left and right ears. *Quarterly Journal of Experimental Psychology, 19,* 59–63.

Shubert, A. 1940. Dinamika dvuiazvchnoi aleksiiiagrafi pri travme golovnogo mozga. *Trudy Tsentral'nogo Instituta Psi Kbologi,* Moskva. 169–175.

Silverberg, R., & Gordon, H. Forthcoming. Differential aphasia in two bilinguals. *Neurology.*

Simecek, V. 1970–1971. Review in Czech: Psikhologicheskaya: methodicheskaya Kharakteristika Druyazychiga: Bilingvizma by Y. Vereschagin. *Cizi Jazyky Skole, 14,* 124–127.

Simonyi, G. 1951. Echolalie im Rahmen der Aphasie bei Pickscher Atrophie. *Monatsschrift fuer Psychiatrie und Neurologie, 122,* 100–120.

Slobin, D. 1968. Antonymic phonetic symbolism in three natural languages. *Journal of Personality and Social Psychology, 10,* 301–305.

Smirnov, B., & Faktorovicz, N. 1949. Kvoprosu ob afazii u poliglotov. *Nevrologiya i Psikhiatriya, 18,* 26–28.

Smith, M. 1933. A study of language development in bilingual children in Hawaii. *Psychological Bulletin, 30,* 629.

Sodhi, S. 1969. Uzandze's set and second language learning. *International Journal of Psychology, 4,* 317–319.

Sokolov, A. 1960. Silent speech in the study of foreign languages. *Voprosy Psikhologii, 5,* 10–14.

Soller, N. 1970. A study of perceptual defense involving bilinguals. *Philippine Journal of Psychology, 3,* 3–17.

Sommerfelt, A. 1945. Un cas de mélange de grammaires. *Auhandlinger utgitt av Der Norske Uidenskapsakademic,* Hist.-Filos, Klusse 4, Oslo, 1926.

Spreen, O. 1968. Psycholinguistic aspects of aphasia. *Journal of Speech and Hearing Research, 11,* 467–480.

Stafford, K. 1968. Problem solving as a function of language. *Language and Speech, 11,* 104–112.

Stafford, K., & Van Keuren, S. 1968. Semantic differential profiles as related to monolingual–bilingual types. *Language and Speech, 11,* 167–170.

Starck, R., Genesee, F., Lambert, W., & Seitz, M. 1977. Multiple language experience and cerebral dominance. In S. Segalowitz and F. Gruber (Eds.), *Language development and neurological theory*. New York: Academic Press.

Stengel, E. 1939. On learning a new language. *International Journal of Psychiatry, 20*, 471–479.

Stengel, E., & Patch, I. 1955. "Central" aphasia associated with parietal symptoms. *Brain, 78*, 401–416.

Stengel E., & Zelmanowicz, J. 1933. Ueber polyglotte motorische Aphasie. *Zeitschrift fuer die gesamte Neurologie und Psychiatrie, 149*, 292–311.

Stevens, H. 1957. Reading epilepsy. *New England Journal of Medicine, 257*, 165–170.

Stieglitz, F. 1971. The effect of stimulus length and grammar structure on repeatability of stimuli by native and foreign speakers of English. *Dissertation Abstracts I, 3-(12a)*, 6417.

Straussler, E. 1912. Ein Fall von passagerer, systematischer Sprachstorung bei einem Polyglotten, verbunden mit rechtsseitigen transitorischen Gehorghall u Zinationen. *Zeitschrift fuer die gesamte Neurologie und Psychiatrie, 9*, 503–513.

Streifler, M., & Hofman, S. 1976. Sinistrad mirror writing and reading after brain concussion in a bi-systemic (oriento–occidental) polyglot. *Cortex, 12*, 356–364.

Stroop, J. 1935. Studies of interference in serial verbal reactions. *Journal of Experimental Psychology, 18*, 643–662.

Swain, M., & Wesche, M. 1973. Linguistic interaction: Case study of a bilingual child. *Working Papers on Bilingualism, 1*, 10–34.

Tarone, E. 1974a. A discussion on the Dulay and Burt studies, with comments by H. Dulay and M. Burt. *Working Papers on Bilingualism, 4*, 57–70.

Tarone, E. 1974b. Speech perception in second language acquisition: A suggested model. *Language Learning, 24*, 223–233.

Tataru, A. 1968. Unusual mistakes in hearing and pronouncing foreign sound-sequences. *Revue Roumaine de Linguistique, 13*, 139–141.

Taylor, G., Latford, J., Guiora, A., & Lane, H. 1971. Psychological variables and ability to pronounce a second language. *Language and Speech, 14*, 146–157.

Taylor, I. 1971. How are words from two languages organized in bilinguals' memory? *Canadian Journal of Psychology, 25*, 228–240.

Taylor, I. 1976. Similarity between French and English words—A factor to be considered in bilingual behavior? *Journal of Psycholinguistic Research, 5*, 85–94.

Taylor, L. 1970. The relationship of personality variables to second language pronunciation. University of Michigan. *Dissertation Abstracts I, 30 (9-B)*, 4384.

Taylor, M. 1974. Speculations on bilingualism and the cognitive network. *Working Papers in Bilingualism, 2*, 68–124.

Terry, C., & Cooper, R. 1969. A note on the perception and production of phonological variation. *Modern Language Journal, 53*, 254–255.

Tesniere, L. 1939. Phonologie et mélange de langues. *Travaux du Cercle Linguistique de Prague, 8*, 83–93.

Thorndike, E., & Lorge, I. 1944. *The teacher's word book of 30,000 words*. New York: Teachers College Press.

Tiglao, A., Capco, C., & Tucker, R. 1971. Filipino and English word associations by Filipino–English bilinguals. *Philippine Journal of Psychology, 4*, 37–43.

Tits, D. 1948. Le méchanisme de l'acquisition d'une langue se substituant à la langue maternelle chez une enfant espagnole âgée de six ans. Brussels: Imprimerie Veldeman.

Travis, L., & Johnson, W. 1937. The relationship of bilingualism to stuttering. *Journal of Speech Disorders, 2*, 185–189.

Treisman, A. 1964. Verbal cues, language and meaning in selective attention. *American Journal of Psychology, 77*, 206–219.

Treisman, A. 1965. The effects of redundancy and familiarity on translation and repeating back a foreign and a native language. *British Journal of Psychology, 56*, 369–379.

Tremaine, R. 1975. Piagetian equilibration processes in syntax learning. In D. Dato (Ed.), *Developmental Psycholinguistics: Theory and Applications.* Washington, D.C.: Georgetown University Press. Pp 255–265.

Trites, R., & Price, M. 1976. *Learning disabilities found in association with French immersion programming.* Ottawa: University of Toronto Press.

Tulving, E., & Colotla, V. 1970. Free recall of trilingual lists. *Cognitive Psychology, 1*, 86–98.

Umiltá, C., Rizzolatti, G., & Marzi, C. 1974. Hemispheric differences in the discrimination of line orientation. *Neuropsychologia, 12*, 165–174.

Uznadze, D. 1966. *The psychology of set.* New York: Consultant Bureau.

Valdman, A. 1975. *Bibliography of language learner approximative systems and error analysis.* Center for Applied Linguistics, University of Indiana.

Van Overbeke, M. 1968a. La description phonétique et phonologique d'une situation bilingue. *La Linguistique, 2*, 93–109.

Van Overbeke, M. 1968b. A propos d'une interférence intonationelle due au bilinguisme. *Revue de Phonétique Appliquée, 10*, 65–79.

Van Overbeke, M. 1972. *Introduction au problème du bilinguisme.* Brussels: Editions Labor.

Velikovsky, I. 1934. Can a newly acquired language become the speech of the unconscious? Word plays in the dreams of Hebrew thinking persons. *Psychoanalytic Review, 21*, 329–335.

Velten, H. 1943. The growth of phonemic and lexical patterns in infant language. *Language, 19*, 281–292.

Vereschehagin, E. 1969. *Psikhologicheskaya i methodicheskaya kharakteristika dvuyazychiya (bilingvism)* [The psychological and methods aspects of bilingualism]. Moscow: Moscow University Press.

Veyrac, G. J. 1931. *Etude de l'aphasie chez les sujets polyglottes.* Thèse pour le Doctorat en Médecine, Paris.

Vidal, F. 1974. Lenguaje y desarollo psicoafective (considerationes psicologices en torno al bilinguismo y emigracion en Galicis. *Archives of Neurobiology* (Madrid), *37*, 123–132.

Vildomec, V. 1963. *Multilingualism.* Leyden: A. W. Sythoff.

Vocadlo, O. 1938. Some observations on mixed languages. In *IVᵉ Congrès International des Linguistes, 1936, Actes Copenhague, 1938*, 169–176.

Vogt, H. 1949. Dans quelles conditions et dans quelles limites peut s'éxercer sur le système morphologique d'une langue l'action du système morphologique d'une autre langue? In *VIᵉ Congrès International des Linguistes, Actes Paris*. 31–40.

Wakefield, J., Bradley, P., Yom, B., & Doughtie, E. 1975. Language switching and constituent structure. *Language and Speech, 18*, 14–19.

Wald, I. 1958. Zugodnienie arozil poliglotow. *Postepy Neurologii, Neurolochirugii i Psychiatrii, 4*, 211.

Wald, I. 1961. Problema afazii poliglotov. *Voprosy Kliniki i Patofiziologii Afazii*, Moskva, 140–170.

Walter, D., & Werzberger, J. 1971. Recognition of Hebrew and English letters as a function of age and display predictability. *Developmental Psychology, 5*, 518–524.

Walters, J., & Zatorre, R. In press. Laterality differences for word recognition in bilinguals. *Brain and Language.*

Wechsler, A. 1977. Dissociative alexia. *Archives of Neurology, 34,* 257.

Weijner, A. 1919. *Tweetaligheid.* Tilburg. (Opuoed Kundige brochurenrecks, No. 139).

Weinreich, M. 1969. Dvuyazychie i mnogoyazychie [Bilingual and plurilingualism]. *La Monda Lingvo-Problemo,*167.

Weinreich, U. 1953. *Languages in contact—Findings and problems.* New York: Publication No. 1. Linguistic Circle of New York.

Weinreich, U. 1957. On the description of phonic interference. *Word, 13,* 1–11.

Weirs, A. 1956. Von Zweisprachigkeit und Sprachbogobury. *Orbis, 5,* 152–163.

Weisenburg, T., & McBride, K. 1935. *Aphasia: A clinical and psychological study.* New York: Commonwealth Fund (Case No. 4). Pp. 160–182.

Weist, R. 1974. Interlingual-facilitation and retrieval processes. *Perceptual and Motor Skills, 38,* 947–952.

Weist, R., & Crawford, C. 1972. Phonological and semantic representations of words, compartments of memory, and rehearsal. *Psychonomic Science, 28,* 106–108.

West, M. 1926. *Bilingualism.* Calcutta.

Whitaker, H. Forthcoming. Bilingualism: A neurolinguistics perspective. In W. Ritchie (Ed.), *Second language acquisition research.* New York: Academic Press.

White, M. 1969. Laterality differences in perception: A review. *Psychology Bulletin, 72,* 387–405.

Whorf, B. 1956. *Language, thoughts and reality.* Cambridge, Mass.: MIT Press.

Winterstein, O., & Meier, J. 1939. Schaedetrauma und Aphasie bei Mehrsprachigen. *Der Chirurg, 11,* 229.

Yadrick, R., & Kausler, D. 1974. Verbal discrimination learning for bilingual lists. *Journal of Experimental Psychology, 102,* 899–900.

Yeni-Komshian, G., & Lambert, W. 1969. Concurrent and consecutives modes of learning two vocabularies. *Journal of Educational Psychology, 60,* 204–215.

Young, R. 1969. Transference and retroactive inhibition in bilingualism. *Revista Mexicana de Psicologia, 3,* 367–375.

Young, R., & Navar, M. 1968. Retroactive inhibition with bilinguals. *Journal of Experimental Psychology, 77,* 109–115.

Young, R., & Saegert, J. 1966. Transfer with bilinguals. *Psychonomic Science, 6,* 161–162.

Zangwill, O. 1960. *Cerebral dominance and its relations to psychological function.* Edinburgh: Oliver and Boyd.

Zierer, E. 1974. Psycho-linguistic and pedagogical aspects in the bilingual education of a child of pre-school age. *Lenguaje y ciencias, 14,* 47–64.

Zirkel, P., & Greene, J. 1974. The validation of parallel testing of aural ability as an indicator of bilingual dominance. *Psychology in the Schools, 11,* 153–157.

Zurif, E., & Bryden, M. 1969. Familial handedness and left–right differences in auditory and visual perception. *Neuropsychologia, 7,* 179–188.

Author Index

Subject Index